DATE DUE

THE PASTORA GOLDNER SERIES
in Post-Holocaust Studies

The Pastora Goldner Series in Post-Holocaust Studies explores questions—
ethical, educational, political, spiritual—that continue to haunt humanity in
the aftermath of Nazi Germany's attempt to destroy Jewish life and culture.
Books in this series, addressing the most current and pressing issues of our post-
Holocaust world, proceed from scholarship undertaken by the Pastora Goldner
Holocaust Symposium, whose membership—international, interdisciplinary,
interfaith, and intergenerational—is committed to dialogue as a fundamental
form of inquiry. The symposium and the series are generously supported by
Pastora Campos Goldner, who has devoted much of her life to working toward
tikkun olam, the healing of our world, and whose vision and courage inspire
the participants in the symposium who contribute to this series.

THE PASTORA GOLDNER SERIES
in Post-Holocaust Studies

After-Words: Post-Holocaust Struggles
with Forgiveness, Reconciliation, Justice
Edited and Introduced by
David Patterson and John K. Roth

Fire in the Ashes:
God, Evil, and the Holocaust
Edited and Introduced by
David Patterson and John K. Roth

Open Wounds: The Crisis of Jewish Thought
in the Aftermath of the Holocaust
by David Patterson

Testimony, Tensions, and Tikkun: *Teaching*
the Holocaust in Colleges and Universities
Edited and Introduced by
Myrna Goldenberg and Rochelle L. Millen

Testimony, Tensions, and *Tikkun*

TEACHING
THE HOLOCAUST
IN COLLEGES
AND UNIVERSITIES

Edited and Introduced by

Myrna Goldenberg
and Rochelle L. Millen

UNIVERSITY OF WASHINGTON PRESS

Seattle and London

© 2007 by the University of Washington Press
Printed in the United States of America
Design by Pamela Canell
12 11 10 09 08 07   5 4 3 2 1

University of Washington Press
P.O. Box 50096, Seattle, WA 98145 U.S.A.
www.washington.edu/uwpress

Library of Congress Cataloging-in-Publication Data
Testimony, tensions, and tikkun : teaching the Holocaust
in colleges and universities / edited and Introduced by
Myrna Goldenberg and Rochelle L. Millen.
p. cm. — (The Pastora Goldner series in post-Holocaust studies)
Includes bibliographical references and index.
ISBN-13: 978-0-295-98687-6 (hardback : alk. paper)
ISBN-10: 0-295-98687-5 (hardback : alk. paper)
1. Holocaust, Jewish (1939–1945)—Study and teaching (Higher)
2. Holocaust, Jewish (1939–1945)—Study and teaching (Higher)—
United States. I. Goldenberg, Myrna. II. Millen, Rochelle L., 1943–
III. Title: Teaching the Holocaust in colleges and universities.
D804.33.T53 2007   940.53'18071173—dc22   2006032917

The paper used in this publication is acid-free and 90 percent recycled from
at least 50 percent post-consumer waste. It meets the minimum requirements of
American National Standard for Information Sciences—Permanence of Paper
for Printed Library Materials, ANSI Z39.48–1984. ♾☉

Illustration (jacket, pp. i, 21, 187, 233): *First Station: Auschwitz-Birkenau,* by Arie Galles
(1998, 47½ × 75 in., charcoal and white Conte on Arches with barbed wire-impressed
wrought-iron frame), from the suite of fifteen drawings *Fourteen Stations/Hey Yud Dalet
(Hashem Yinkom Daman),* the latter phrase meaning "May God avenge their blood."
The title of the suite refers both to the Stations of the Cross and to the fact that the
Nazi concentration camps and killing centers were near railroad stations. Galles's
drawings are based on Luftwaffe and Allied aerial photographs of those sites. Within
this drawing and all the others are invisibly embedded, hand-lettered phrases
from the Kaddish, the ancient Jewish prayer for the dead.

Contents

Foreword

HUBERT G. LOCKE

The essays in this volume are the work of teachers from a wide range of backgrounds, interests, and approaches, teachers who—some for only a few years, and others for considerably longer—have been engaged in a task that is both impossible and imperative: that of confronting students with the grand horror of the twentieth century, commonly termed "the Holocaust." Each of the essayists acknowledges the impossibility of the task—"teaching something that cannot be taught," as David Patterson puts it (chapter 7). They recognize the enormous limits—of language, thought, imagination, and comprehension—that necessarily thwart any attempt to grasp and express the story they seek to tell. Yet all are linked by the conviction that they are pursuing an effort of uncommon importance, one that is pivotal not only to our understanding of the past but also to whatever prospects there may be for a more decent and humane future.

No other topic or subject matter in teaching is fraught with such limitations, nor are teachers in any other field confronted by such a pervasive sense that what they seek to accomplish may be well nigh unattainable. For most purveyors of the profession, teaching is a treasured opportunity to impart knowledge that enlivens or enriches the human experience—as do the arts and literature—or that cultivates expertise, as in mathematics and the sciences, intended to increase competence as well as the contributions that can be made to the community and the larger society. Teachers value their work because they see their efforts as part of the fundamental responsibility and commitment of each society to expand and improve the cultural, social, and intellectual horizon of its citizens.

Why, then, teach a topic so laden with the malevolent—subject matter that does not elevate but depresses, a history that is not inspiring but rather is filled with accounts of the worst of which the human species is capable? Various answers to this question are to be found in these pages. For the most part, however, these teachers—and their countless associates—who dutifully offer courses in Holocaust studies do so because they have a keen sense that the story of the Holocaust is one that the modern world will fail to master at its own peril.

It will surprise some, no doubt, to find that not all the essayists are Jewish—a fact that cuts the ground from under those who wish to portray the Holocaust as predominantly or exclusively an event in Jewish history. Jewish citizens of Europe did perish in numbers that are staggering, but the madness that swept across the European continent crushed Gypsies, Jehovah's Witnesses, Polish intellectuals, and an inexplicable assortment of other victims as well. Therefore, the field of Holocaust studies examines a range of problems and issues that are universal in their reach and implications. These essayists, not only in what they have to say but also in the differing perspectives from which they write, make an invaluable contribution to our understanding of how the transmission of a painful chapter in human history can best be accomplished.

Teachers are nominally expected to be paradigms of objectivity, dispassionately conveying information and insights about the subjects that are their academic specialties. But every teacher who has ever excited students, no matter what the field, has been one who has cared deeply about the subject taught, a person who has managed to convey to students a sense of the crucial and the compelling. At the college and university level, where dispassion and objectivity are most highly prized, it is often forgotten that the very term "professor" denotes, in its most elemental form, someone who has something to profess—something worth declaring, and worth consideration by those who hear it.

This fact suggests that teaching, in the final analysis, is testimony. Teachers of the Holocaust attest to the event by providing the irrefutable evidence of its occurrence—the records of the perpetrators, the testimony of the victims who survived, the accounts of bystanders. These teachers support the evidence with the work of scholars who have patiently sifted through the accumulation of more than half a century's traces of the Holocaust, weaving an incontrovertible narrative that constitutes the main contours of an annihilation that, although there have been similar episodes of mayhem and mass murder, stands alone in the annals of human depravity. Teachers of the Holocaust also affirm, in the stories of those few who are considered rescuers, that some found it possible, even during such a grim epoch, to rise above the massive brutality and to manifest what the world would like to believe is human instinct at its best. And these teachers verify, every time they teach, that this catastrophic moment in twentieth-century history remains one of the defining events of the modern era.

Here, then, are the stories of a very special group of teachers whose efforts help to instill in the modern conscience a story that many would just as soon forget, but one that the world must remember if there is to be any possibility of a future better than the recent past.

SEATTLE, WASHINGTON

Acknowledgments

This book owes its origins to the Pastora Goldner Holocaust Symposium, whose founders and participants encouraged its development and supported its publication. The generosity of spirit and depth of intellect of the symposium participants inspired and fostered this work. While we appreciate the involvement of all those who contributed to the book, we thank in particular Leonard Grob and Henry F. Knight for their leadership, energy, persistence, wisdom, and warmth.

This book was strengthened by the contributions of several members of the summer seminar titled "Post-Holocaust Ethics and Religion," sponsored by the Center for Advanced Holocaust Studies, United States Holocaust Memorial Museum, and most ably and sensitively led by John K. Roth.

Myrna Goldenberg wishes to acknowledge and thank Neal, her life partner, for his unwavering devotion and sharp eye. His attention, caring, and love enrich not only her life but also her work. He makes things possible and good.

Rochelle L. Millen wishes to acknowledge and thank Henoch, her life partner and best friend, for helping to weave the tapestry of their shared journey. With him, life is rich, deep, and challenging.

Testimony, Tensions, and *Tikkun*

Introduction

MYRNA GOLDENBERG AND ROCHELLE L. MILLEN

"Why," our students ask, "do you choose to teach a subject as depressing as the Holocaust?"

"To change the world," we respond, "one person at a time."

Their eyes widen quizzically, they nod absently, they shift in their seats, and they settle into silence. They ask again several times during the semester, but perfunctorily, because they are beginning to acknowledge the urgency of the subject as well as its moral weight. Within several weeks, their questions become slightly more sophisticated: How can we, students and instructors alike, sleep? Don't the images from books and films turn dreams into nightmares? Is it possible to believe in inherent goodness, in the face of so much evil? What are the real goals for students in the course? And so on.

Like all teachers, we turn the questions back to them: "Why do you choose to take the course?" Students' responses are predictable and run the gamut from "I'm a European-history major" to "I've always been curious about the subject" to "I needed three more credits, and this course is being offered at a convenient hour." Occasionally students offer more serious reasons, or personal ones: they may be the grandchildren of survivors, or the descendants of Germans, or even the grandchildren or great nephews or nieces of Nazis. Inevitably, their comments at the end of the course are always more thoughtful than at the beginning. The students are changed, and they end the semester with heightened sensitivity and a commitment, at some level, to respond actively to injustice. For example, they volunteer to share their books with whoever will borrow them, or they pledge to identify with social-justice issues, to speak out for human rights, to become a force for change (at an acceptable level of discomfort). On the basis of students' stated commitments, we consider the semester a success. But we are left somewhat depleted. In addition to feeling the usual mixture of relief, exhaustion, and angst associated with finishing a semester, we find it necessary to reinforce our own faith in humankind. There are many proofs—the news of persistent if not constant violence, mass murders, and genocide around the globe; the bombing of the Pentagon and the World Trade Center on September 11, 2001; the regularity of suicide/homicide bombings in Israel, even after Israel's disengagement from Gaza; the alarming, dramatic rise of antisemitism in Europe and Africa—that the lessons of history have not been learned well, if at all. With the completed course's assigned texts fresh in our memories, we reevaluate the effectiveness of teaching the Holocaust for the purpose of motivating our students to become better citizens, better people, and more engaged activists. We wonder whether other teachers of Holocaust studies feel as we do, and so we seek their company, and we learn that their responses usually parallel our own.

This book is an exploration of the experience of teaching the Holocaust. It focuses on the impact on the teacher, the agony of confronting the material, the struggle to balance intellectual and emotional responses to the course content and to students, the challenge to refrain from imposing personal values, and the teacher's difficulty in dealing with an abundance of complex, painful content. This book is also a unique addition to Holocaust educational material in that its contributors are experienced scholars who grapple with the weighty importance of the subject and with the intensity inherent in teaching or presenting it. Representing different disciplines, the contributors share their insights, which in turn reflect religious, ethnic, and geographic diversity as well as unique teaching environments. They explore the effects of the subject on their students and on themselves, and, in doing so, they work to gain insight into the development of teaching strategies and techniques

that can encourage students to become more engaged human-right:
cates, if not activists.

As we move ahead into the twenty-first century, the Holoca
become something of a flash point, inflaming latent and overt antise
and simultaneously arousing passionate arguments—theoretica
tential, and political—in defense of Jewish existence. Increasingly,
of the Holocaust's historical connection to the birth of the state o
and to the alarming persistence of genocide, learning about the He
is slowly becoming a required or unavoidable element of educa
the Western world, more noticeably in Europe than in the Unite
In the decades immediately following World War II, European c
focused largely on their own suffering, and on building nation;
of spiritual and physical resistance.[1] In Europe, particularly in G
the need to address the topic of the Holocaust had its roots in tl
tion given by the media to the Adolf Eichmann trial, in 1961.[2]
sequent confrontation with the personification of evil in the p
this German SS officer—who, twenty years after the fact, expr
regret at not having killed more Jews—turned that nation's pr
tion away from its own suffering and toward the challenge of fa
understanding the conditions that had led Germany to the so-ca
Solution: namely, racial discrimination, antisemitism, and intol
minorities. Yet another impetus for teaching the Holocaust in
schools was the airing of the American docudrama miniseries
on German television in 1979 and 1980. Although German ed
decentralized, the requirement to teach the Holocaust is imp
through textbook oversight and through guidelines from the n
education. Moreover, German students are continually remin
Holocaust through research, educational materials, the resou
Wannsee House, memorial sites at major concentration ca
numerous other memorials scattered across Germany.[3] The
memory of National Socialism, or Nazism, although nearly
erations removed, is unavoidable.

According to Hanns-Fred Rathenow, a German Holocaus
"the memory of National Socialism was usually suppressed" un
1960s. Change began with the Eichmann trial, continue
Auschwitz trial in Frankfurt (1963–65), grew during the stu

ments (1967–68), and reached a peak with the broadcasting of the docu-drama *Holocaust* in 1979. Rathenow points out that the trend toward local history ("dig where you are standing") has inevitably yielded results: "Cognitive and affective ways of learning were connected by linking scientific analyses with the circumstances of the ordinary people . . . and the people's everyday life experiences during National Socialism. The emphasis on events of local history and biographical approaches (eye-witnesses) led to a number of programmatic approaches in historical and political classes."[4] "The demand that Auschwitz must never happen again is the most crucial education. It is so much more important than anything else that I don't feel I should have to justify it," Rathenow writes, and he questions the approach of "shared suffering," characterizing it as counterproductive if it is excessive, and seeing great need for Martin Buber's dialogic approach: "symmetrical communication between teachers and students . . . no losers or winners."[5] He goes on to explain that Holocaust education is "not about preserving Nazi horror but about learning from history to provide the basis of hope for the future."[6]

Other European countries, such as Austria and Poland, have taken similar steps to educate their children about the Holocaust. Poland, however, while requiring primary and secondary students to study the Holocaust in units about World War II, has not, in keeping with the practice of other Catholic countries, integrated the topic into its religion curriculum. In the mid-1980s, however, Jagiellonian University and the University of Warsaw established, respectively, a research center on Jewish history and culture and the Mordechai Anieleqicz Center for the Study and Teaching of the History and Culture of Jews in Poland. Such steps contrast conspicuously with France's ambiguous response to its own World War II–era Nazi occupation and collaboration. By the mid-1980s, however, France had incorporated the study of the Holocaust into its secondary and university-preparation courses: the Klaus Barbie trial, in 1987, and Claude Lanzmann's documentary film *Shoah* triggered increased interest in France's role during World War II.[7]

Curiously, it was not until the 1990s that Great Britain required the study of World War II, along with the Holocaust, in its secondary school curriculum, although individual teachers had always been free to include it in their courses. There is also an increasing presence of Holocaust

courses, as well as courses on modern antisemitism, at the college and university levels. Both in England and in Germany, courses on the Holocaust are apt to examine the complexities of legitimizing intolerance through the rule of law.[8] According to John P. Fox, "The prodigious amount of authoritative scholarly publication[,] . . . especially by German authors," is evidence of the presence and importance of Holocaust education in European schools.[9]

In the United States, Holocaust education is decentralized and eclectic, to say the least. The United States Holocaust Memorial Museum, reporting on 135,000 U.S. teachers of social studies and history in grades 7 through 12, found that fewer than half made any mention at all of the Holocaust in their teaching, and that the "overwhelming majority" devoted no more than three lessons to information about the Holocaust.[10] Holocaust educators in the United States include classroom teachers like those just described, in addition to staff members in Holocaust resource centers, special programs, foundations (such as the Facing History and Ourselves National Foundation), and museums as well as college and university faculty and other teachers. This rather inchoate array of pedagogical options is compounded by the dismal reality that about half of America's public school students take no courses at all on world history or Western history and therefore have no context in which to place a subject as complex as the Holocaust even if they are exposed to it. Moreover, isolated instructional units, such as discussions of Anne Frank's diary, reinforce an ahistorical approach to the topic. According to Samuel Totten, there has been no systematic study so far on "the extent and quality" of what is being taught in units, courses, or programs on the Holocaust.[11]

In the United States, as in Europe, the Holocaust had no part in the curriculum during the twenty years after World War II unless teachers themselves chose to introduce it and to develop or find teaching materials on the subject. A popular teaching tool during that period was *Anne Frank: The Diary of a Young Girl*, published in 1957, but neither the book nor its successors on stage and on film was formally included in U.S. middle school curricula until much later. The Eichmann trial in 1961 did bring some attention to the Holocaust; but, Totten argues, it was the twentieth anniversary of the Warsaw Ghetto uprising, marked by the National Council of Jewish Education in 1963, that stimulated not only interest in the Holocaust but also the development of appropriate teaching materials.[12] At the same time, memoirs and gatherings of survivors provided additional sources of information. All these sources influenced Jewish education, but not public education.

The civil rights movement in the United States also helped bring attention to the Holocaust, through a focus on its victims and survivors and on their having lost their human rights in the highly accomplished and cultured German nation. Thus, by the 1970s, when genocide became a legitimate (though not yet widely accepted) subject of scholarly attention, the Holocaust as genocide was becoming a field of intellectual inquiry. For example, one of the "deans" of Holocaust studies, Raul Hilberg, asserted that the Holocaust was "an American subject; the demand for knowledge about it came from students searching for the certainties of moral choices in the late 1970s after the United States' withdrawal from Vietnam."[13] It should also be noted that at Emory University, almost twenty years earlier, in 1959, Franklin H. Littell had introduced the first U.S. undergraduate course on the Holocaust. Dr. Littell saw a natural connection between the academic world and the Holocaust in that teachers, professors, and other intellectuals had been among the first to join the Nazi Party. Moreover, he explained, students were "especially attracted to Nazism," and university faculty "planned, rationalized, staffed, and supervised the key positions" in the regime.[14]

During the same period, and in the context of diminishing racial and religious prejudice, some U.S. school districts made Holocaust-related curricular materials available to classroom teachers. By 1977, Holocaust education was mandated in New York City schools through a unit called "The Holocaust: A Study of Genocide." Other school systems across the nation, although they do not necessarily require teaching about the Holocaust, have adopted or endorsed curricular units on the Holocaust. These school systems include those in Atlanta, Baltimore, Des Moines, Los Angeles, Milwaukee, Minneapolis, Philadelphia, and Pittsburgh. By the end of the twentieth century, five states—California, Florida, Illinois, New Jersey, and New York, all of which have substantial Jewish populations and, presumably, significant communities of survivors— had mandated teaching about the Holocaust. Other states—Connecticut, Georgia,

Indiana, Maryland, Nevada, North Carolina, Ohio, Pennsylvania, South Carolina, Tennessee, Virginia, and Washington—encourage the inclusion of Holocaust education as part of the curriculum.[15] Independent bodies also provide systematic and accurate information on the subject. These include the Holocaust Educational Foundation's summer seminar on the Holocaust and Jewish Civilization, founded and organized by Theodore (Zev) Weiss; the Lest We Forget summer study tours, organized and conducted by Marcie Littell as part of the master's degree program in Holocaust and genocide studies at Richard Stockton College, New Jersey; and the Teacher's Summer Seminar on Holocaust and Jewish Resistance, organized by Vladka Meed and sponsored by the Jewish Labor Committee, the American Federation of Teachers, the Education Committee of the American Gathering of Jewish Holocaust Survivors, and the National Catholic Center for Holocaust Education. In spite of the available opportunities, however, challenges remain in the United States at the precollege level. They include teacher preparation, decentralization of the curriculum, and the development and distribution of accurate, interesting, and accessible teaching materials. The profusion of teaching units and opportunities has not ensured quality or even accurate teaching.

Nevertheless, there have been several far-reaching influences in recent years, including the establishment of the United States Holocaust Memorial Museum, the opening of the Museum of Tolerance, the growth of local and regional Holocaust resource centers (often in university settings), the Holocaust Educational Foundation's Lessons and Legacies Conference, and the Annual Scholars' Conference on the Holocaust and the Churches. These initiatives have directed scholars' attention to the Holocaust and encouraged the inclusion of papers on the Holocaust in a variety of academic conferences, among them the annual meetings of the Association for Jewish Studies, Modern Language Association, the American History Association, the American Academy of Religion, and the National Women's Studies Association. In 1970, the Scholars' Conference, though more focused on theological than on political or historical issues, began a tradition of sophisticated academic analysis of the Holocaust. Its published annual proceedings exemplify a growing body of scholarly work that stems from the experience of Holocaust teaching at the college and university level.[16] The scholarship is prodigious, and the effect on university education is noticeable. Not only are courses on the Holocaust taught in a variety of academic departments (German, history, literature, political science, psychology, religion), but endowed chairs and notable programs have also been established in several universities. Not surprisingly, Yeshiva University led the way with the first chair, in 1976. Clark University followed twenty years later, offering a doctorate in Holocaust history. In 1997, the Richard Stockton College established the National Academy for Holocaust and Genocide Teachers Training as the core of its master's degree program. These accomplishments—along with the work of the University Programs Division of the United States Holocaust Memorial Museum, which offers rigorous summer seminars and prestigious fellowships—reflect serious attention to Holocaust and genocide studies. Nevertheless, a study of university courses on the Holocaust revealed that undergraduate courses on the subject are generally elective, that they focus on either the perpetrator or the victim, and that they pay little or no attention to the more complex and difficult issues of Holocaust denial, antisemitism beyond the Third Reich, gender, non-Jewish Holocaust victims, Jewish culture prior to 1933, and other genocides.[17] Indeed, a 1995 pronouncement in the *New York Times,* that "academic study of the Holocaust is slow to gain a foothold at American colleges and universities," is reinforced by the low number of endowed chairs in Holocaust studies: there are still only six, as was the case in 1996, and the number of endowed chairs is not increasing appreciably.[18]

On a broader scale, the relatively simplistic 1979 miniseries *Holocaust* spurred interest in the subject and generated a steady flow of popular works on the Holocaust that has lasted to the present. In the United States, the proliferation of Hollywood films and television docudramas, miniseries, and documentaries on the Holocaust has had interesting consequences. On the one hand, this popularization has led to oversimplification of the subject and to a sense of familiarity that promotes desensitization; on the other hand, this familiarity—even at a superficial level—prepares the public for more serious and accurate study.

At all levels of Holocaust education, there is a uniform challenge: to determine the purpose or rationale for courses on the Holocaust. According to Margaret Crouch Weiss, the 1979 *Report of the President's*

Commission on the Holocaust, authored by Elie Wiesel, cites three reasons for studying the subject: forbidding a posthumous victory to the killers, ensuring that the survivors' wish to bear witness is fulfilled, and enabling the rest of us to remember the Holocaust for our own sake.[19] Colleges and universities, of course, must give rationales more specific than those found in a broad policy statement, but instructors clearly can use such statements to support their courses or instructional units. Nevertheless, the disparities between and among courses on the Holocaust are manifold. There is virtually no agreement on what or how to teach in a Holocaust-related course, or even on the discipline in which it should be taught.[20] In history courses that focus on the Nazi period, the Holocaust, even though it is taught, is approached for the most part as a secondary issue; the presentation of a body of political, military, social, and intellectual content overrides other rationales for the course. But all such courses do cover a body of material for a particular purpose, and the Holocaust does provide a rich source of material that lends itself to teaching courses—in history, ethics, literature, political science, sociology, and religion—that fall under the disciplines included in the humanities and the social sciences. Most instructors of Holocaust courses cite loftier goals—to make students aware of state-supported injustice, to heighten students' readiness for activism, to teach moral decision making at the personal and political levels, and so on—than those entailed in simply teaching courses in particular humanistic disciplines, but the media we use to access these more abstract and critical issues are historical texts, memoirs, and artistic expressions. It is this set of idealistic reasons for teaching the Holocaust that both intensifies the passion the teacher brings to the subject and simultaneously makes the effort impossible, and thus frustrating. Indeed, one constant or principle both motivates and challenges many instructors: Holocaust courses are about the future more than the past.[21]

There are thorny issues in Holocaust-related courses. These include uniqueness versus universality, teaching about antisemitism in non-Jewish classroom contexts, Jewish teachers addressing antisemitism in classes of non-Jewish students, and teaching about the Holocaust in the current anti-Israel political climate. Teachers are faced with unsettling questions: If the Holocaust is so egregious, and so sharp and clear an example of "moral outrage," then is it really helpful to use as a resource for teaching? Is it so far from recognition that it becomes unthreatening and ineffective as a teaching tool?[22] Another recent issue in Holocaust education centers on technology and distance learning: the possibility of earning a graduate or undergraduate certificate in Holocaust studies through a program of online courses introduces pedagogical questions that complicate standards of rigor that are already problematic.

What does Auschwitz ultimately teach us? According to Krystyna Olesky, we learn that the "moral order around us is fragile," that some "institutional forms of community life can lead to genocide," and that "ordinary people established an Auschwitz"—and that these ordinary people are like those who preceded and followed the generation that built Auschwitz.[23] If we use the Holocaust to foster individual moral development and, ultimately, communal or societal moral progress, we can use two categories of texts: literature that seeks to explain how the Holocaust happened or could have happened, and literature that "looks to the significance of the Holocaust for us as human beings, individually and socially, as we struggle precariously to live with each other."[24] How, then, can the Holocaust be taught? Ian Gregory argues that if it is really incomprehensible, we cannot use it to teach peace, justice, and morality. If it is "so far removed from our normal moral experience and expectations," how can we adequately understand and analyze it?[25] How can we bridge the gulf between the language of the familiar and the language of the unthinkable so that we can describe the evil that defined the Holocaust?

Another issue can surface as well: Do we teach the Holocaust for what it "tells us about humans as moral and political creatures—how we conduct our lives at the individual and social level with reference to others and their independent interests"?[26] Ultimately, if the goal of moral progress governs our reasons for teaching this subject, we work from the premise that such progress is possible. Will a greater awareness of our capacity for inhumanity "diminish the amount of violence"[27] among human beings? Moreover, a belief in moral progress is challenged by the very reality of the Holocaust, which "forces us to confront the complex of issues surrounding responsibility . . . [and] moral indifference."[28] But, realistically, can the subject of the Holocaust be an appropriate vehicle for teaching morality? Is it reasonable to instrumentalize the Holocaust as a vehicle for teaching ethics? At what point do we diminish its historical substance by using it to teach other disciplines?

If we believe that education can help prevent mass murder and genocide in the future, how can we explain the fact that educated Germans gave enthusiastic support not only to such butchery but also to the manner in which it was committed?

> How can one come to terms with men eagerly swinging young children around in front of the parents and dashing their skulls against walls, with drowning humans in pits of human excrement and urine, with telling a father to shoot his sons, bury their bodies and then instructing him to carry on digging despite one of the children still being alive, or throwing live children into the crematoria? . . . Knowing [that these things] happened, however, poses the task of coming to understand how they could [happen].[29]

The literature on the Holocaust is vast and growing but relatively recent, and the amount of violence that we and our students encounter is stunning.[30]

It has been said that teaching the Holocaust is both dangerous and controversial. Its dangers are felt by the teacher who continually explores the evil that defines the Holocaust, and who can easily become depressed and even cynical. Yet many teachers teach the subject in order to stimulate student activism through a commitment to justice, to help create memory in the context of Jean Améry's statement that "no one can become what he cannot find in his memory." A profound problem thus emerges when we recognize the limits of education. According to Gregory, "to understand how to pre-empt the radical evil that can accompany this disdain for other humans might be a task beyond us"; to take such a "consequentialist approach—teaching a subject because of its expected outcomes"—is to "ransack the Holocaust simply in order to highlight some point about historical method or explanation, even to highlight a point about prejudice and its role in human affairs," and that, in turn, is "to be disrespectful of the victims of the Nazi genocide."[31] In addition, and ironically, to teach the Holocaust as a way of encouraging tolerance where tolerance is clearly inappropriate is to subvert our stated purpose.[32] For example, the evil of the Holocaust and, more recently, the bombing of the Pentagon and the World Trade Center, as well as repeated attacks by suicide bombers in Israel and elsewhere, cannot and should not be tolerated, and yet we live in a society that preaches and values tolerance. In the face of moral outrage, is tolerance a desired goal?

In the hope that study of the past will illuminate the present, we study the Holocaust as the most cataclysmic event of the twentieth century—for Gregory, the "most important single" event of the past century.[33] Thus we teach it to learn and to gain "understanding of how it came about and what its significance was and, importantly, might be to us at the present time."[34] We want our students to learn the historical chain of events that led both to Adolf Hitler's political success and to his military defeat. They need to learn about the subject of the Holocaust, but, they say, they also want to "understand" it. Ultimately, however, they say that they cannot understand such single-minded hate, even though we point out the nearly ubiquitous character of nonrational political behavior since the Holocaust. Ironically, it may be useful to cite Emil Fackenheim, who famously claims that one cannot comprehend the Holocaust but can only confront it and object. If Lawrence Langer's dark view—asserting "the impotence of the humanistic vision in an age of atrocity"[35]—is right, then there is no hope for the human condition, and teaching about the Holocaust is pointless. Indeed, it is likely that mere intellectual study of the Holocaust is insufficient, but we still must make students confront the consequences of moral indifference and extreme discrimination. *We must bring home the point that the Holocaust was not inevitable.*

Sweden's prime minister, Goran Persson, concerned that memories of the Holocaust were beginning to fade, and that young people in Sweden were not even sure that it had occurred, organized an international task force to address Holocaust education. By the year 2000, the prime minister had convened the Task Force for International Cooperation on Holocaust Education, Remembrance and Research, thus creating a forum that, by virtue of having been organized, established the issue in a definitive manner. Forty-six countries were represented at the first conference, which included twenty heads of state and government. Four conferences later, the agenda and participation had broadened, but the question remained: "Can conferences change the 'real' world?"[36] Alyson J. K. Bailes,

Introduction

British diplomat and director of the Stockholm International Peace Research Institute, argues that "they can and must . . . but each success is only an interim gain because the problems have a way of evolving as fast—or faster—than international society can find solutions."[37] Yet, for Bailes and the task force's members, as well as for scholars, academics, politicians, and other committed individuals and groups, "giving up is not an option."[38]

The symposium, rooted in the belief that teaching and study can and do encourage moral progress, was convened for the first time in June 1996 by two university professors whose organizational and intellectual skills brought a vision to fruition. Henry Knight of the University of Tulsa and Leonard Grob of Fairleigh Dickinson University were responsible for the initial call for papers that resulted in what has become an international, interdisciplinary biennial symposium composed of nearly forty scholars who focus on the response of higher education to the Holocaust. Meeting in small and large groups in the idyllic environment of Wroxton Abbey, a campus of Fairleigh Dickinson University in Oxfordshire, England, the participants confront multiple complex issues and opportunities: the contributions of various scholarly disciplines to the subject of the Holocaust; varying and often conflicting points of view among people of different ethnic and religious backgrounds; points of theological and discipline-based difference; areas of common ground among the assembled scholars; reasons for teaching the subject of the Holocaust; complementarity between scholars and directors of museums or resource centers; and other abstract and concrete topics that arise. The idea for this book emerged from the first symposium group, taking its shape from discussions during subsequent symposia and from further interaction of the editors with scholars and teachers at a summer seminar on post-Holocaust ethics and religion at the Center for Advanced Holocaust Studies of the United States Holocaust Memorial Museum. Thus the contributors address the subject of their teaching through a very wide lens focused on a common subject. They are all intensely involved in research and teaching and passionately committed to helping their students accept responsibility for building a more just, peaceful world—for *tikkun olam*. Their breadth of experience informs this book.

Introduction

The variety of approaches presented in this volume illustrates how profoundly educators are engaged by the moral dilemmas posed by the Holocaust. We find ourselves confronted by two additional factors: the inevitable influence of personal experience on our relating of historical events, and the impossibility of conveying both the experience and the memory of unimaginable horror through "normal" syntax and vocabulary.[39] These concerns demonstrate the search for language that is both personal and discipline-based, and they point to the struggle not only with the question of what to teach but also with the question of how to transmit course content, and to what ends. The methodological and substantive issues that confront those who teach the Holocaust compel us to deal with complexities more easily overlooked in the study of other historical periods. An example of these challenges is the need to consider the ethical and theological implications of the Holocaust, which forces us to focus on large and significant questions: What makes us feel at home, and from where do we derive our sense of right and wrong? Can our notions of right and wrong be universally persuasive? Indeed, philosophy is unavoidable in serious encounters with the Holocaust. How does one stand in the darkness and still go on? This is a difficult question for educators who guide their students in a confrontation with the "kingdom of night." It has been argued that an authentic encounter with the Holocaust leads to a shift in one's own morality and at the same time provokes silence, utter speechlessness; but teachers have lessons that they want students to learn. Is this didactic aim a betrayal of the material? How does one handle the dialectic of silence and derived ethical judgments? Teaching the Holocaust must invoke silence in the classroom, but silence is not enough—it must be broken.[40] Both teacher and student must use words to break the silence, even if the words lead back to silence once again. Confronting Holocaust material in its historical particularity offers many possibilities for nuanced learning.

Given this conceptual framework, this volume is divided into three sections. Part One, "Course Content," contains ten chapters, each written from a different perspective. The authors teach the Holocaust from the vantage points of architecture, art history, business ethics, composition, German studies, history, literature, religious studies, philosophy, and theology. The three chapters in Part Two, "The Process and Nature of Student Learning," are authored by writers whose main disciplines are philosophy, education, and theology. Part Three, "Progress and Process: Higher Education, Museums, and Memorials," relates the work of a humanities scholar, a university chaplain, two historians, philosophers, and museum founders and staff.

It is our hope that the chapters in this volume will stimulate, inform, guide, and challenge those who, like the contributors, labor in the university setting to teach the Holocaust and educate toward goodness.

NOTES

1. See John P. Fox, "Holocaust Education in Europe," in Walter Laquer and Judith Tydor Baumel, eds., *The Holocaust Encyclopedia* (New Haven: Yale University Press, 2001), 301–5.

2. Ibid., 301.

3. Ibid., 303–5.

4. Hanns-Fred Rathenow, "Teaching the Holocaust in Germany," in Ian Davies, ed., *Teaching the Holocaust: Educational Dimensions, Principles, and Practice* (London: Continuum, 2000), 68–69.

5. Ibid., 73–74.

6. Ibid., 75. Rathenow cites Theodor W. Adorno, "Erziehung nach Auschwitz," in Hans-Joachim Heydorn et al., eds., *Zum Bildungsbegriff der Gegenwart* (Frankfurt: Diesterweg, 1967), 111.

7. See also Fox, "Holocaust Education in Europe."

8. Ibid., 303–4.

9. Ibid., 305.

10. Samuel Totten, "Holocaust Education in the United States," in Walter Laquer and Judith Tydor Baumel, eds., *The Holocaust Encyclopedia* (New Haven: Yale University Press, 2001).

11. Ibid., 305.

12. Ibid., 306.

13. Cited in Margaret Crouch Weiss, "The Holocaust in Undergraduate Education: A Status Survey and Interpretative Synthesis of Topics, Textbooks, and Resources" (Ph.D. diss., Wilmington College, 1996), 4.

14. Ibid., 5.

15. Totten, "Holocaust Education in the United States," 307.

16. See, for example, the section on education in Michael Hayse, Didier Pollefeyt, G. Jan Colijn, and Marcia Sachs Littell, eds., *Hearing the Voices: Teaching the Holocaust to Future Generations* (Merion Station, Pa.: Merion Westfield Press International, 1999). The volume is the published proceedings of the 27th annual Scholars' Conference, held in March 1997 at Tampa, Florida.

17. See Margaret Crouch Weiss, "Holocaust Education in American Colleges: An Overview," in Michael Hayse, Didier Pollefeyt, G. Jan Colijn, and Marcia Sachs Littell, eds., *Hearing the Voices: Teaching the Holocaust to Future Generations* (Merion Station, Pa.: Merion Westfield Press International, 1999), 239–41. Weiss analyzed Holocaust course offerings in four-year baccalaureate degree–granting colleges and universities of the mid-Atlantic region. Of 273 schools surveyed, 26 percent offered one or more courses, with New York offering the most. Courses were listed or cross-listed in ten different departments; their syllabi revealed a dramatic lack of uniformity and topics, but the two texts most frequently listed were Elie Wiesel, *Night,* and Primo Levi, *Survival in Auschwitz.* See also Totten, "Holocaust Education in the United States," 310.

18. Weiss, "The Holocaust in Undergraduate Education," 4.

19. Ibid., 24.

20. Ibid., 4.

21. Sue Foster and Carrie Mercier, "The Jewish Background and the Religious Dimension," in Ian Davies, ed., *Teaching the Holocaust: Educational Dimensions, Principles, and Practice* (London: Continuum, 2000), 25.

22. Ian Gregory, "The Holocaust: Some Reflections and Issues," in Ian Davies, ed., *Teaching the Holocaust: Educational Dimensions, Principles, and Practice* (London: Continuum, 2000), 37.

23. Krystyna Olesky, "The Education Centre at the Auschwitz Birkenau Memorial and Museum," in Ian Davies, ed., *Teaching the Holocaust: Educational Dimensions, Principles, and Practice* (London: Continuum, 2000), 78–79.

24. Gregory, "The Holocaust," 38.

25. Ibid., 45.

26. Ibid., 40.

27. Ibid.

28. Ibid.

29. Ibid., 45.

30. Ibid., 38.

31. Ian Gregory, "Teaching about the Holocaust: Perplexities, Issues, and Suggestions," in Ian Davies, ed., *Teaching the Holocaust: Educational Dimensions, Principles, and Practice* (London: Continuum, 2000), 49–50.

32. Ibid., 51–52.

33. Ibid., xx.

34. Ibid., 52–53.

35. Ibid., 56. Gregory is citing Lawrence Langer, "The Writer and the Holocaust Experience," in Henry Friedlander and Sybil Milton, eds., *The Holocaust: Ideology, Bureaucracy, and Genocide* (Millwood, N.Y.: Kraus International Publications, 1980), 310.

36. See Eva Fried, ed., *Beyond the "Never Agains"* (Stockholm, Sweden: Aug. 2005), 125. The volume is the published report of the Task Force for International Cooperation on Holocaust Education, Remembrance and Research.

37. Ibid., 149.

38. Ibid., 162.

39. For further discussion, see Ziva Amishai-Maisels, "The Visual Arts as an Aid for Teaching About the Holocaust," in Gideon Shimoni, ed., *The Holocaust in University Teaching* (New York: Pergamon Press, 1991), 4.

40. John Roth, "Ethics after the Holocaust: Key Issues for Philosophy and Religion," seminar presented at the Center for Advanced Holocaust Studies, United States Holocaust Memorial Museum, Washington, D.C., July 2001.

PART ONE

COURSE CONTENT

The broad, almost generic term "Holocaust course" refers to an instructional offering that may fulfill one or more functions. It may focus entirely on the Holocaust. It may serve as a touchstone in a larger program of genocide studies. It may be a unit within a wider curriculum that includes art, literature, ethics, history, religious studies, jurisprudence, philosophy, theology, film studies, Jewish studies, German studies, composition, urban studies, or architecture. Or it may constitute one of the main threads of an interdisciplinary course. Because the Holocaust was a political, cultural, social, ethical, and theological upheaval, the very fact of its being, in the opinion of the contributors to this book, has exerted a profound influence on our knowledge base since the middle of the twentieth century. Sensitive scholars have reflected on their individual fields of study to assess the impact of the Holocaust on their disciplines.

The extent of the Holocaust's reach into virtually all disciplines in the humanities, the arts, and the social sciences is not surprising in light of the fact that the Nazi regime controlled nearly every facet of life in the countries it occupied; it was, as all totalitarian governments aim to be, pervasive. The government reached into family life in the most basic sense, regulating birth, life, and death. While war obviously affects the civilian populations it involves—and increasingly so since World War II—Hitler's unrealistic and unthinkable goals, coupled with his maniacal anti-semitism, imposed a catastrophe that afflicted Germans as well as non-Germans, perpetrators as well as victims, and even bystanders. Virtue was redefined. Literature and the other arts became instruments of the state. Nazism morphed into a religion. History was conveniently adjusted to glorify Hitler and the Third Reich. Most of all, language was perverted to reflect Hitler's vision and version of reality. Life in its most quotidian details changed.

As a result, faculty in the humanities, the social sciences, and the visual and performing arts[1] have had reason to reconsider the content of the courses they teach, especially if their syllabi cover the twentieth century. For example, to teach twentieth-century history of the Western world and not attend to the Holocaust is to distort that history. However, inclusion of or emphasis on Holocaust content is not without controversy, nor, as the writers of this section imply, is it a neutral, benign endeavor. Moreover, faculty are also faced with the question of "handling" content that may challenge their students' beliefs and will certainly challenge their complacency.

Stephen Feinstein, in chapter 1, reminds us of the impact of atrocity on the arts. He raises issues of representation, memory, and imagination. His discussion of five contemporary artists and their responses to the Holocaust presents perspectives that we seldom use in the classroom. Here, however, his clear explanations of artistic interpretation suggest ways to incorporate the visual arts into our courses without compromising our disciplines, and his work reinforces an argument made by Ziva Amishai-Maisels: that the visual arts, as a tool and a resource, are underused in teaching about the Holocaust.

In chapter 2, Rachel Rapperport Munn guides us into areas not yet explored in any depth. She describes the representation of memory in the so-called built environment. We travel with her through Berlin as she translates events into places. She brings narrative to urban sites and exposes the Nazis' use of space and materials to facilitate murder and aggrandize the state.

Beth Hawkins Benedix, in chapter 3, shows us how to demonstrate the Nazis' intentions by analyzing their language. "Words have consequences," she reminds us, and they are weapons. She shows how the Nazis used language carefully to implement the Final Solution, and how survivors use language explicitly to represent their experiences and implicitly to convey their feelings. Moreover, we learn how words, in both memoir and fiction, have limits.

In a unique course on business ethics, Donald Felipe explores the moral choices that faced individuals and corporations in the Nazi era (chapter 4). Rooting his course in history, survivors' memoirs, and the film *Conspiracy* (a re-creation of the Wannsee Conference), Felipe asks his students to think like the German businessmen of that period and to explain their choices and motives for choosing one action over another. He models the assignments by sharing his responses with students in the form of a journal.

In her course on the Holocaust and ethics, discussed in chapter 5, Tam Parker explores the ethical dilemmas and challenges facing teacher and students alike. In connection with presenting and then judging the narratives of victims and perpetrators, she raises issues of moral responsibility, moral responses, and moral relativism. Citing a response by one student, Parker deconstructs the "response of no response" and its "moral failing." She develops assignments to encourage her students to respond morally to injustice and indifference.

Paul A. Levine, in chapter 6, defends his argument that teaching the history of the Holocaust is the basis of all further study of the subject. His demands for particularity and accurate chronology, as well as for a healthy respect for the complexity of the subject, are fundamental in preparing students to learn and teach Holocaust history. Levine cautions us that "genuine emotional pain" is part of the process of teaching and learning about this "horrible chapter of human history." (Indeed, as Marla Morris has cautioned elsewhere, studying the Holocaust is "difficult knowledge."[2])

"You cannot teach the Holocaust without teaching something about life and meaning," says David Patterson in his philosophical inquiry into the epistemological, religious, and, hence, ultimate meaning of the Holocaust (chapter 7). Patterson argues that the metadisciplinary nature of the Holocaust commands us to pay close attention to the details, nuances, and spiritual dimensions of survival and nonsurvival. As a consequence of knowing and witnessing, he goes on to say, we oblige ourselves to try to understand the profound impact of the Nazis on the values derived from a belief in God and humankind; thus do we accept our responsibility for one another.

Timothy A. Bennett and Rochelle L. Millen, colleagues at a Lutheran university, describe in chapter 8 the course they developed on Germans and Jews, a course that interrogates easy and familiar stereotyping. They guide students into the tensions of asking discomfiting questions about their religious and cultural traditions, and they simultaneously examine the historical contexts that have shaped the actions of individuals and of nation-states. They probe historical, literary, and religious texts to understand the relationships among the three, and hence the influences on the German people of the Nazi period.

In chapter 9, David R. Blumenthal outlines his responsibility as a teacher of the Holocaust to examine the complexity of the catastrophe and to inculcate the habit of doing Good. Through discussions of the historical, sociological, theological, and political aspects of the Holocaust, Blumenthal challenges "ethically neutral" or "objective" responses to injustice, apathy, or other types of oppression. One of the legacies of the Holocaust, he proclaims, is that social action is required of us all.

In his religion, ethics, and Holocaust courses, Didier Pollefeyt asserts that the Holocaust was, at bottom, the result of people turning their faces away from the Other. The Holocaust as a subject, he explains in chapter 10, breaks disciplinary boundaries and expands across categories of knowing. For example, the study of the Holocaust demands knowledge of Jewish history and of the history of the Third Reich. Pollefeyt opens his students' minds to the complex ambiguities involved in determining and analyzing the influences on the Holocaust of theology, history, religious practice, and modernity, and of the ideological, political, and social contexts that provided the background and foreground for this atrocity.

We might well read this entire section on course content as an injunction to teach and act in a manner consistent with the cautionary message that there is no tolerance for moral neutrality with regard to the Holocaust and, further, that there appears to be no subject in the humanities or the social sciences where the impact of this cataclysmic event has not been felt.

NOTES

1. See Ziva Amishai-Maisels, "The Visual Arts as an Aid for Teaching about the Holocaust," in Gideon Shimoni, ed., *The Holocaust in University Teaching* (New York: Pergamon Press, 1991), 1.

2. Marla Morris, *Curriculum and the Holocaust: Competing Sites of Memory and Representation* (Mahwah, N.J.: Lawrence Erlbaum Associates, 2001), 6. Morris cites Deborah Britzman, the source of the quoted phrase.

Uses of the Arts in the Classroom

An Unexpected Alternative

STEPHEN FEINSTEIN

> I did not realize it then, but through art, we might
> have understood why.—Edith Hahn Beer, *The Nazi*
> *Officer's Wife* (New York: Harper Collins, 1999), 127

The use of documentary film, photographs, and even fictionalized films or mixed fiction-and-nonfiction films is often taken for granted as being useful in the classroom or in other venues for teaching about the Holocaust.[1] There is another area of visualization within Holocaust pedagogy that has been recognized in certain contexts but also neglected. That area is the plastic arts—painting, sculpture, and memorials. In the future, all these forms of representation may become increasingly significant for creating an understanding of the Shoah as well as for conveying the story to a future era, when the story will have become routinized. First, as we move away from historical events, even those of momentous and traumatic nature like the Holocaust, the tendency of historical texts is to narrow the scope of the story. The condensation of historical epochs that is found in standardized texts is sometimes disquieting by reason of what is left out. Second, memories of certain big events are often known to us through the visual, particularly paintings, bas-reliefs, and friezes on public monuments.[2] One might refer, for example, to the major events of Roman or early modern history or in the tradition of mythology, all of which have been well represented by artists: the Arch of Titus (81 C.E.), in Rome, contains the best-known image of the Romans carrying away the ritual objects from the Second Temple in Jerusalem in the aftermath of the Jewish War (66–70 C.E.).[3] Picasso's *Guernica* (1937), the most heralded painting of the twentieth century, is better known than the chronology of the events associated with the destruction of the Basque town by the German Luftwaffe on April 26, 1937, during the Spanish Civil War. Here, art might be said to have triumphed over narrative: the painting has become the narrative and the memory as well. With respect to American history, the same may be said of Ben Shahn's *The Passion of Sacco and Vanzetti* (1931–32), which became not only a comment on the executions of two convicted anarchists but also a terse commentary on the American judicial system.

Most scholars are familiar with the often quoted comment of the philosopher and literary critic Theodor Adorno, who saw writing lyric poetry after Auschwitz as "barbaric."[4] Although he later reversed this view, his remarks about lyric poetry have been used time and time again to refer to the visual arts and to suggest the impossibility of representation. The quest for writers and artists alike has been for a new language, one with new symbols and new metaphors. Primo Levi understood this well when he was writing about his own experiences: "Daily language is for the description of daily experience, but here is another world, here one would need a language 'of the other world.'"[5] Art is also a form of memory that treads on sacred soil: "In the Jewish tradition, death is a private, intimate matter, and we are forbidden to transform it into a spectacle. If that is true for an individual, it is six million times more true for one of the largest communities of the dead in history."[6] Rebecca Abrams, commenting on David Edgar's play *Albert Speer,* is quite critical of the play's ending, which depicts Speer alone on the stage protesting his innocence while a film showing British soldiers at Bergen-Belsen, pushing corpses into mass graves, is projected over him. Abrams asks of this scene, "Is it acceptable or necessary or useful to exploit horror in this way? Is there something morally indecent about using such grotesque, quasi-pornographic images to twist a certain reaction out of the audience?"[7] A recent play and film by Tim Blake Nelson, *The Grey Zone,* raises the same questions in attempting to deal with the ethical issues surround-

ing the twelfth Sonderkommando at Birkenau and its rebellion of
October 7, 1944.

Thus an important question that runs through art related to the Holocaust is the scope of interpretation and the issue of the necessity of "realism." Primo Levi discussed the need for precise narratives in contrast to
more interpretative ones: "Emphatically renouncing any regulative, pro-
hibitive or punitive claim, I would like to add that in my opinion one
should not write in an obscure manner, because a piece of writing has
all the more value and all the more hope of diffusion and permanence,
the better it is understood and the less it lends itself to equivocal interpretation."[8] Levi was also concerned about excesses in visualization, especially in film. According to Myriam Anissimov, he was "deeply shocked"
by Liliana Cavani's *The Night Porter,* to which he responded, "Please,
you film producers, leave the women of the camps alone. . . . They were
not sexy actresses; people suffered there, but in silence; and the women
were not beautiful, on the contrary they aroused an infinite compassion, like defenceless animals."[9] However, films like *The Night Porter*
and plays that may be described as "on the edge" continue to be made,
and they even reveal a bit of unearthed truth. Therefore, the question
for the artist or filmmaker focuses on the ethics of a particular form of
representation. On the question of poetic representation, which
approaches the issue of the visual arts, especially with respect to scope
of interpretation, Levi wrote:

> I am a man who has little belief in poetry, yet goes in for it. There is cer-
> tainly a reason. For instance, when my verses appear in *La Stampa*'s "La
> Terza Pagina" I receive letters that express agreement or disapproval. When
> I publish short stories, the reactions are less sharp. I have the impression
> that poetry in general has become a vector of human contact. Adorno
> wrote that after Auschwitz there could be no more poetry, but my hope
> has been just the opposite. In 1945–46 it seemed to me that poetry would
> be better suited than prose to explain what was weighing inside me. When
> I say poetry, I have nothing lyrical in mind. In those days, I would have
> reformulated Adorno's remark like this: After Auschwitz, there can be no
> more poetry, except about Auschwitz.[10]

If one can write poetry and make films about Auschwitz, one can also produce paintings depicting it. However, one must be clear that representation is not re-creation; and, like a monograph, one painting, even a series of paintings, cannot tell the whole story. Nor should one try to do so, as demonstrated by several attempts at "comprehensive" projects that have been disappointingly simplistic and often misdirected.[11] A formulation that should be accepted, therefore, seems to be that art and public monuments (another form of art, although governed by conceptual principles specifically related to commissions and public space) can be important and powerful tools for teaching about the Holocaust.[12]

HOLOCAUST ART: THE ISSUES

Art is important on several levels. To begin with, the idea of unrepresentability must be challenged. At the same time, the Holocaust, like other major issues or earth-shattering events, must be placed in a framework of learning. The use and misuse of art was pervasive during the Third Reich. Bodily and artistic aesthetics, for example, are concepts that run through the Nazi regime, and issues of eugenics and racism were often expressed in art. Hitler himself aspired to become an artist but failed admission to art school. In *Mein Kampf,* his 1925 plan for himself and the world, Hitler denounced modernism, as well as abstract and "Dadaist" art, as affronts to civilization. His artistic tastes can be judged by his favorite works of art, which were realistic military paintings. Paintings depicting six hundred such heroic themes were hung for the Great German Art Exhibition, which opened in Munich on July 18, 1937. A day later, the first of many "Degenerate Art" (*Entartete Kunst*) shows was opened just across from the Great German Art Exhibition. These shows, which may have drawn the largest crowds in museum history, juxtaposed "degenerate" art influenced by "the Jews" with the Aryan ideal as expressed in painting and sculpture. Many important avant-garde works from the Weimar period were destroyed as part of Hitler's war on culture. The campaign continued and later focused on "degenerate music," also called "Afro-Judaic" music, and was particularly linked to the jazz motifs of Benny Goodman and Louis Armstrong. A good deal of the Nazi attack on culture might be called a war against imagination, foreshadowing the genocide that was to take place on a larger scale.[13]

The attempt by artists to grapple with the Holocaust is nothing new. It is a movement that was visible during Hitler's rise and concentration of power, and it was continued during World War II by artists in camps or in hiding. In the past sixty years, artists have produced a vast number of visual works that deal with Nazism and with what became known as the Holocaust—a flow of work that seems unabated, even in the first years of the twenty-first century. If there is such a vast number of working artists and available visual works, it seems reasonable to assume that some of this production will become a visual resource for remembrance and teaching. Marc Chagall's *White Crucifixion,* a response to the German Kristallnacht ("night of broken glass") in 1938, remains iconic among many paintings that represent Jewish suffering before 1939. Unlike artists who merely depicted suffering, on many occasions Chagall used the theme of a crucified "Jewish" Jesus set against vignettes of Jewish persecution that unfolded in the Nazi era. Why did Chagall have such an obsession with the crucifixion motif? The art historian Franz Meyer explains that Christ became a universal symbol for Chagall by virtue of having more than one meaning: "He is the Jewish martyr and the Jewish prophet; he is the 'revolutionary' who shares man's fate to the bitter end. He is creative man who pays for every prize with pain. He is also and always simply man in his loneliness and isolation."[14] Meyer, analyzing *Yellow Crucifixion*—a 1943 painting by Chagall that includes an image of the sinking of the *SS Struma,* a ship of immigrants torpedoed in the Black Sea—suggests that a mystical interpretation is in order, one stemming from Chagall's emphasis on mystical themes, which he talked about frequently in 1943:

> In this way we can follow, through the horrors of war, a process that involves man and nature: the transition from night to day, from covert to overt, from the depths of the psyche to the fulfillment of spirit. Thus the picture celebrates the rebirth of life, in the vegetative and spiritual sense, the ever recurrent victory over death. The dreadful events on earth—murder and persecution, torture and rape—are part of a general and far more vital process.[15]

The Lithuanian-born American artist Ben Shahn also produced strong responses to the persecution of Jews and others during World War II. While working for the U.S. Office of War Information, Shahn created a series of famous posters dealing with the destruction of the Czech village Lidice and the occupation of France. As the war ended, he painted scenes that evoked metaphors of destroyed Europe, dead children, and lamentation over what came to be known as the Holocaust. He returned to the theme of the Warsaw Ghetto uprising several times, as if he was attempting both to work through the past and to place the destruction of the Jews into some historical context. For example, *Warsaw,* a serigraph from 1963, has as a central image a man with his head in his hands, as if in lamentation. However, his clenched fists also suggest resistance. Underneath the image is the full text of "Elah Eskerah," a prayer from the Yom Kippur martyrology service that was written in the Middle Ages to lament the murders of ten rabbis who were killed by order of the Roman emperor Hadrian. Thus the juxtaposition of Nazi atrocities with Roman revenge seems to attempt both linkage and context. Within the rabbinic tradition, the prayer also has a relationship to the story of Joseph sold into slavery by his brothers, and to their guilt, presumably carried forward to future generations. Chagall and Shahn are both artists whose works, reaching as far back as the Hebrew Bible and the New Testament as sources for understanding, are easily accessible and useful for integrating visual art into the narrative text of classroom learning.

Non-Jewish as well as Jewish artists were interned in concentration camps. Some in both groups survived and others were killed, but survivors in both groups produced artistic legacies of their victimization, and those who were Jews have provided visions of how Jews saw their diminishing horizon. For example, Felix Nussbaum's self-portraits from 1943 and 1944, painted after his escape from French camps and before his ultimate deportation to Auschwitz, reveal isolation, fear, contempt, and hopelessness as his last works become surrealistic landscapes of a skeleton orchestra amid a wasteland (*The Dance of Death,* 1944). Even more complex is Charlotte Salomon's *Life or Theatre?*[16] This work is a series of more than one thousand gouaches, documenting personal history, feminine concerns, and family problems and set in the landscape of declining German-Jewish fortunes as Nazism came to power. In his discourse about this work,

Ernst van Alphen correctly indicates that there has been more interest in Salomon because of these paintings' framework of Jewish history than because of their purely aesthetic qualities. To limit one's encounter with Salomon to only the historical or the aesthetic sphere is, according to van Alphen, "to profoundly misread the work." The narrative aspect of the work has hitherto been relatively inaccessible because of the problems in presenting art as a diary. Van Alphen also makes the important point that Salomon's "life story in art seems to tell the story of the impossibility of the female artist." Death is the other powerful force that runs through *Life or Theater?* That is, death not only hovers over Charlotte Salomon's family history and the conditions of all European Jews but also becomes the point of departure for artistic creativity.[17]

An immediate and strong postwar response to the Holocaust appeared from the palettes of many important artists. Rico LeBrun, for example, insisted that the Holocaust was "a subject that no serious artist could neglect."[18] The American painter Leonard Baskin, LeBrun's colleague and friend, described LeBrun's approach to the subject as confronting "the mind-curdling reality of the least human of human endeavors," adding that "in paintings and drawings of dissolution, dismemberment and incineration he is saying, all is not vanity, all is horror."[19] After 1950, the issue of the Holocaust in art was not avoided altogether, but it appeared infrequently except in the realm of public memorials, principally at the sites of destruction in Europe. Many artists who were survivors stayed in their native countries; for example, Jozef Szajna, a Polish Catholic, and Janusz Stern, a Polish Jew, focused much of their work on memories of atrocity and destruction linked to the war. The Argentine-born artist Mauricio Lasansky shocked New York audiences at the Whitney Museum in 1965 with his horror-laden series *The Nazi Drawings.* Lasansky, who lived in Iowa but understood fascism because of his earlier life in Argentina, was impelled to do this exceptional series of paintings and collages after reading about the 1964 Frankfurt trial of the Auschwitz SS. Many other artists, however, responded in very much the same way as those survivors who decided against talking about the event. Nevertheless, from the 1970s through the beginning of the first decade of the twentieth-first century, literally hundreds of artists have grappled with the difficulties of art after such a monstrous period of destruction.

The use of art is a critical question that is much less concerned with the historical narrative as we know it than with how the Holocaust will be remembered one hundred years hence. Both memory and forgetting will influence remembrance. Van Alphen, for example, notes that his responses to learning about this subject during his youth in Holland "almost dulled" him because a predictable empathy for the victims was expected of him by his teachers. Narratives, to him, seemed "hypocritical" because of the juxtaposition of the horror of mass death with stories of national heroism. Van Alphen felt that the Holocaust did not make sense in the context of World War II as it was explained, and it was certainly devoid of the heroic masculinity related as part of the national story in Holland. But when he became "hooked" on the Holocaust, it was through representations in the realm of the visual rather than in the historical or literary.[20] His monograph *Caught by History* suggests that the Holocaust will be fully integrated into society not through being taught at every place and on every occasion by way of narrative but rather through art and what he calls "Holocaust effects" and an "indexical language."[21]

A critical aspect of the issue of art and the Holocaust is that of the permanence of artistic materials. In reality, nothing about the Holocaust itself seems permanent except the extent of the Jewish absence and the futile attempts to understand the behavior of the perpetrators. Documents decay, photos fade, film crumbles, and videotape can deteriorate (although newer DVD technologies are said to be more lasting), just as memory itself and written history go through alterations. With art, styles of representation always change, and in this respect the visual arts may be the most unstable and also the most challenging of forms of memory. Another concern related to permanence is that every exhibition has its birth and its death, with a five-year life expectancy for a traveling exhibition. The great paintings of the masters may be hung as classics in museum galleries; lesser works rarely endure in this way.

Visual art has been the most challenging medium for representing the Holocaust, and the challenges seem particularly strong for viewers who were not "there." Therefore, relatively easy access to Holocaust art can raise the questions of why an artist creates work about the Holocaust and what dangers may be inherent in dealing with the subject. Virtually every artist who works with a Holocaust theme has a story to tell; but Valerie Jacober

Furth, for example, a New York artist and Holocaust survivor, was told by her art instructor in an M.F.A. program that she "shouldn't be doing painting like that." According to Arie Galles, his dealers at his New York gallery asked him "what they were supposed to do with works on the Holocaust," since, they said, the purpose of the gallery was to sell art, not simply display art about a controversial subject. Yet one sees a certain logic in using the medium of painting with respect to the Holocaust. One reason is the artist's need to witness or affirm the event by repetition of the Holocaust theme in visual art. Another reason is what might be called "working through the past" in the only way the artist knows—the visual. A third possible reason is the sense that art can provide some insights, especially when combined with the mythic and poetic visions that escape the historian. For those who have worked in a theological context, the reasons may include the artist's need to understand how the horror of the Holocaust relates to the broad body of Christian art (which deals with a horrible yet redemptive subject) as well as to the Judaic concept of *tikkun olam,* repair of the world in the aftermath of Shoah. The survivor artist Samuel Bak explains this idea as follows:

> Sometimes the very word *Tikkun,* weary with the way the world goes, sinks into disrepair; its Hebrew letters fall apart. My small series of *Tikkun* paintings tries to put them back together. As I painted these works, I thought they were very far from the cubist adventure. But looking now with fresh eyes, I see that we had much in common after all. Our world is composed of broken thing—things with bruises, cracks and missing parts—and we must learn to live among them. Of course people, too, can be broken—in body or in spirit, or both. One may even attempt to repair the soul. I have lived for many years among victims of the Shoah, broken individuals and their recomposed families. A continuing effort to mend is what made our lives possible.[22]

STRATEGIES FOR INCORPORATING ART INTO COLLEGE COURSES

There are relatively easy ways of integrating art into a curriculum in Holocaust studies. However, finding sources adaptable to the classroom

which depicts, in large part, the arrival of Hungarian Jews on the ramp at Auschwitz-Birkenau during 1944. A third such source is the legendary prewar shtetl and city photos of Roman Vishniac,[28] which occasionally shade into artistic works as reminders of a lost world. Such repetition goes to the heart of the problem of Holocaust imagery: it is sometimes too familiar.

It is important yet difficult to distinguish great, even good, art from the mundane. The answer here must be subjective, but repetition of the same symbols by many artists probably reveals a simplistic reading of the complexity of the Holocaust as a subject. The best art seems to revert to complex visual idioms that are accessible and comparable within the traditions of Western painting. Thus Samuel Bak uses theological images as well as references to such well-known European painters as Michelangelo, Albrecht Dürer, Andrea Mantegna, Max Ernst, René Magritte, Hieronymus Bosch, and Joan Miró.

SOME IMPORTANT CONTEMPORARY ARTISTS

A glance at the work of five artists—Samuel Bak, Ron B. Kitaj, Alice Lok Cahana, Anselm Kiefer, and Christian Boltanski—provides a starting point for incorporating art into a course on Holocaust representation. Bak's entire postwar life has been involved with difficult memories of the Holocaust. He survived the ghetto in Vilna, but his vision of the post-Holocaust world is one of disturbance—and, for many, it is indeed disturbing. As early as 1974, Jean Aberbach called Bak a "guardian of human conscience"[29] for not permitting the memory of the Shoah to disappear from common memory. Bak's *Self-Portrait* (1995–96) is, in a way, the signature piece for understanding his own biography, his worldview, and the images of the Holocaust that return to him constantly.

The major focus of his oeuvre is a serious attempt to deal with his survival and to tell the story. His work may be likened to a healing art or may be seen as reflective of the deep tragedy and powerlessness of ghetto existence. *The Family* (1974), perhaps the strongest painting of this period, does not show "the family of man" as one, with unity of purpose, but rather as a group of dysfunctional figures, victims, and onlookers. Some have turned into statues, set against the backdrop of a burning city and

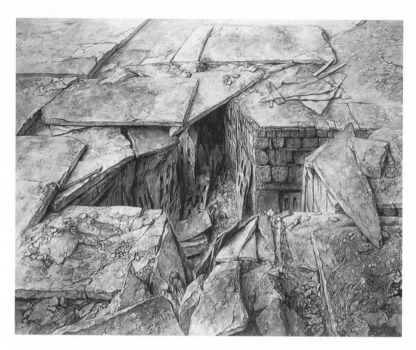

Samuel Bak, *The Ghetto of Jewish History,* 1976. Oil on canvas, 52 × 48 in. From the series *Landscapes of the Jewish Experience.* Pucker Gallery, Boston, Massachusetts; reproduced by permission of the artist.

a long row of survivors. In this monumental painting, the background sky is darkened with smoke. The faces depicted, according to the artist, were guided by memory. Some are two-dimensional, while others are incomplete monuments. The dominant figure is the artist's blind great-grandfather. He and the rest of the family lived

> in their pre-war paradise, quite eyeless as to the fate that awaited them [and] are surrounded by those who were destined to become targets for captivity, pain and extinction. They are all there in various degrees of "alive-ness." Hiding among the great figures of the past are others in dirty army fatigues, who seem doomed to live in a state of eternal alert.[30]

Bak's art may be said to be archival in that he returns to themes on a repetitive basis to work out his understanding of the past. The themes are easy to distinguish visibly but perhaps more difficult to decipher. These themes include the creation of the human being by a present God, the absence of God during the Shoah, the destruction and isolation of the Jewish people and Jewish life, the possibility of renewal when the tree has been cut at the roots, chess and pears as metaphors, and the conflict between technology with a progressive aim and humanity's misuse of it. Bak's paintings, particularly a commissioned series of immense works titled *Landscapes of Jewish Experience*,[31] are ideal in the classroom, not only for their mysterious themes but also for their absence of answers.

The American-born artist Ron Kitaj (R. B. Kitaj) has made the Holocaust and his own theory of representational art ("Diasporism") the focal points for a good deal of his painting, which has brought much acclaim, possibly because the Holocaust themes are generally obscure in his paintings. He has written, "I, who was warm and safe in America, can't keep away from some oblique engagement with what happened all those years. I believe something awful will happen again."[32] Kitaj seems to be asking whether a painting should carry within it the same power as theological discourse or ethical debate. A cursory viewing of his own paintings suggests that this may indeed be the case because the artist refuses to separate Jewish identity from antisemitism.[33] But his Diasporism is an artistic theory that affects not just Jews but others as well. Kitaj came face to face with this issue during the 1980s and developed a response in his book *The First Diasporist Manifesto*.[34] He comments that the *Manifesto* "was meant as a summing up of my erratic Jewish obsessions, but I came to regret its hasty publication" because it appeared unfinished.[35] Kitaj's concept—that a "diasporist" lives in two societies at once—places the Jew conceptually, after the Holocaust, in perhaps not just two but three places: where he is, where he once was (Jerusalem, and places in the Diaspora), and where he might have been (Auschwitz). A series of descriptive words and phrases has emerged—absence of specific place, rootlessness, dislocation, ambiguity—that can describe Kitaj's painting and thus Diasporism itself. Kitaj has suggested, appropriately enough, that because Jews are the Diaspora people par excellence, "the threatened condition of the Jews witnesses the condition of our wider world. It is a radical witness."[36] Diasporism is neither melancholia nor lamentation; it has the potential to be uplifting. Diasporist painting is contradictory, inconsistent, tense, historical, mythological, and homeless, and it is essentially Western because it is a product of Jews living in the West. It is also assim-

Ron B. Kitaj, *If Not, Not,* 1975-76. Oil on canvas, 60 × 60 in. Scottish National Gallery of Modern Art, Edinburgh; reproduced by permission of the artist.

ilationist and modernist. Above all, for Kitaj, the style is defined in a most significant way by the events of the Holocaust.

During 1975–76, Kitaj painted what may be his most significant painting, *If Not, Not,* a large oil on canvas. Based partially on T. S. Eliot's poem "The Waste Land" and Joseph Conrad's novel *Heart of Darkness,* it evokes the terrain depicted in Eliot's poem as the antechamber of hell, and passages regarding death by water as allusions to the Jews. The landscape depicted in this work is the epitome of Diaspora space, as it is not the Jews' own land. At the top of Kitaj's painting is an image of the entrance and SS barracks at Auschwitz-Birkenau, with a chimney in the foreground, abstract and almost figurative forms at the left that might represent people, and a fire-orange sky and smoke to the right. That Auschwitz dominates the painting is a reflection of the artist's perception of its importance to Judaism and to the world as a whole. Kitaj has said of the painting that it is "a piece of rhythmical grumbling . . . but the grouse here has to do with what Winston Churchill called 'the greatest and most horrible crime committed in the whole history of the world' . . . the murder of the Jews."[37] Many of Kitaj's other works have indirect references to the Holocaust, and these have to be decoded by the viewer.

Alice Lok Cahana is a native of Sarvar, Hungary, and was deported to Auschwitz during the late summer of 1944. She survived Auschwitz, Guben, and Bergen Belsen.[38] Cahana came from a religious family, and her abstract painting and mixed-media works reflect themes of a religious nature as well as her attempt to convey the blackness of deportation and victimization at Auschwitz. A redemptive feature of her oeuvre is a series of paintings that pay homage to Swedish diplomat Raoul Wallenberg, who was responsible for her father's survival in Budapest.

For Jews deeply imbued with faith in God, the concept of the spiritual may have strong links to the belief in the proximity of the Jews to God and in the notion that the Jews represent God's stake in the world. Therefore, in the most adverse circumstances, a Jew who is observant must remember the grandeur of creation even if it is juxtaposed against human free will—which, admittedly, God cannot control. Cahana's paintings, which originally followed what one might suggest is allegiance to the second commandment (forbidding images of God) and were abstract color fields, later became more expressionist with the use of collage. Generally, her canvases are autobiographical, using such items as a school photograph and, occasionally, some photos from the broader assemblage of recognizable images from either German or allied sources.

One of Cahana's most interesting paintings is *Sabbath in Auschwitz*, based on her memory of a Friday evening when her sister Edith commemorated the Sabbath with other women in a latrine. The focus on Shabbat, the Jewish Sabbath, provides what may be termed a feminine perspective on Holocaust representation because the Sabbath is usually ushered in by the women in the family through the lighting of candles. *Sabbath in Auschwitz,* a large acrylic work conceived as a tablecloth with

Alice Lok Cahana, *Shabat in Auschwitz*, Acrylic on canvas. 42 × 85 in.
Collection of the Skirball Museum of Art, Los Angeles; reproduced by permission of the artist.

formal edges and colored in a green-tinted white, recalls not only the events in the hellish situation of Birkenau but also the festive Sabbaths of Cahana's home in Sarvar. In this painting, the artist also evokes another key Jewish festival, Passover. In the context of Auschwitz, Passover—the universal commemoration of the liberation of the Jews from Egyptian bondage, through the miraculous intervention of God—becomes a poignant source of memory of both the intervening and the absent God. While the artist's focus is indeed the Sabbath and the memory of creation, this work also unleashes some probing and difficult questions about prayer during and after Auschwitz.

The images in this painting suggest ghostlike apparitions that fail to disappear with time. In Jewish worship, the Sabbath is seen as a "queen" ushering in the day of rest. The word *Shabbat* is inscribed in Hebrew ("SHIN/BETH/THET") on the bottom right, in red, as if written in blood and perhaps with an unsteady hand. Diagonally to the left in the upper part of the painting is a mutilated red swastika, which in its destruction appears as if it is being reformed into the Hebrew letter *shin,* the letter of God, hence affirming for the believer God's presence and power in Auschwitz. The whiteness of the canvas not only serves as a transparent curtain across these memories but also suggests the absence of time during the Holocaust. Within the painting, Cahana has placed four distinct torn pages from Hebraic texts, but these contain questions from the Passover Haggadah rather than excerpts from the Sabbath liturgy. While both the Sabbath and Passover are occasions for remembrance, Sabbath memory is related to remembrance of the creation and the goodness of it, whereas Passover memory is about the freedom of the Jews from Egyptian bondage through intercession of the deity. The Sabbath prayer over the wine, however, also contains the memory of the intercessional God who delivered the Israelites from bondage. Thus the Sabbath and Passover are interrelated. In the context of Auschwitz, the Passover question ("Why is this night different from all other nights?") is related to the positive memory of being able to commemorate the Sabbath, even in horrible circumstances where even the existence of God is questioned.

By the 1980s, the German artist Anselm Kiefer had become known for his immense paintings that represent a working through of the past by a child of perpetrators. His early works, beginning in the late 1960s, examined Nazism, the romanticized myths of German history, and the absence of the Jews. There is no doubt that Kiefer, like many other Germans, was influenced by Paul Celan's famous poem "Todesfugue," which established the metaphor of the German woman, Margarite, living in the home of the Jewish woman Shulamite, who becomes ash during the Holocaust. Because the ashes of the people of Israel fall on German soil, the physical absence of the Jews does not lead to loss of the memory of this destroyed people.

Kiefer's interest in this subject led to a series of paintings that may be linked to the tradition of alchemy, the second commandment's injunction against representation, and the history of the Jewish victims. Lisa Saltzman suggests that Kiefer's large paintings from the late 1970s and the early 1980s, such as *Iconoclastic Controversy* (1977, 1980) and *Aaron* (1984–85), represent a discourse on the problems of representing the Holocaust. According to Saltzman, "the prohibition on image making" also "points to the political uses and abuses of both representation and iconoclasm."[39] Kiefer went on to produce many paintings with themes derived from the Kabbalah: *Lilith; The Daughters of Lilith; Sefiroth; Emanation; Zim Zum;* and *Merkabah.* In addition, he produced a 1990 artist's book titled *The Heavenly Places: Merkabah.* Each of Kiefer's titles reflects an issue or approach to texts found in the Kabbalah. Although Kiefer's work is seen as somewhat off-base by some, he has had several important installations that must be seen in the context of his earlier ruminations about the German past. *The Breaking of Vessels* (1990), a large (17 feet high and 36 feet long) conceptual sculpture of iron, lead, copper, wire, glass, charcoal, and aquatec is set in a room at the St. Louis Museum of Art. It draws its inspiration from the Kabbalistic conceptualization of creation and *shivrat hakelim,* the breaking of vessels. On the simplest level, the sculpture can be read as a representation of Kristallnacht. On a deeper level, one asks whether humanity can read and learn, comprehend, and contain the evil that has spilled out to consume the Jews of Europe. Do Kiefer's representations suggest a way to find understanding, repentance, and closure regarding the Holocaust? In the most formal sense, Kiefer is also suggesting that nonfigurative, hence spiritual, vision is the best way to comprehend the Holocaust. Cahana and Kiefer can both be viewed as artists who have created midrashic visual texts that link traditional theological issues to an attempt to understand the Holocaust.

An exceptional presence in the world of installation art is a Parisian, Christian Boltanski, who emerged during the 1980s as an important conceptual artists. Lynn Gumpert has suggested that "for Boltanski, the Holocaust was synonymous with the very notion of death itself."[40] Boltanski has elaborated on the theme of death: "Our relation to death has changed over the last few years. It is increasingly denied. . . . The outward signs of mourning, even the idea of monument, have disappeared. . . . We have a problem with death."[41] Boltanski was born in 1945 to a Corsican-Catholic mother and a Jewish father whose parents had come from Odessa. The elder Boltanski converted to Catholicism in Paris before World

Christian Boltanski, *Jewish School of Grosse Hamburgerstrasse in Berlin in 1939,* 1994. Installation: moving photographs, fluorescent lamps, fan; dimension variable. Courtesy of Marian Goodman Gallery, New York

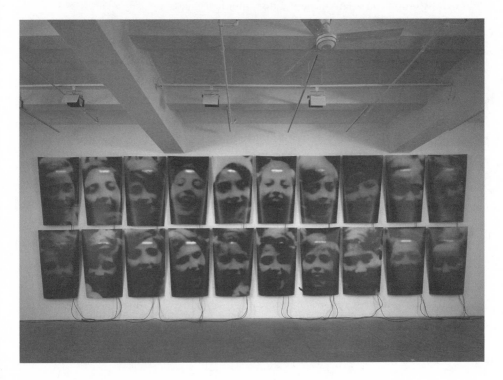

War II, and yet he had to hide for a year under a floor to avoid being rounded up by the French police and the Gestapo: according to the race law, he was a Jew despite his conversion. Boltanski was named "Christian Liberté," allegedly because he was born on the day of Paris's liberation.

Leçons de Ténèbres/Lessons of Darkness, Boltanski's most ambitious installation series, evolved during the period 1984–1992. It actually appears as seven different installation works, linked aesthetically and in terms of their subject matter. On an individual basis, all these works can be said to have references to the Holocaust. Collectively, they stand as a major reflection of the Holocaust while maintaining an independent aesthetic that makes the works attractive to an uninformed viewer, and yet they subtly evoke anxiety because of a certain historicism in the work. Andrea Liss believes that the artist has achieved a level of methodological success by "his picturing of victims outside of the traditional documentary photographic rhetoric of victimology. In his refusal to depict the victims as victims, Boltanski's methodology challenges the documentary photograph's ability to function as an authentic document."[42]

His installations can be discussed in a limited perspective. *Les Enfants de Dijon* (1985) was based on an earlier photographic installation, *Portraits des élèves du C.E.S. des Lentillères,* for which Boltanski had obtained photos from two hundred children in 1972. Speaking of the use of these photographs from Lentillères for *Les Enfants de Dijon,* Boltanski noted: "Ten years later, all these children's faces really seemed to me to be like corpses. Those pictured are dead forever, since they are now adults"[43]—as if photographs have a life equivalent to that of the person himself. Boltanski rephotographed fifty black-and-white photographs as close-ups, framed with strips of Christmas wrapping paper. They were arranged on a long wall, connected with electrical wires, and lighted with one hundred fifty exposed light bulbs. The overriding image conveyed to the viewer was that the children of Dijon were indeed dead. In the United States, the installation was almost universally interpreted as a Holocaust display, with the message that there was no way to bring these children back, and that the photograph was a monument to their memory, nothing more. The display was also very consistent with a Holocaust/postdisaster motif in displaying photographs of "victims." Americans especially can relate to this form of memorialization, which they witnessed in the aftermath of the September 11 attack on the World Trade Center in New York. Boltanski commented that the images "were all similar, yet different. Each had its own life. . . . Everybody was somebody."[44] What he was attempting to convey was the individuality of each life—what Judith Miller, in describing the Holocaust, has called "one by one."[45] Again, Ernst van Alphen describes Boltanski's technique as "indexical." The tension exists to fight this specific interpretation while at the same time acknowledging that it exists.

In 1988, Boltanski became more directly concerned with the Holocaust through his installation *Canada,* which appeared in several versions. *Canada* was the name given to the large warehouses at Auschwitz-Birkenau used to store the clothing and other durable goods confiscated from inmates and from those who had been gassed. "Canada" was apparently a camp metaphor for a land of unlimited wealth. Boltanski's installation of *Canada* at the Ydessa Hendeles Art Foundation, in Toronto, used six thousand second-hand garments and, in terms of evoking a specific memory, suggested the similarity between the power of the photograph and that of discarded clothing: "What they have in common is that they are simultaneously presence and absence. They are both an object and a souvenir (or memory) of a subject, exactly as a cadaver is both an object and souvenir of a subject."[46] A variation of *Canada,* retitled *Réserves: La Fête de Purim* and exhibited in Basel, used more than one thousand pounds of clothing on the floor, lighted with lamps. Viewers of the installation had to walk over the garments, "and with each step they felt increasingly as if they were walking on human bodies."[47] Speaking of the Basel installation, Boltanski noted:

> So, I turned them all into murderers. There was also a certain pleasure in walking on all that clothing, which they felt, so they were completely implicated in it. They were murderers. . . . I think the Holocaust showed us . . . that we can be killers and that the people we love the most, who are closest to us, are almost always killers too. Germany was the country with the most culture and philosophy in Europe. Maybe having that knowledge about ourselves could make us a little less killers. So, the clothing was a kind of parable.[48]

Andrea Liss believes, I think correctly, that Boltanski's installations, unsettling as they are in a museum setting, are more effective than the installation of shoes at the United States Holocaust Memorial Museum, where the perpetrators, the "them" of history, never touch the "us."[49]

Art has one final role to play in Holocaust education: helping to define the nature of the perpetrators, their methods, and the aftermath of their acts. The last frontier in understanding the role of art during the grim Nazi period is an examination of what art was stolen and the attempts to retrieve it. Many monographs and commission reports have been written about stolen art and the restitution process, which has come to involve even countries that were neutral during World War II and now, in the twenty-first century, museums around the world. The Nazis were not the first to plunder. Many came before. However, the scale of Nazi plundering was beyond any formerly seen, and the paper trail left behind has created a multitude of legal cases that are now outstanding. The complexity of recovering lost artworks means that the process will probably go on for many years. It has already has involved attempts to bring governments, private parties, and museums together to resolve outstanding claims involving artworks.

There is obviously much more than can be said about the nature of Holocaust-related art. The conceptual overviews given here, as well as the few examples from contemporary artists, suggest that there is much to discuss when art is joined to the issue of Holocaust representation and its memory. It may be difficult to construct an entire course around painters and sculptors, but it should not be forgotten that artists have developed substantial interest in the Holocaust as a subject for painting. Their approaches, while sometimes failed, can also lead to interesting breakthroughs dealing with questions of identity, theology, and modernity and may stimulate a conversation about the most basic question: why the Holocaust happened.

NOTES

1. The tradition of historical research has always favored the document. Oral histories of survivors, liberators, and, occasionally, perpetrators, especially when they are documented for posterity via videotape, have entered the archives, but

there is a sense of uncertainty regarding how videotaped oral histories will be used in the future, beyond the realm of serious scholarship. The concern, often heard in academe, is about the future of telling the story when the last survivor of the Holocaust has passed away. The answer, it seems, is relatively easy. Big video projects, such as the Yale Fortunoff Archive and the Survivors of the Shoah Oral History Project, will provide a video-based vision of survivors' testimonies. Researchers may use the full tapes, but it is doubtful that any class situation will tolerate a full, unedited narrative. The bottom line, however, is probably that the subject of the Holocaust eventually will be evaluated in the same way that all other history is evaluated: objectively, with distance, and on the basis of documents and testimony.

2. For general observations about representation, see Rebecca Abrams, "Showing the Shoah," *New Statesman* 17 (July 2000), 43–46; Saul Friedlander, ed., *Probing the Limits of Representation* (Cambridge, Mass.: Harvard University Press, 1992); Berel Lang, *Holocaust Representation: Art within the Limits of History and Ethics* (Baltimore, Md.: Johns Hopkins University Press, 2000).

3. See also Poussin's or David's *The Rape of the Sabine Women,* Brueghel's *Massacre of the Innocents,* or Goya's representations of the horrors of the Peninsular War in Spain during the Napoleonic Period.

4. Theodor Adorno, "Cultural Criticism and Society," in *Prisms,* trans. Samuel and Sherry Weber (Cambridge, Mass.: MIT Press, 1984), 43; Theodor Adorno, *Negative Dialectics,* trans. E. B. Ashton (New York: Seabury Press, 1973), 362. An interesting series of reflections on Adorno is found in Matthew Baigell, *Jewish American Artists and the Holocaust* (New Brunswick, N.J.: Rutgers University Press, 1997), 114.

5. Primo Levi, quoted in Michael Kimmelman, "Horror Unforgotten: The Politics of Memory," *New York Times,* March 11, 1994.

6. Elie Wiesel, "Art and the Holocaust: Trivializing Memory," *New York Times,* June 11, 1989.

7. Abrams, "Showing the Shoah," 44.

8. Primo Levi, "On Obscure Writing," *La Stampa,* Dec. 11, 1976, quoted in Myriam Anissimov, *Primo Levi: Tragedy of an Optimist* (Woodstock, N.Y.: Overlook Press, 1998), 323.

9. Anissimov, *Primo Levi,* 332.

10. Ibid., 369.

11. I have in mind Judy Chicago's *The Holocaust Project,* a large installation of paintings done in conjunction with the artist's husband, Donald Woodman. *The Holocaust Project* ultimately became an avenue for exploring every aspect of injustice in world history. Added to this is the imposition of a feminist ide-

ology, which appeared in the entry of *The Fall,* executed as a tapestry and representing "the historic defeat of matriarchy and the rise of patriarchy." From there the story unfolds simply: the conquest of women leads to genocide, and antifeminism leads to antisemitism.

12. See Shari Rosenstein Werb, *Teaching and Studying the Holocaust* (Boston: Allyn and Bacon, 2001), 239, which is helpful in using art in the precollege classroom.

13. See Sander L. Gilman, *Making the Body Beautiful: A Cultural History of Aesthetic Surgery* (Princeton, N.J.: Princeton University Press, 1999); *Degenerate Art,* videotape based on the exhibition "Degenerate Art" curated by Stephanie Barron at the Los Angeles County Museum of Art.

14. Franz Meyer, *Marc Chagall* (New York: Harry N. Abrams, 1963), 490.

15. Ibid., 448.

16. The full edition is Charlotte Salomon, *Charlotte: Life or Theater? An Autobiographical Play by Charlotte Salomon* (New York: Viking Press, 1981). See also Mary Lowenthal Felstiner, *To Paint Her Life: Charlotte Salomon in the Nazi Era* (New York: HarperCollins, 1994).

17. Ernst van Alphen, *Caught by History: Holocaust Effects in Contemporary Art, Literature, and Theory* (Stanford, Calif.: Stanford University Press, 1997).

18. Quoted in Leonard Baskin, *Iconologia* (London: Harcourt Brace Jovanovich, 1988), 22.

19. Quoted in ibid., 23.

20. Van Alphen, *Caught by History.*

21. Ibid.

22. Samuel Bak, "An Introduction to the Notes on My Paintings" (unpublished manuscript, 2001).

23. The only reasonable way to build a collection of usable slides for the class is to make color slides or PowerPoint presentations from books. Usually an audiovisual department can do so by using macro lenses on a 35–millimeter camera, high-intensity Tungsten lighting, and Tungsten-rated film (in general, T-160). Sources include exhibition catalogues, books about art and the Holocaust, biographies, monographs on individual artists, and art magazines that may carry some art about the Holocaust without necessarily labeling it as such.

24. See Stephanie Barron et al., *"Degenerate Art": The Fate of the Avant Garde in Nazi Germany* (Los Angeles: Los Angeles County Museum of Art, 1991); *From the Bitter Earth: Artists of the Holocaust,* produced and directed by Paul Morrison (London: Shooting Star Productions, 1988); Jewish Art and Architecture Partners, *Tradition and Transformation: A History of Jewish Art and Architecture*

(Pepper Pike, Ohio: Jewish Art and Architecture Partners, 1989), especially chap. 9B, "From Holocaust Art to Abstract Expressionism"; Monica Bohm-Duchen, *After Auschwitz: Responses to the Holocaust in Contemporary Art* (Sunderland, England: Northern Centre for Contemporary Art, 1995); Stephen Feinstein, ed., *Witness and Legacy: Contemporary Art About the Holocaust* (Minneapolis: Lerner Publications, 1995). The most encyclopedic book on the subject, and one that should be a mandatory addition to any university library, is Ziva Amishai-Maisels, *Depiction and Interpretation: The Influence of the Holocaust on the Visual Arts* (Oxford: Pergamon Press, 1993).

25. For example, the photography of the American Civil War by M. B. Brady, Alexander Gardner, George S. Cook, and the E. & H. T. Anthony Company was revolutionary in that it brought the battlefield home to viewers who were not there and who had nurtured romanticized visions of war.

26. Jurgen Stroop, *The Report of Jurgen Stroop: Concerning the Uprising in the Ghetto of Warsaw and the Liquidation of the Jewish Residential Area* (Warsaw, Poland: Jewish Historical Institute, 1958).

27. Peter Hellman and Lili Meier, *The Auschwitz Album: A Book Based upon an Album Discovered by a Concentration Camp Survivor* (New York: Random House, 1981).

28. Roman Vishniac, *A Vanished World* (New York: Farrar, Strauss and Giroux, 1983).

29. Jean Aberbach, *Bak: Oils, Watercolours, Drawings, 1972–1974,* exhibition catalogue (New York: Aberbach Fine Art, 1974), n.p.

30. Letter to Jean Aberbach from Samuel Bak, quoted in ibid., n.p.

31. See Lawrence L. Langer, *Landscapes of Jewish Experience: Paintings by Samuel Bak* (Boston: Pucker Gallery/University of New England Press, 1997); Lawrence L. Langer, *In a Different Light: The Book of Genesis in the Art of Samuel Bak* (Boston: Pucker Art Publications, 2001).

32. Interview with R. B. Kitaj in Julian Rios, *Kitaj* (London: Hamish Hamilton, 1994), 55.

33. Kathy Deepwell and Juliet Steyn, "Readings of the Jewish Artist in Late Modernism," *Art Monthly* 133 (Feb. 1988), 8.

34. R. B. Kitaj, *The First Diasporist Manifesto* (London: Thames and Hudson, 1989).

35. John Northey, "Chronology," in Richard Morphet, ed., *R. B. Kitaj: A Retrospective* (London: Tate Gallery, 1994), 64.

36. Kitaj, *First Diasporist Manifesto,* 21.

37. Interview with R. B. Kitaj in Morphet, ed., *R.B. Kitaj,* 120.

38. For a biography of Cahana, see Steven Spielberg and Survivors of the Shoah Visual History Foundation, *The Last Days* (New York: St. Martin's Press, 1999), 59–74.

39. Lisa Saltzman, *Anselm Kiefer and Art After Auschwitz* (Cambridge, England: Cambridge University Press, 1999), 26.

40. Lynn Gumpert, *Christian Boltanski: Lessons of Darkness* (Buena Park, Calif./Chicago: Gardner Lithograph/Museum of Contemporary Art, 1988), 53.

41. Interview with Beatrice Parent in Christian Boltanski, *Dernières Années* (Paris: ADAGP, 1998), 4.

42. Andrea Liss, *Trespassing Shadows: Memory, Photography, and The Holocaust* (Minneapolis: University of Minnesota Press, 1998), 44–45.

43. Quoted in Gumpert, *Christian Boltanski,* 84.

44. *Christian Boltanski,* videotape produced and directed by Gerald Fox (London: Phaidon Press Ltd./London Weekend Television, 1995).

45. Judith Miller, *One, by One, by One: Facing the Holocaust* (New York: Simon and Schuster, 1990).

46. Gumpert, *Christian Boltanski,* 110.

47. Ibid., 118.

48. Georgia Marsh, interview with Christian Boltanski, in Liss, *Trespassing Shadows,* 80.

49. Ibid.

2

History, Memory, and the City

Case Study–Berlin

RACHEL RAPPERPORT MUNN

The upper-level seminar "History, Memory and the City: Case Study—Berlin," taught through the Department of Architecture at the Wentworth Institute of Technology, in Boston, was developed to promote understanding of the connections among the Holocaust, political ideology, architecture, and urban design. We study the past and contemporary built environment of Berlin to reveal the relationship of architecture and urban design to history, place, memory, and the ongoing legacy of the Holocaust. The course's approach emphasizes a multidisciplinary understanding of Berlin as it is embedded in Germany's history and in the history of the Holocaust. The course material encourages students to struggle with ethical themes that the Holocaust raises and to heighten their comprehension of the relevance that these issues have to contemporary society.[1]

The seminar's interdisciplinary approach to the study of Berlin introduces students to four major themes:

1. The question of how architecture and art are influenced by and reflective of the ideological time and place in which they are created
2. The idea that "place" is both a social and a physical construction, part of a community's ongoing and constantly renegotiated relationship to history and to historical memory
3. The idea that a city's monuments and memorials are a significant

part of continuing, communitywide dialogue, debate, and self-examination about history

4. The idea that the built environment, including urban designs, buildings, streets, and memorials, can be interpreted as layers of a historical, cultural, and social map

All four of these themes are related, through the prism of the built environment, to the Holocaust, the political ideology of the Third Reich, and continuing discussions of the Nazi legacy in Berlin. The use of texts in history, urban design, architecture, the visual arts, and literature, combined with visual material (from architecture, film, fine arts, and photography), allows the use of overlapping methods for fostering understanding of the physical city and the layers of history, memory, and meaning that inform perceptions and understanding of Berlin, of Holocaust history, and of ourselves.

The seminar is not envisioned as linear or chronological; instead, it is intentionally interdisciplinary and multidisciplinary so as to encourage alternative approaches to comprehending the Holocaust. Each discipline offers a distinct way of understanding the four central themes, and each lecture, conceived as one spoke of a wheel, contributes in a different way to the journey of exploration. During the semester, guest lecturers from different disciplines are invited to speak, including specialists in German history, German art history, architectural preservation, and other fields. The pedagogical intent rests on a collective spirit of inquiry and shared responsibility for assembling the course material rather than reliance on a single professor who is seen as the expert.

Primary sources, including original manifestos written by Walter Gropius, founder of the Bauhaus, and autobiographical accounts from Albert Speer's diary, provide a window into the emotional tone of the period. Secondary sources help students understand historical events, contextualize artistic movements, and raise ethical issues. A number of secondary sources that examine the Third Reich's ideological connections to the built environment have also been particularly useful.[2]

Art films, documentary films, and commercial movies are also an essential part of the seminar. Documentary films include *A Letter without Words*, historical footage of a wealthy Jewish family's experiences in wartime Berlin; *Architecture of Doom,* on the architecture and art of the Third Reich; and *The Wonderful, Horrible Life of Leni Riefenstahl,* on Hitler's propagandist filmmaker. Wim Wenders's film *Wings of Desire,* set in divided Berlin, is a moving testimony of loss that touches on many of the themes of the course. All these materials convey, in emotional and visual terms, a different experience of the Holocaust's impact from what textual accounts alone can provide. Newspaper articles, such as a discussion of the Vienna memorial to Austrian Jews who were murdered in the Holocaust, have been used as well, to show students how relevant and inflammatory the issues they are debating continue to be.[3] Especially for students who have never seen Berlin, my own slides of the city also lend immediacy and reality to class discussions.

We begin the course with an introduction to German history, since a fundamental understanding of history is imperative in understanding both the meaning of the built environment of Berlin and the intensity of the current debates over preservation and memorial issues. We focus on the period from 1920 through the end of World War II but also include introductions to postwar divided Berlin and to the current rebuilding of the unified city. For students who do not have a comprehensive background in liberal arts, the historical overview, particularly of the Holocaust, is eye-opening and invaluable. For example, as a class, we read about and debate the morality, individual responsibility, and opportunistic behavior of Albert Speer in his ascent to the post of chief architect and, later, minister of armaments and war production under Hitler, and of Leni Riefenstahl's decision to make propaganda movies for Hitler. We discuss whether people such as Speer were too young at the beginning of their careers to be held morally accountable for their actions, eliciting the students' self-examination (for example, they ask themselves whether they, at almost the same age as Speer, should be held accountable for their actions). Where Leni Riefenstahl is concerned, we ask whether her artistic virtuosity can be seen as separate from her political involvement with the Reich. We explore the incremental nature of the descent into genocide, including the roles of German education, of bystanders, and of propaganda. A feeling for the times is evoked through readings of works like Christopher Isherwood's *Goodbye to Berlin,* which describes with great immediacy the texture of daily life in Berlin on the brink of war. Many of the students at Wentworth Institute have never before heard ethical questions discussed in a classroom setting, and I find their struggle to think and articulate ethical dilemmas moving and important. I make it a fundamental aspect of the course to highlight my argument that ethical questions cannot be separated from the worlds of art, architecture, and urban design.

Many students asked very basic, difficult questions after learning more about the Holocaust: "How could this have happened?" "Why did the Germans hate the Jews so much?" "How could other Germans have let this happen?" "Why was there such strong antisemitism in Germany?" "Why didn't the Jews fight back?" These are not simple questions to address, but the asking is critical. I encourage group discussion, in contrast to an authoritative "answer,"[4] and feel that having a group discussion of these themes is an invaluable start in being able to form and articulate moral positions.

With a background in the history and zeitgeist of Berlin, we look at how architectural and artistic movements of the period were tied to political ideology. We examine the progressive, modern ideals of the Bauhaus, look at why it was political and revolutionary, why it was reviled and shut down by the Nazis, and the more traditional architectural and artistic movements that Hitler supported and why he did so. We work to decode the intentions behind the architecture and urban planning of the Third Reich, especially architectural and urban design schemes for the new Berlin, which was to have been completed in 1952 and renamed Germania. Extensive urban design plans were developed for Germania that would have widened major thoroughfares for military parade routes and built enormous new governmental structures designed to intimidate crowds and glorify Hitler. By examining these plans carefully, we see that the new city was not envisioned through a theory of city planning based on life and on an active world of streetscapes, parks, stoops, and the vibrant texture of a healthy metropolis, such as would later be described by the architectural commentator Jane Jacobs.[5] This was the city planning of a death machine, the reflection of a maniacal war-and-power ideology that can be read through careful study of the urban design schemes developed by Hitler and Speer.

We also examine how Nazi governmental buildings, designed in a pared-down neoclassical style that was meant to evoke the power and glory of ancient Rome, were rigidly symmetrical, with huge, intimidating portals and windows. We learn that these structures were deliberately designed to fall eventually into glorious ruins that would memorialize the Third Reich, a fact highlighting that these buildings were concerned with death and immortality rather than with the healthy growth of a culture and a metropolis. We look at the design of some of the slave labor and concentration camps, particularly Sachsenhausen, outside Berlin. Sachsenhausen was built by slave labor as a model prison camp and was originally intended to provide the bricks for building the new Germania. The camp was a model of the one-point guard surveillance techniques that were emulated at other camps, and it remains a powerful marker of the horrors of the Holocaust. It is also an example of the physical layering of history, since it was taken over and used as Special Camp 7 by the Soviets in East Germany after the war. As we trace the ideological intentions that can be read in the urban planning schemes for Germania, in the architectural styles of the immense Nazi governmental buildings, and in the slave labor and concentration camps' machinery of terror, the web of horror that was the Holocaust takes on a reality grounded in the physical world of the built environment.

We examine the connections between propaganda, art, and ideology. We study the folk emphasis and realism of the artwork encouraged by Hitler, including the pervasive portrayal of traditional family and gender values. We examine how modernism in both art and architecture was labeled "degenerate" (along with the liberal individuality, women's emancipation, and independent thinking that it represented) and how it was ridiculed by the Nazi regime and directly tied to descriptions of physically "deformed" individuals and Jews. We explore how much a part of their times these progressive movements were, why they were controversial, and how they proved so threatening to Nazi ideology that they had to be systematically discredited and eradicated by the Nazis. We discuss the effects of the Nazis' having forced many of the leading architects and artists of the Bauhaus and modern movements to flee Germany. These members of the cultural elite took these movements to the United States and other countries, tremendously expanding the influence abroad of Bauhaus thinking and educational style (for example, Walter Gropius became chair of the Department of Architecture in Harvard University's Graduate School of Design).

By continually referring to the built environment of Berlin, our physical map of the city, and its traces and layers of history, we sustain a sense of immediacy and physical reality in connection with the themes being discussed. We look at figure-ground illustrations of Berlin, where buildings are shown in black and open space in white. Illustrations from before the war reveal a traditional European city of defined street walls and squares. Illustrations from after the war show the appalling gaps and empty spaces that reveal the enormity of wartime destruction in Berlin. We also see that as the postwar city was divided into east and west and rebuilt, the new modern urban patterns, such as West Berlin's "Kulturforum" and modern mass-housing projects, did not follow the pattern of Berlin's streets but instead set housing blocks in open space. We discuss these changes as products of new political and planning ideologies from the Bauhaus, which were intended to provide a new spiritual beginning for Berlin. The depth of the feeling that preceded these changes is shown in the following statement, written in 1947 and signed by leading architects who had returned to Berlin:

> The collapse has destroyed the visible world that constituted our life and our work. When it took place we believed, with a sense of liberation, that now we should be able to return to work. Today, two years later, we realize how much the visible breakdown is merely the expression of a spiritual devastation and we are tempted to sink into despair. We have been reduced to fundamentals and the task must be tackled afresh from this point.[6]

The theme of architectural preservation is a major topic of the course as we discuss what has happened, and what should happen, to historically significant sites related to the Holocaust. In Berlin, for example, Hitler used buildings in the area around Wilhelm Strasse (equivalent to London's Downing Street) as a center for torture and interrogation. These historically significant buildings survived the war, but during the 1950s they were purposefully neglected or demolished, a reflection of the community's desire to erase physical reminders of the Nazi era. Later, the community began to change how it viewed this area. A temporary exhibit was created to show what had happened at this location. With intensive preservation efforts, the exhibit was then developed into a permanent installation, *The Topography of Terror,* augmented by a comprehensive effort to document the past and create a museum. We discuss how that kind of evolution in the community's attitude occurred and how, in current society, historical information about the Holocaust is debated through the built environment. We discuss the role of such debates in reconciliation and historical understanding, and we ask whether sites like this should focus on education or memorialization. We also ask what should be preserved from different eras—from old Berlin, from the Nazi era, or from postwar divided Berlin—and why. Discussions about what should be saved lead to questions about what is considered historically important and how its importance should be communicated to future generations. While the focus is on the built environment as a vehicle for debate, the discussion is also about why the history of the Holocaust is important to learn and transmit to future generations.

Having established a base of historical knowledge and an understanding of the architectural, urban design, and artistic movements of the period and how they are tied to ideological positions, we consider contemporary memorials to the Holocaust in Berlin. We study memorials created on specific sites of importance, including concentration camps, deportation sites, formerly Jewish neighborhoods, and destroyed synagogues, and we discuss the power of these places and memorials. We trace how different memorials or museums seek to heighten the realization that it happened *here* rather than that it simply happened. For instance, we look at recent photographs of Sachsenhausen, with the peeling paint of its wooden structures, and at historical photographs showing the same structures with rows of men confined in near-death conditions. We discuss how this place should be preserved, how its existence serves as a memorial, and what the message of the memorial is.

Another example of a memorial involves the deportation of Berlin's Jews from Grunewald, a nondescript suburban train station, one of three points in or near Berlin to which some 55,000 Jews, starting in October 1941, were marched through the streets. They were taken first to the ghettos of Lodz, Riga, Warsaw, and elsewhere in the east. Most were then killed there by the SS, and the rest were sent to death camps. Within a year, all were transported directly to Auschwitz. At the Grunewald station, the abandoned track 17 is now covered with metal pavers, arranged chronologically and showing the dates of the transports and the number of Jews in each one. One slide that I project of this memorial shows a small white flower set by a specific transport date. The station at Grunewald is a quiet, chilling memorial that silently states the facts of the draining of Berlin's Jewry.

We also study actual and proposed Holocaust memorials in Berlin that are not related to specific historic sites, and these present different challenges and opportunities. They include the controversial "memorial to the murdered Jews of Europe" and the recently completed Jewish Museum of Berlin, designed by Daniel Libeskind. The plan for another memorial that we discuss, called *Bus Stop,* features a central bus station in Berlin and proposes to run bright red buses to important Holocaust sites in Berlin, elsewhere in Germany, and elsewhere in Europe. The proposed destinations also include concentration camps, which are often difficult to get to on public transportation. This memorial was not ultimately realized, but it did have vigorous popular support. The concept emphasizes the web of complicity in the Holocaust that reached across not only Berlin but also the rest of Germany and Europe, and it implies that the notion of a central memorial does not make sense. It shows that the memorial should actually be the real places of memory and horror, and it says that the continuous visibility of the bright red buses crisscrossing Berlin, and emblazoned with the names of destinations like Auschwitz, would be the most appropriate way to acknowledge the memorial sites and honor the murdered Jewish population.

The use of architecture and art as vehicles to discuss the Holocaust, memory, ideology, and ethics is compelling. The integration of history, political culture, ethics, and the visual arts keeps discussion from focusing only on stylistic aspects of design and illuminates how the visual arts and architecture are integral elements in shaping and reflecting culture. Nor are historical texts left in a vacuum of text-based analysis; rather, they are integrated with material culture and an understanding of the physical and emotional worlds. How we are affected by the built environment (urban designs, buildings, street names, memorials, important sites) and the visual arts (painting, photography, and film) is different from how we are affected by historical accounts. The built environment and the visual arts convey an emotional connection as well as an immediate visceral connection to a different time and place.

The seminar at its most radical challenges students to think about how and why the different disciplines have been separated and asks them what is gained or lost by this approach. It challenges the notion that learning about the history of the Holocaust should take place only through a tracking of its political or historical means. What happens when you start with a city and develop a thematic understanding of its culture, politics, history, architecture, and artistic milieu? What happens if you start from the visual, emotional, and built worlds, and how does this approach ground an intellectual, abstract understanding of the complexity of the Holocaust? How does this approach help one understand a foreign time and place and relate it to our contemporary world? The full panoply—emotional experience fused with historical facts—is what creates a richly understood and felt picture of history and an understanding of how the historical record of the Holocaust is carried into the present.

We examine Daniel Libeskind's design for the Jewish Museum both as a powerful symbol for the new Berlin and as one of the only new buildings to take on the depth of this city's history in the very fiber of its architecture. The museum's architecture abstractly expresses the loss and what should have been the unimaginable absence of the once thriving Jewish community, a community that was the intellectual heart of Weimar Berlin. The museum's broken plan and façade express the shattered history of Berlin's Jews as well as the immense, continuing impact of their absence. It is a complex, brilliant contribution to the city's architecture, and I use it in bringing together many of the themes of the course.

Many of the Holocaust memorials that we study are extremely moving to students, particularly once they have acquired the historical background to appreciate the memorial debates and symbolism. Learning about the memorials has helped students deepen their understanding of the Holocaust and of the intense emotions that its history leaves in its wake. For example, one memorial in a formerly Jewish district of Berlin comprises ordinary-looking street signs on lampposts throughout the neighborhood; each of the signs reproduces an edict of the anti-Jewish laws of the late 1930s and early 1940s, with the date of each pronouncement printed below.[7] A sign within sight and earshot of a church playground reads: ARYAN AND NON-ARYAN CHILDREN ARE NOT ALLOWED TO PLAY TOGETHER, 1938; another sign down the street reads JEWS MAY NO LONGER OWN HOUSE PETS; and, further down, JEWISH DOCTORS MAY NO LONGER PRACTICE MEDICINE. The project brilliantly illustrates the pervasive, public, subtle, incremental, insidious, and complete stripping of Jewish citizens' civil rights. The prohibition of house pets for Jews has an even more sinister quality when one realizes that Nazi officials did not want to have the disturbance and unease that would be caused by abandoned pets roaming the streets after the Jews were deported. Contemporary inhabitants of the neighborhood called the police when the signs first went up, thinking they were neo-Nazi propaganda. As a result, smaller explanatory signs were posted by the artists, who also pointed out that no one had called the police when the edicts were announced in the 1930s and early 1940s. This memorial encourages the realization that the culture of the time was imbued with antisemitism; the edicts were not simply elements of an isolated, higher-level political decision making. Students find the memorial very moving, and it prompts discussion about the ongoing process of remembering history and incorporating it into daily modern life.

The class also examines and discusses the aesthetic elements of memorial designs and the question of how to represent a society struggling to come to terms with the historical legacy of the Holocaust and its horrors. We discuss how debates around memorial design are a crucial and productive part of ongoing dialogue and understanding of the Holocaust. How and why does a culture remember such an event? How does one give form to a memorial to an "absence"—a murdered people or culture? How much of a memorial of this kind should be educational, and how much artistic or emotional? How are negative experiences memorialized? How does art transform memory? What should be done with the ground on which important events have occurred? How can the community constructively discuss such a painful history? These are some of the questions that we address in the last third of the course, and that form the intellectual heart of the seminar. The students' engagement with them continues as they study these issues further in their final projects.

An area of this seminar that I would like to expand in the future is study of the gender-related messages that are encoded in many of the themes that are presented, such as the strict gender roles dictated through propaganda of the Reich; the gender codes of a military machine; the place of homosexuality; the gendered nature of architectural buildings and urban design; the different experiences of women as victims or perpetrators of the Reich; the Nazi Party's symbolism of health, hygiene, and body image; and the involvement or exclusion of women in contemporary decisions about memorials. All these areas are important and currently insufficiently discussed in this course.

As I teach about Berlin, I find myself less and less interested in the purely formal qualities of the newly emerging built environment of the city—the technological wonders, the scale, and the specific elements of shiny new office buildings designed by international "star" architects. These topics are important and have a place, but they remind me of watching films about the new Potsdamer Platz in the Info Box in Berlin—being inundated with facts and astounding technology, with almost no mention of the historical importance of the ground on which I was standing. The silence with respect to history was, in this instance, deafening. I find myself increasingly drawn to the emotional history of place, of stone and of buildings—drawn to how the built environment is a visual map of a worldview. I admire Alan Balfour's[8] deep analysis of Berlin's historic Leipziger Platz over time, and of how, if one looks closely and deeply enough, and with enough wisdom and breadth of knowledge, the stories of Berlin, of the rest of Germany, and of the rest of Europe are in evidence here—in the rise, clash, and fall of ideas and ideologies. Balfour's study reflects how, in the pathos, suffering, darkness and hope of Berlin, both our collective history and our dreams for the future are revealed.

NOTES

1. Parts of the course have also been adapted to a multidisciplinary graduate seminar titled "The Politics of Traumatic Memory: History, Place, and Art in Societal Examinations of Memory," offered by the Graduate Consortium for

Women's Studies at the Radcliffe Institute for Advanced Study, Harvard University.

2. See Alan Balfour, *Berlin: The Politics of Order, 1737–1989* (New York: Rizzoli, 1990); Brian Ladd, *The Ghosts of Berlin: Confronting German History in the Urban Landscape* (Chicago: University of Chicago Press, 1997). See also Facing History and Ourselves National Foundation, *Facing History and Ourselves: Holocaust and Human Behavior* (Brookline, Mass.: Facing History and Ourselves National Foundation, 1994), an excellent resource for ethical discussions centered on the Holocaust, and Dolores Hayden, *The Power of Place: Urban Landscapes as Public History* (Boston: MIT Press, 1995), which provides background for the concept of a social construction of place. Two books that provide necessary background for examining questions of memorialization and the Holocaust are James Young, *At Memory's Edge: After-Images of the Holocaust in Contemporary Art and Architecture* (New Haven, Conn.: Yale University Press, 2000) and James Young, *The Texture of Memory: Holocaust Memorials and Meaning* (New Haven, Conn.: Yale University Press, 1993).

3. See Michael Kimmelman, "Behind Sealed Doors, Opening up the Past: After a Long Delay, a Stark Memorial in Vienna Confronts a Dark Legacy," *New York Times,* Oct. 30, 2000.

4. See Leonard Grob, Peter J. Haas, David H. Hirsch, David Patterson, Didier Pollefeyt, and John Roth, "Emmanuel Levinas and the Primacy of Ethics in Post-Holocaust Philosophy," in John K. Roth, ed., *Ethics after the Holocaust: Perspectives, Critiques, and Responses* (St. Paul, Minn.: Paragon House, 1999), 1–48.

5. See Jane Jacobs, *The Death and Life of Great American Cities* (New York: Random House, 1961).

6. Balfour, *Berlin,* 158.

7. Project by the Berlin artists Renata Stih and Frieder Schnock; see the article in the Harvard University Graduate School of Design magazine by James Young, "Memory and Counter-Memory: The End of the Monument in Germany," *Constructions of Memory: On Monuments Old and New* (Fall 1999), 11, 12.

8. Balfour, *Berlin.*

3

Looking for Words

Teaching the Holocaust in Writing-Intensive Courses

BETH HAWKINS BENEDIX

Let me begin with an apologetic of sorts: I do not teach a course on the Holocaust or one dedicated solely to the Holocaust. Rather, I have incorporated units of Holocaust-related literature into two courses, both of which are writing-intensive. The first is a college writing course; the second, a course in modern continental European literature. It is my belief that such units, in the context of writing or writing-intensive courses, shed light on the surrounding course material, challenging us, as readers and writers, to confront the urgency, fragility, and precariousness of the written word. In writing, perhaps more than in any other academic act, we are forced to commit ourselves to the consequences of our speech and to make ourselves vulnerable, known, exposed to those we write to. If indeed our words have consequences, if words are indeed the impetus for action, then we have the responsibility as writers to exercise extreme caution and take nothing for granted about the way we place our words upon the page. Though it is perhaps a painful and graphic lesson for students to learn, and though they may feel at times overwhelmed and paralyzed by the weight of their own words, it is my strong belief that part of what we do in writing classes is instill a healthy fear in our students that they can, in fact, say the *wrong* thing, that the words they use have political, ethical, and cultural implications, and that they need to be aware of these implications when they voice their thoughts. Writing is a fundamentally social act, a communicative act, and an act that gestures outside itself—however hermetic or closed or strictly personal a given text may seem. In my writing classes, I stress to students that, however implicit, subtle, or hidden this outward gesture may be, we as readers and as writers are tied to one another, in a relationship with one another; we need to take great care, then, to recognize the dynamics of power inherent in this relationship, and to acknowledge that this relationship can easily become a manipulative or hostile one if we allow it to become so.

To the above apologetic I add a disclaimer: both of these courses are very much works in progress as well as works in process; much of what I will go on to say about these courses, particularly the composition course, is based on my experience in the classroom and on my speculations and projected hopes concerning the material.

THE COMPOSITION COURSE

My choice to include a unit of Holocaust-related material in the composition course was largely driven by external factors. During the semester when I introduced this unit, we were lucky enough to bring to campus two speakers who prompted me to consider teaching Holocaust-related material: Art Spiegelman and Berel Lang. Wanting to take advantage of the opportunity to introduce students to two equally effective strategies of presenting and describing the unimaginable, I decided to use these guest lectures as the pivot point for our discussion. The composition course is as much about critical thinking as it is about writing; our focus often involves deconstructing the materials before us, digging into the way in which an argument has been constructed, and then attempting to reconstruct how form and content work together. As the overarching rubric for the course, and with the intention of encouraging this multilayered process, I've chosen "subtlety, subversion, subjectivity," a rubric encompassing three characteristics that challenge an intended audience to question its beliefs and values, that test the limits of conventional literary forms, and that may work to convince an audience to accept a given set of premises, which it might never accept under different conditions. I've shifted the content from semester to semester, but the design remains the same; the tripartite theme provides the freedom necessary for keeping the material fresh and current, but it also serves as a leitmotif of sorts, an echo that we can return to throughout the semester to test the legitimacy, artistry, and/or merit of the material and its claims. We talk a good deal about agendas in this course, about the hidden forces that drive the spoken voices of the texts we encounter, about the layering of said and unsaid, and about the ways in which the lie comes both to bolster and to represent truth. Such a framework, it seems to me, provides an appropriate backdrop for a discussion about the Holocaust, and, more specifically, about how language—in the form of rhetoric and propaganda— was instrumental in constructing, perpetuating, and, ultimately, activating a fatal set of premises.

To accompany the guest lectures, I chose these materials:

> The *Wannsee Protocol,* the only existing written record of the January 20, 1942, conference at Wannsee, where the so-called final solution was confirmed and sealed
>
> The film *Conspiracy*
>
> Art Spiegelman's two-part graphic novel *Maus*
>
> Franz Kafka's "In the Penal Colony"—not, strictly speaking, a Holocaust piece, but one that is often considered eerily prophetic of the graphically violent, bureaucratic Nazi machine[1]

My intention was to use these materials as a way of exploring our three-part rubric and pushing students to think about precisely how and when effective rhetoric becomes devastating, how and when words themselves not only describe but also create whole worlds of meaning—worlds that are internally consistent and, for this reason, logically impenetrable.

The unit began with the *Wannsee Protocol.* The document is short (fifteen pages) and intensely gripping in its stark clarity. On the day the reading was assigned, the students came to class having read the *Wannsee Protocol.* I asked them first to free-write about their responses and reactions to the transcripts. The class was divided on the subject. Many admitted to being bored by the material, not understanding what the situation was about, and not being drawn in by the text. Another group was disturbed by the simplicity of the language being used to describe such horrific acts. I then divided the class into three groups and assigned a specific task to each. The first group was asked to identify and list all instances of euphemism and understatement and to equate these terms with what they really signify. The students in this group treated the task exhaustively; when they reported back to the whole class, their findings— phrases such as "enforced, accelerated emigration" and "elimination by natural causes"—covered the blackboard completely. The second group identified and listed the ways in which language was used to make the subject "legal." I suggested that they use as the point of departure for their list the discussion of the Nuremberg Laws that was included in the transcript of the *Wannsee Protocol*. The result was that the group was confused but intrigued by the complexity of this discussion and was able to show how this complexity—the act of making complex, that is—governed the overall logic of the Wannsee Conference. They were also able to demonstrate how the language of the transcript depicted Jews as both subhuman and criminal and therefore as a credible threat to the German public. The third group was assigned the task of distinguishing the personalities and agendas of the conference participants. I expected the students in this group to have some difficulty with the task because the information provided in the transcript of the *Wannsee Protocol* is quite hazy and sketchy, but I was surprised by their findings. They were able to pinpoint the major lines of argumentation and the underlying subtleties of these arguments. For instance, they noted that some participants in the Wannsee Conference had cited political and financial expedience as the major factor in the decision to "evacuate" the Jews, that others were in favor of sterilization rather than the so-called evacuation, and that the latter preference indicated a deeper hatred of Jews than that shown by their expedience-minded counterparts.

The group work set the stage for *Conspiracy*. In our viewing and discussion of the film, we concentrated most on the ways in which the movie made *explicit* the implicit (subtle, suggestive) language of the transcripts, on how what had merely been hinted at was fleshed out in the movie's characters and setting, on the dynamics of power, and on the increasingly tangled interplay of rhetoric and the precise action that this rhetoric enforced. We were careful to deal with this film as a speculative account, that is, as an account with its own failings regarding the truth of the Wannsee Conference. The students were especially taken with the way in which the movie called attention to language itself—with how the conference participants, in this rendition, continued to call each other to task for what they were saying and continued to force each other to clarify and explicate their terms. The students contended that the clarification process depicted in the film had the paradoxical effect of presenting a more complicated spectrum of responses than could be found in the transcript's reductive account. They suggested that, in the film, lines between arguments had begun to blur, and that only shades of meaning could be distinguished between arguments based on expedience and those based on hatred. In turn, their own reactions to the Wannsee Conference became more complicated. Having now seen filmed depictions of the participants—several of whom are shown voicing concern, anxiety, and disgust—the students attempted to sort them out in terms of whose arguments were more or less egregious. A veritable mess ensued as students first defined their criteria for judgment and then came to recognize that the criteria differed greatly from student to student. Some students lauded the ability to wield power, others the "integrity" to speak in no uncertain terms, and still others the choice to quietly demur. We concluded our discussion with a question of practical ethics: What type of argument, if any, could have been launched against the arguments presented at the conference? The students' responses were disappointingly similar: no argument, they suggested, could have made a difference in this setting; the balance of power was too far skewed, the decision-making process was a farce, and everything had been decided before the Wannsee Conference had even begun.

How to express to them that—although history confirmed their own sense of inevitability, and although those who were involved in carrying out this "solution" justified themselves by closed and, in many ways, circular arguments—there is a more crucial ethical and existential imperative at work here? How to make them see that it is not enough to plead "no contest"—that, in effect, to resign themselves to a lack of sufficient argument is to be complicit in the outcome of a decision that goes unchallenged? I thought it best to highlight two crucial lessons that the transcript and the movie present with regard to writing. The first is that personalities and agendas, though seemingly hidden in the written text of the transcript, were all too well represented at the Wannsee Conference.

Our own biases, similarly, cannot be erased or extracted from anything we write. It is our responsibility, therefore, to be aware of these biases and how they inform what we say—to be aware that sometimes, despite our best intentions, what we depict as fact may be, in fact, only opinion. The second lesson is that the most powerful weapon in the room at the Wannsee Conference was language. By means of language, the conference participants were able to carefully craft a basis for the annihilation of millions of people. By extension, we, as writers, need to acknowledge the power—potentially destructive—of our words. We need to become fully aware of the implications and consequences of what we say; we need to recognize that we are accountable not only for what we say but also for how we say it.

This pairing of "what" with "how," of content with form, paved the way for *Maus,* the next portion of this unit. It was my hope, in teaching this book in conjunction with the *Wannsee Protocol* and *Conspiracy,* that students would be introduced—by means of a poignant, graphic, painful example—to the reality enforced by the words spoken at Wannsee. I wanted students to see, literally, an abstraction take on concrete, indelible form. In contrast to the sterile atmosphere of the *Wannsee Protocol,* Spiegelman's *Maus* offers an account of an intensely real and palpable relationship (between Vladek and his son, Artie). In contrast, too, to the hidden agendas of the participants in the Wannsee Conference, in *Maus* we have a self-proclaimed and indisputably subjective account. I wanted students to grapple with how these distinctions, as encapsulated in the telling of the story, affect us as readers. The pseudoscientific, legalistic rhetoric of the Wannsee Conference transcript presents itself as true, as given, natural, and uncontestable; this mask of truth insidiously and intentionally subverts the categories that we have come to trust, in effect using our tendency toward categorization, our need for order, against us, lulling us by our own devices. In contrast, *Maus* immediately jars its readers out of complacency; it directly confronts and thus subverts our expectations and assumptions with regard to form and representation. The language of the *Wannsee Protocol* aims for acceptance; it is manipulative, deliberate, and circuitous. The language of *Maus* (and here, graphic representation is inseparable from the written text) aims for revolt, for rejection of established norms; it is confrontational, stark, and self-aware.

We started our discussion of *Maus* with another free-writing session. This time, the students were asked to think about ways in which we might begin to make connections between the *Wannsee Protocol* and the first section they had read in *Maus*. They suggested that while both were subjective accounts—meaning that they were governed by the opinions of those who had constructed them—the account we are presented with in *Maus* is filtered through several layers of subjectivity and is described in everyday language. Vladek's account is filtered through Artie, but we always read Artie's account with an eye to how it reacts to or against that of Vladek. Here, an intense relationality—not present in the *Wannsee Protocol*—becomes a function of the language. Where we, as readers, were forced to pay close attention to what was really being said in the *Wannsee Protocol*, in *Maus* we are challenged to look at each particular moment of the text—written and graphic—in terms of its connectedness to other moments. The structure of the piece is narrative, but not merely in a linear or sequential way; the narrative folds over itself, subverts itself by means of interruption and interjection.

To continue this discussion, and to encourage more detailed reading of the text, I broke students into groups, assigning each group one of the three chapters that we had prepared for the day. The students were asked to address several issues in their groups:

How does the chapter title help frame the content of the chapter?[2]
How are layers of time represented, and how do they interact with each other? What is depicted as memory here? What is present-day account? Are there memories within memories? When memories occur, how do they affect or respond to the present-day narrative?
How do Artie and Vladek relate to one another? How do they interact? What issues trouble their relationship? How have their experiences informed their stances in the world and against each other?

Of these questions, the one that proved the most fruitful was the third. The students contended that the characters are portrayed so realistically (to support this claim, they pointed to Vladek's accent and Artie's uncensored thought processes) that the reader is forced to care about them. The reader is forced to see Vladek and Artie as three-dimensional figures, consumed and battered by their pasts, anguished in the present. Whereas the *Wannsee Protocol* eliminates all feeling, in *Maus* feeling is precisely the mechanism used to engage the reader. Such personal investment, the students suggested, works to subvert the *Wannsee Protocol*'s attempts at dehumanization and the numbing effects of its pseudoscientific rhetoric.

The second of the three questions, regarding narrative structure as an element of time, was the most difficult one for the students. They were resistant to the layering of time, not wanting to push past the fairly simple description of the narrative as a present-day obsession with the past. In my mind, this question is the most important of the three because it forces us to see not only relationality among all the parts of the narrative but also intentionality behind the construction of the narrative. The intention on Spiegelman's part is to construct a world that operates according to the premise of a relation—a dialogic model where past and present are engaged in a relationship of reciprocity, mutually and continuously informing each other (again, a subversion of the logic of the *Wannsee Protocol*)—in which the future is marked by a vehement and violent break with the past. Choosing a relational narrative, Spiegelman challenges us, as readers, to locate the present in the past, to recognize the indelible mark of the past on the present, to rethink the past in terms of the present, and to use the interconnectedness of present and past to speculate about the future. One panel of *Maus*, one narrative moment seemingly frozen in time, is by no means frozen; rather, one panel represents a living entity, reaching back to other moments of the text, and straining forward to what is to come. For the culminating essay assignment in this unit, students had the opportunity to address this topic at greater length:

> Select a moment in *Maus* that you find particularly striking, interesting, important, troublesome, or relevant to the whole narrative (both parts). Beginning with this moment, analyze how Spiegelman constructs his narrative. What kind of sequence does your chosen moment reveal? Where does this moment occur in the context of the whole piece? What does it have to do with the beginning(s) of the piece? With the end(s)? With the middle? (Note: you'll want to be thinking about how the two parts of *Maus* relate to one another in order to talk about beginning, middle, and end as well as about what you mean in your selection of a moment.) How

does isolating a moment in the text help us, as readers, to understand Spiegelman's choices with regard to his subject matter?[3]

A few students chose this option over the other three and were able to show in their essays how a particular moment functioned as a microcosm of the text as a whole, not only foreshadowing an event to come, or echoing a scene already past, but also forcing the reader to reread and rethink what had already been read and to prepare for what was to come. These students suggested that *Maus* was, in this sense, an unfinished text because one could never be satisfied that any reading was the definitive one. They suggested, too, that there are implied lessons in *Maus,* that the narrative is not only subjective but also prescriptive, if only in a completely understated way. Spiegelman, forcing us into the text, as the students agreed he does, also forces us to participate in its outcome.

This seemed to me to be an issue well worth taking up with the entire class. I wanted students to see if they could move from reading for description to reading for prescription. To facilitate this move, I chose a particularly troubling sequence in *Maus II* in which Vladek displays his own deep-seated prejudices and bigotry when Artie and his wife stop to pick up an African American hitchhiker. Aloud, Vladek refers to the man as a *shvartser* (a pejorative Yiddish term used to refer to a black person); the narrative displays the unspoken thought process in Vladek's head, which is conducted in Vladek's native Polish. The sequence culminates in a heated exchange between Vladek and Françoise, his daughter-in-law (99–100):

> *Vladek:* I had the whole time to watch out that this *shvartser* doesn't steal us the groceries from the back seat!
>
> *Françoise:* What?! That's *outrageous*! How can you, of all people, be such a racist? You talk about blacks the way the Nazis talked about the Jews!
>
> *Vladek:* Ach! I thought really you are more smart than this, Françoise. . . . it's not even to *compare,* the *shvartsers* and the Jews!

Artie stays virtually silent throughout the exchange, resignedly saying only this to his wife: "Forget it, honey . . . he's hopeless."

Around this sequence I staged a debate between the students, assigning to one side the proposition that racism is inevitable and to the other the proposition that we are making progress with regard to racism. Both sides were asked not only to argue their case but also to use their assigned proposition to construct a view of human nature supportable with evidence from the text. The first side's argument was, tellingly, much stronger than that of the other side. The students on the first side forced the issue to its breaking point, stating about halfway through the debate something to this effect: *We need to define our terms here. If we take "racism" to mean a deeply felt sense of self, fixed by virtue of opposition against the "other," mired in both fear and ignorance, and exhibited on the level of preverbal, preconscious thought, then we have to agree that Spiegelman suggests that, despite everything, even for those who have experienced the most fatal and obliterating brand of prejudice, prejudice will continue to hold sway.* I wanted them to take it to the next level—to the level not only of description but also of prescription, so that we could consider what Spiegelman may be implicitly promoting by choosing to include such an honest rendition of such a troubling moment in the text. Their response: *We have to be aware of such prejudices before we can have any control over them.* Spiegelman's choice to include this moment, they suggested, amounts to forcing on the reader an awareness of the pervasiveness of prejudice. Here, in this moment that comes late in the text, when we have moved so far and so closely with these characters, we are jarred violently into our own present. A nightmarish world, a world by no means extinguished by the passing of time, is thrust upon us in all its relevance and urgency. We're called to an accounting. We're brought into relation with this text.

In addition to the issue of relationality, we also dealt with the question of form. Why does Spiegelman choose the form of a comic book? Is a comic book an appropriate means of approaching/representing the Holocaust? What do we even mean by "appropriate"? How does this form of representation challenge our expectations? Why do we have these expectations in the first place? To help students begin thinking about these questions, I asked them to free-write on a series of related issues, beginning with the first question: Why a comic book? What forms other than a comic book might Spiegelman have chosen? What would the implications of these other forms be? Brainstorming produced several responses.

Many students felt that the pictures helped them understand the situation on a literal, almost visceral, level. They interpreted the representation of "types" by means of animals—for instance, Jews as mice, Nazis as cats, Poles as pigs, and Americans as dogs—at once as a self-appropriation of the perceptions and prejudices of others, as a perpetuation of stereotypes, and as an allegorization of the dynamics of power. They suggested that the form could have been more "objective"—the story itself could have taken the form of a historical account—or perhaps even more "subjective," as a journal or autobiography. They contended that the form of a comic book was an interesting mix of objectivity and subjectivity—that the visual representation lent a greater degree of credibility to the personal account. The other possible forms, they suggested, all fell short of producing the startling immediacy for the reader that *Maus* is able, by virtue of its form, to produce.

Curiously, no one felt that such a form trivialized its subject, and, when I hesitantly admitted to feeling uneasy the first time I encountered *Maus,* my confession was met with somewhat surprised glances. I suppose that, while I do agree with the students that *Maus* is effective precisely because it forces us to look at a subject that we may rather leave to abstraction, I wanted the *issue* of looking to be more troublesome for them. To complicate the question of form a bit more for them (not to win them over to my uneasiness, but to help them recognize the complexity of the problem of representation), I offered this topic as one of four choices for an essay:

One of the issues we've been dealing with in *Maus* is Spiegelman's choice of representation. His use of a comic strip to approach the Holocaust presents a jarring and vivid contrast between form and content. This essay consists of several parts: (a) First pinpoint a panel or set of panels (probably one page from the text is a fair estimate) from *Maus* that you find particularly interesting. Include this page in your essay. (b) Then briefly discuss the major issues addressed by the panel(s). (c) Next, "translate" the panel(s) into some other medium (poetry, prose, song lyric, and so on). You have several options with this step: you may either literally create this "translation" or speak hypothetically about what other possible "translations" might look like. (d) Now consider these questions: How

has the new form changed the meaning of the piece you've chosen to "translate"? Why did you choose the medium you chose?

Many of the students who chose this topic used poetry as their form of
"translation." They concentrated, for the most part, on carrying over the
emotions that they felt were portrayed in a particular panel or sequence
of panels. The most interesting and creative "translation" took as its subject a sequence in the first volume of *Maus*. In this sequence, Vladek,
having been in hiding in a woman's cellar in Poland, decides to go to
Hungary, where, he has heard—falsely—conditions are less dangerous
for Jews. His decision takes him out into the street, in disguise (indicated by a mask, which serves as a symbol of Vladek's attempt to "pass"
as non-Jew), in search of transportation to Hungary. On the street, some
children who are playing recognize him as a Jew and, in their fear, begin
screaming, "Help! Mommy! A Jew!!"[4] After Vladek approaches the growing crowd of concerned mothers with a "Heil Hitler," the mothers apol-
ogize for their children's behavior, and Vladek is allowed to move on,
though the experience has cost him "really a lot of hairs."[5]

The student who chose this sequence identified freedom and identity
as the most central issues here. In his "translation," he wrote a first-person
narrative account of a prisoner who had escaped from jail. The prisoner
rejoices at his newfound freedom, thirstily drinks in the air around him,
and sees the beauty of the world as if for the first time. He stops at a
roadside diner, at which point a young child, there with his mother, asks
him about his past. The prisoner creates a story for the child's benefit as
well as the mother's, and he gains their respect rather than their contempt.
In his "translation," the student pursued an equation that is both subtle
and insightful in the context of Holocaust studies: freedom is contingent upon how others perceive and define us; it is limited and precari-
ous, bound up with the wishes of others, out of our control. Identity,
likewise, is externally imposed: both Vladek and this prisoner were able
to survive only by convincing others that they were who those others
wanted them to be. In many ways the analogy the student promotes here
falls short. It is problematic to equate Vladek (and, by extension, perhaps
Jews in general) with an escaped convict, particularly if this convict has
been legitimately convicted for a crime that he committed. The situa-

tions are also not directly comparable: the prisoner takes back his freedom, whereas any such freedom that Vladek may enjoy is largely due to circumstance. Nevertheless, this student points directly to the horrifying condition for Jews during the Holocaust: identity meant, in fact, absolute, ultimate loss of freedom; it meant death. This "translation" helped the student recognize how such pervasive loss of freedom became an identity for those persecuted in the Holocaust.

Unfortunately, the question of how change in medium (or form) enforces change in meaning went largely unaddressed by the students who chose this essay topic. Indeed, what seemed to be the unintended result of this assignment was the conclusion that, because students found it possible to "translate" the panel(s) from one form to another, the form itself became accidental, negligible. There was very little accounting for what had been lost in translation, very little sense that anything *had* been lost in translation.

The final piece in this unit is Kafka's intensely disturbing story "In the Penal Colony." I have taught this story in other courses and other contexts. Here, I use the piece as a way of reminding students of the graphic and violent world we glimpsed at Wannsee, the world in tatters that *Maus* represents. "In the Penal Colony" is paired on the syllabus with another of Kafka's stories, "The Judgement." In our discussions, we focused on the power of the spoken and written word to produce nightmarish and incomprehensible results. The "Harrow," the instrument of punishment in the penal colony, painfully and fatally inscribes the condemned one's transgression upon his flesh. The so-called transgressions are unintentional, and the inscription remains illegible until the moment when death becomes inevitable. Understanding cannot be paired with action; the "word" itself serves as a vehicle of execution. Similarly, in "The Judgement," Herr Bendemann pronounces judgment over his son—"I sentence you now to death by drowning"—and the mere pronouncement is suitable for its realization. He breathes life, gives existence, to these words simply by uttering them. Once uttered, they can neither be taken back nor disempowered. In both stories, *words kill*, literally and figuratively. We have seen a world in which words have killed, I reminded the students, a world that was all too real, a world that Kafka somehow sensed was emerging, a world that would eventually murder Kafka's own sisters. Had he lived to see his nightmarish vision take form, he most probably would not have escaped it.

MODERN CONTINENTAL EUROPEAN LITERATURE

My course in modern continental European literature is also a writing-intensive course; students can gain writing competency by taking this course. Here, in contrast to the composition course, emphasis is placed more heavily on content than on the process of writing, though the process is still strongly enforced by means of peer review, multiple drafts, and free-writing exercises. The overarching rubric for this class is "transition, identity, and the limits of language." The Holocaust is, in many respects, the specter that looms over the material we cover in the course. "Transition," here, is meant both as a literary and a historical term; one of the more relevant functions of this term, in the context of Holocaust studies, involves how ideology is filtered through and espoused by literary and philosophical texts. The course culminates in Marguerite Duras's gripping testament to the mass horror of World War II, *Hiroshima, Mon Amour.* Everything we read during the semester can, in some respects, be seen as leading up to this horror; inadvertently or anachronistically, for the most part, the works we read trace a line, albeit a circuitous one, from the imprisonment of the individual soul (Gustave Flaubert, Charles Baudelaire, Fyodor Dostoevsky) to the freeing of this soul in a cataclysmic rupture (Friedrich Nietzsche, Sigmund Freud, the symbolist poets, Thomas Mann) to the nightmarish pictures of this new world order governed by the unconscious (Kafka, Bruno Schulz) to the loss of purely individual expression as self is joined to other (Jean-Paul Sartre, Albert Camus, Samuel Beckett, Eugène Ionesco) and, finally, to the aftermath of the Holocaust (Nelly Sachs, Paul Celan, Ingeborg Bachmann, Duras).

The works directly relating to the Holocaust are Schulz's *Street of Crocodiles* (Schulz was gunned down by a Nazi officer in the streets of the ghetto in Drohobycz), the poetry of Sachs and Celan, and, a bit less directly, Bachmann's short story "The Barking," an eerie piece that challenges the audience to accept the premise that "fascism forms the basis of every relationship between a man and woman" when an academic psychologist, specializing in post-traumatic stress disorders in camp survivors, terrorizes his mother and his wife (the latter mysteriously disappears and dies at the end of the piece). One of the major components of the discussion surrounding these works is the question of language. What kind of language can be used to describe, in Schulz's case, a drastically changing world that retains a spark of the sacred, but in which that very spark is crushed? What words, in the cases of Sachs and Celan, heed Theodor Adorno's warning that it is "barbaric" to write poetry after Auschwitz at the same time that these poets are driven by the urgency to bear witness?

Schulz becomes in many ways the pivotal voice for this discussion. For Schulz, language serves to reflect the interdependence of natural and inanimate objects; it uncovers a world of mystery, connection, vitality. *Street of Crocodiles* is Schulz's contribution to Jewish mysticism, his own kabbalistic rendering of the universe. This richly layered culture, this lush and labyrinthine world, was virtually extinguished by the Nazis, and it is a world to which most students have had precious little exposure. Without coming into contact with the life of this world, with the living, breathing vibrancy of this culture, it is difficult, I think, for students to feel the impact, the tragic magnitude, of the annihilation of this culture. I want them to see and to feel a bit—if only a small bit—of what was lost. To help students enter into the complexity of Schulz's language, of his descriptions that playfully endow the inanimate with life and mechanize the living, one day I brought in several props: a birdhouse, a marionette, a teapot, and various stuffed animals. I asked the students to write, in a way that Schulz might, descriptions of these objects. We then used their descriptions as a point of departure for a discussion of what it means to connect the natural and the inanimate in such a way. What, if we might speculate, is Schulz's vision? What kind of world promotes such a connection? What kinds of action, behavior, ethics does such a world entail?

With this exercise, I hoped to stress to students that the way a world looks is intimately connected to the type of action this world promotes. Later in the semester, we saw the extended horrors of a worldview that promoted, through the rhetoric of its most articulate adherents, extermination on a scale so massive as to be almost unimaginable. In this "before" space, occupied by Schulz, we saw a worldview equally invested in the power of language, but a worldview grounded in the kabbalistic belief that language is endowed with the spark of the divine; by extension, this worldview promotes an intense relationality and connectedness among all things. Whatever language touches here, it renders sacred. Schulz, in effect, offers, through the sheer beauty and richness of his voice, the possibility that language can be—*should* be—creative, that it should be in the service of celebrating and affirming life and in the service of relation, in sharp opposition to the cold, sterile, deadly use the Nazis made of language. Schulz offers an alternative worldview: a world that combats, by power of example, the rigid, impenetrable, and thus "inevitable" logic of Wannsee. Students need to see these alternatives; they need to see examples of those who choose to embrace a logical paradigm that, if they were given the chance to argue on the basis of logic alone, would shatter the "logic" of the status quo.

Less directly but still integrally related are the pieces by Kafka, Sartre, Camus, Beckett, Luigi Pirandello, and Ionesco. The question of identity is raised again and again in these works, in ways that help us talk about, and that provide us with a frame of reference for the Holocaust pieces. What does it mean to say "I" when the other defines me? We do not read Sartre's *Antisemite and Jew,* but it becomes an important touchstone for our conversations about existentialism, and for our discussions of those authors directly affected by the Holocaust. Several of the dramas we read in this course—Sartre's *No Exit,* Beckett's *Waiting for Godot,* Pirandello's *Six Characters in Search of an Author*—are guided by a pervasive anxiety that identity is a construct, imposed externally, situated in conflict and violence. Sartre's contention, in *No Exit,* that "we are each other's torturers," and the increasingly sadistic relationship between Pozzo and Lucky in *Waiting for Godot,* painfully chronicle how cruelty has come to stand in for true connection, and how it has literally become a diversionary tactic in a bleak and abandoned world. The sparse and empty landscape that Sartre and Beckett depict provides a vivid corollary to the ashen terrain of Celan's "Todesfuge"; the same indictment, the same judgment, reverberates here as in Sachs's "You Onlookers."

Both in this course and in the composition course, a central focus has been to look for words that might begin to approach the Holocaust. Such words require a kind of hesitation, a cautious deliberation, a subtle power that strains both toward and against silence. My writing-intensive courses aim to help students find their own voices and to recognize how they might use their voices as a force for change and/or resistance. At the same time, I remain ever mindful that there are no easy formulations or ways to "teach" the Holocaust. I am uncomfortably and consistently aware of my own ambivalence in teaching this material. Though compelled to teach this material—to recite *Kaddish,* really, by way of this material—I am also extremely reluctant to force a normative and/or reductive structure on these works and on my students. Their experience with these texts, with this material, the language they choose to express their experience, must be their own. To navigate this space of ambivalence and discomfort—a space that, in my deepest hopes, my students begin to feel is an authentic space for them as well—I gesture to Paul Celan, who offers us a necessarily hazy "prescription" for writing, elastic in its applicability, vigilant in its demands:

> Speak, you also
> speak as the last,
> have your say.
>
> Speak—
> But keep yes and no unsplit.
> And give your say this meaning:
> Give it the shade.[6]

NOTES

1. See *Wannsee-Protokoll/The Wannsee Protocol, and A 1944 Report on Auschwitz by the Office of Strategic Services,* introd. Robert Wolfe (New York: Garland, 1982); *Conspiracy,* directed by Frank Pierson (Los Angeles: HBO Films, 2001); Art Spiegelman, *Maus: A Survivor's Tale* (New York: Pantheon, 1986); Art Spiegelman, *Maus II: A Survivor's Tale: And Here My Troubles Began* (New York: Pantheon, 1991); Franz Kafka, *The Judgement and In the Penal Colony,* trans. Malcolm Pasley (New York: Penguin, 1995).

2. Spiegelman provides clues with the chapter titles, choosing titles that are not immediately apparent but that, with some analysis, help us to coax out their symbolic functions for the chapters.

3. For his assistance and suggestions in writing this assignment, I am indebted to Professor Mel Wininger of the English Department at Indiana University–Purdue University Indianapolis.

4. We are told at this point of how mothers have always warned their children to be careful lest a Jew catch them and eat them.

5. Spiegelman, *Maus,* 149.

6. Paul Celan, "Speak, you also," in *Poems of Paul Celan,* trans. Michael Hamburger (New York: Persea Books, 1972), 101.

4

Teaching Business Ethics and the Holocaust

DONALD FELIPE

No one would deny that a business ethics course should aspire to make people better than they are. But how can that be achieved?[1] In what ways can an ethics course actually make students better? A lot of ink has been and continues to be spilled on these questions in business ethics. Despite the complexity of the debates and arguments, there is a fair amount of general agreement in the business ethics literature on how to account for and measure moral development, and there is a thriving business ethics textbook market that exhibits a high degree of uniformity in methods and materials.[2] I propose a method to teach business ethics through a study of business and the Holocaust. This method aims to promote respect and care for persons as well as moral courage—high, elusive goals of any ethics course. I argue that the method can be used to overcome some limitations of orthodox pedagogy in business ethics.

COMMON APPROACHES AND LIMITATIONS

The general assumption underlying the common approach to teaching business ethics is a fundamental principle of modern constructive-developmental moral learning theory: that becoming a better person, or attaining higher levels of moral development, is related to cognitive development. This assumption leads to theory-characterizing concepts, cognitive skills, and/or knowledge that indicate higher moral development. It also assumes that the development and evaluation of teaching methods will cultivate the requisite skills and traits in students. In business ethics, despite high levels of debate, especially concerning pedagogy, we can discern some common perspectives that seem to be generated by the implicit demands of business education. An ethics course that thematically and methodologically fits into a business curriculum naturally emphasizes certain aspects of the study of ethics over others. Moral questions tend to concern organizational issues and managerial decisions. There is a tendency to treat the identification and resolution of these issues with analytical methods that stress the analysis of facts and variables and the application of quasi-objective moral principles or professional codes of ethics. Finally, the assessment of teaching methods is expected to rely on the use of reliable empirical methods and on quantifiable results, measured according to standards that may lay some claim to objectivity.[3]

This approach to teaching and evaluating ethics courses places great emphasis on analytical and reasoning skills. From a theoretical perspective, the so-called postconventional levels in Lawrence Kohlberg's theory of moral development are extremely well suited to these methods of pedagogy and assessment, providing fairly well defined, empirically grounded, and measurable standards of reasoning skill as well as an arguable claim to moral objectivity.[4] In the many studies that have been done to measure the effectiveness of business ethics courses,[5] the Kohlbergian categories of moral development are, at the very least, considered useful tools in ranking the responses of subjects with regard to moral development. The Defining Issues Test (DIT), developed in the early work of Rest, which explicitly ranks principled responses according to Kohlberg's postconventional categories, is paradigmatic of this approach.[6]

The content of most business ethics textbooks—outlines of rudimentary moral theory; discussions of analyses; moral reasoning; and, most important, presentation of many case studies—also reflects the stark emphasis on analysis and reasoning in teaching ethics. The case-study analysis methodology encouraged in textbooks seeks to enhance levels of cognitive skill in handling the types of moral problems faced by managers.

Learning objectives include development of the ability to distinguish and analyze relevant issues, principles, facts, and variables and the ability to find solutions to moral problems in coherent, consistent reasoning that attends to the facts and flows from acceptable moral principles.

But does the development of reasoning, and of analytical skills and practice, lead to the formation of rational responses to moral crises? And does this process of thinking and problem solving make students better people? Does the ability to conceptualize and reason about a moral issue in postmodern terms really get to the heart of what makes people live moral lives? Teachers and theorists have noted many problems.[7]

First, there is a certain distance between reasoning and action, sometimes referred to as the problem of moral courage.[8] Not only does sophistication of reasoning not guarantee moral action; highly developed reasoning skills may also serve to fortify moral failure through the rationalization of immoral conceptual frameworks.[9]

Second, there is the question of what being good actually amounts to. As Carol Gilligan and many others have pointed out, Kohlberg's theory does an inadequate job of accounting for how caring, feelings of concern for others, and personal relationships figure in moral experience and living a moral life.[10] Rest, Thoma, and other proponents of Kohlberg's view have come to acknowledge that Kohlberg's theory is better suited to accounting for the development of conceptions of justice and norms of social discourse than to accounting for the kinds of traits that make a person good in a full moral sense.[11] But becoming a good person, whatever we take that to mean, has a great deal to do with developing a sense of social responsibility and moral awareness—the very ideals that often surface in appeals for integrating business ethics into the curriculum of the business school. Acknowledgment of the limitations of traditional methods of teaching business ethics is inescapable.

Third, some psychological studies have shown a relationship between the development of a sense of care for others and a tendency to engage in moral action.[12] The research of Ervin Staub, for instance, seems to support the idea that the most certain road to moral action runs through the heart. Martin Hoffman's work on empathy and moral development also indicates that feelings of empathy and care are instrumental not only in the development of moral character and prosocial behavior but also in the evolution of one's entire conceptual moral apparatus.[13] Teaching students to approach moral issues and problems "with the heart" is a substantial challenge for ethics pedagogy. Among the available methods, which ones amount to more than sensitivity training? How can such teaching maintain a sense of academic integrity and avoid the charge of attempted indoctrination? How can one influence moral sensibilities and still maintain at least some quasi-objective principles and learning objectives that allow for reliable assessment?

ASSUMPTIONS AND METHODS

The assumptions and methods of the teaching module proposed in this chapter suggest a few ways to address at least some of these questions. The purpose of these suggestions, of course, is not to advocate the wholesale rejection of traditional or even current methods but to explore new, creative ways to teach ethics that may prove useful in reaching some challenging learning objectives. The proposed module is based on three assumptions about teaching care and respect for persons and moral courage in an academic setting.

First, *in an environment of moral humility and honesty, intimate exposure to and contact with the experience of victims of atrocity can make significant psychological inroads in the development of these same feelings, emotions, and character traits.*[14] Establishing strong perceptions of identity as well as relationships between students, on the one hand, and victims and perpetrators of atrocity, on the other, is effective in nurturing this kind of moral development. The particularity and reality of the experience of the victim must become available to students and instructors in meaningful ways. An important factor in realizing this experience is the personal involvement of the instructor in a supportive environment. These relationships are crucial to the mentoring role of the instructor.[15] As a mentor and moral example, the instructor must visibly share the experience of identity and relationships with suffering victims. This assumption leads naturally to the Holocaust for several reasons. Not only do enormous resources exist for meaningful historical study, it is also true that in Western culture the Holocaust is without question the most horrific atrocity in recent history, and that there are ample and well-documented relationships between business and the Holocaust that can be used as points of departure in the study of business ethics. The requirement for careful, particularized history is unusual in a business ethics curriculum. In the teaching module, I suggest ways to phase in this kind of study.

Second, *assertions of moral confidence and moral objectivity by the instructor or students can be counterproductive in the development of care, respect, and courage in students.*[16] The desired condition in instructor and students alike is moral humility, personal acceptance of human limitations, and honest readiness to explore and interpret cases and literature from points of view that attend to the realities of human experience and to the particularity of history. I recommend readings from Charlotte Delbo's *Auschwitz and After* and Elie Wiesel's *Night* for their clarity, immediacy, and power; readers are inevitably drawn into the nightmarish experiences of the authors and are compelled to confront the horrors of the narrative.[17] Delbo's and Wiesel's vivid depictions of cruelty by the SS at Auschwitz are fertile ground both for openness to experiences of suffering and the attendant responses of care and for emotional condemnation. Common gut responses to these readings are "What monsters!" and "Those people are evil!" These kinds of reactions are natural and perhaps healthy in some sense, but teaching that encourages these kinds of assertions of confidence and objectivity runs the risk of demonizing perpetrators with anger and even hatred and of suppressing sensitivity to the experiences of the victims, perpetrators, and bystanders. In reading Delbo, for instance, students who cannot move beyond perceptions of absolute evil will not come close to grasping nuances of experience in the narrative and memories that Delbo attempts to evoke in her art. Anger and hatred may be justified in certain circumstances, but in moral education we must treat manifestations of these emotions as surreptitious enemies of moral learning. We must be ever vigilant against the invitation to treat "the Other" as evil and thus fortify our blindness to our own weaknesses and failures.

Third, *setting and following a moral example in an appropriate context is essential in helping others develop responses of care.* In business schools, such a process is called "mentoring." I propose that if mentoring is to achieve success, then instructors and the institution must visibly and earnestly accept the responsibility of moral activism and actively seek to nurture moral awareness. Moreover, the instructor's development in the classroom of the role of mentor is dynamic and should expose the vulnerability of the instructor. An instructor cannot lead the way in moral education without engaging moral issues in the same ways that students should. This process entails the instructor's showing, to the extent possible in a college setting, at least the same care, integrity, and courage that are being presented as goals to students. At the very least, showing these traits of character involves instructors trying to communicate justice and care in what they say and do. Instructors should share with their students stories about who they are, and those stories should reveal instructors' strengths, their frailties, and the depth of their commitments. In the teaching module, I recommend that the instructor share personal thoughts in a journal as a way to express these commitments and help students nurture identifications and reflections that can produce responses of care and respect. I provide an example of an instructor's journal later in this chapter.

These three assumptions, if they have even a bit of merit, carry significant implications for the institutional and cultural setting in which we teach. Some of these implications may place stress on the way administrators, teachers, and students conceptualize a business education.

A primary goal of business education is the development of skills and knowledge that will lead to a successful career in business. Success, of course, is measured, for the most part, in terms of the creation of wealth. From an institutional point of view, congruence between the study of ethics and monetary success is of enormous importance for the support of an ethics curriculum. Business ethics textbooks are keen to argue that ethics is good for business. These arguments certainly have a role to play in teaching business ethics, and the assumptions of this module do not imply that the study and practice of ethics will be mostly or even sometimes at odds with profitable business practices in contemporary culture. Nevertheless, these three assumptions do carry grave implications for how we should view the relationship between profit and moral education and for how we should engage in the endeavor of moral education. Not only must the pursuit of self-interest and profit remain outside the boundaries of this phase of moral education, institutions and instructors themselves must also forcefully and publicly embrace a moral purpose, an educational mission that relegates the self-interested pursuit of profit to secondary status. Humble openness to the experience and reality of Holocaust victims, and to whatever moral significance can be learned from such openness, should preclude a preconception (or even the desire to argue) that there exists coextensive harmony between what is good and what is "good for me" from a business perspective. Furthermore, these three assumptions imply that a real and visible institutional commitment to the priority of moral purpose over business interests is a precondition for achieving the high ambitions of moral education. The integrity of institution and instructor alike must provide the groundwork for teaching business ethics.

RATIONALE AND USE OF THE TEACHING MODULE

An entire course devoted to teaching about the Holocaust is politically and pedagogically unrealistic in business education. A module of reasonable duration should not absorb more than six weeks of class time. Study of Holocaust experiences and atrocities is also quite unusual for a traditional business ethics course; it requires creative integration with the traditional themes and concepts of business ethics. I propose the following threefold approach (this is obviously not the only way to attempt this integration):

1. General study of the history of the Holocaust, followed by a study of relevant, concrete cases in business that attempt to stay true to assumptions of historicity and particularity

2. An intimate study of the experience of Holocaust victims that engages students and the instructor in the experience of Holocaust atrocity (in this phase of the module, the teacher's journal becomes a particularly relevant tool)

3. A discussion of issues related to contemporary business practice that is relevant to material covered in the first two phases of the unit

Studies of business, industry, and the Holocaust tend to be voluminous, specialized, and detailed. It is extremely difficult to penetrate to levels of particularity in the few weeks available in a business ethics course. In the first phase of the module, I use a general source on the history of the Holocaust for initial background, followed by some accessible materials that provide general background on the relationships between German business and the Holocaust as well as concrete historical work on the evolving role of IG Farben.[18] These historical components help students achieve some understanding about the historical context of the Holocaust as well as knowledge about a few of the ways in which the largest German corporation, IG Farben, became involved. This first phase of the module ultimately aims at nurturing some level of identification with IG Farben as a company and with some of the actors in the company, such as Carl Bosch, the chief officer from 1925 to 1935. While still in the first phase, points of departure are established for the second through students' and the instructor's reflections on how they are relating to the circumstances and issues confronting IG Farben and to the functioning of the IG Farben facility at Auschwitz.

The second phase of the module—the study of Holocaust experiences and atrocities—is, in light of the three assumptions discussed earlier, extremely important. There is, of course, a wealth of material that can be used in this kind of study, including literature and films. Apart from the inescapable power of the works by Delbo and Wiesel, the setting for both is Auschwitz. As one moves from a study of the horrific day-to-day life in the camp to the vivid experiences narrated in the essays, the importance of the second assumption becomes apparent: heated moralizing or detached historical commentary about events at Auschwitz or the work of Delbo and Wiesel may distract from the brute realities of their experience and that of other victims. The moral message, if one exists, is communicated in the transparency of the history and the narration of the experience itself. The module does minimize the study of perpetrators and bureaucratic/organizational issues in the Holocaust, often considered the aspects of Holocaust study that are most relevant to business ethics. The reasons for this neglect of organizational issues are simply lack of time and relative importance. Studies of perpetrators and organizational issues, I believe, are more likely to leave intact perceptions of difference between students and their instructor, on the one hand, and the experience of the Holocaust, on the other. This is not to imply, of course, that such studies should be neglected. That is why the film

Conspiracy has been added to the first phase of the module, and it can be supplemented by study of the Milgram experiments, authority in organizations, and group psychology.[19]

The third phase of the module attempts to bring the study of the Holocaust back to contemporary issues of business ethics. Given the emphasis of this module on Holocaust experience, moral courage, care, and respect for persons, the most relevant issues concern virtue and character in business. Robert Solomon is considered a pioneer in this area. His book, *A Better Way to Think About Business,* presents a very readable discussion of virtues, and their relationships to negative and positive perspectives on business practice, that is quite relevant to our study.[20] His discussion of "ways not to think about business," which includes treatment of dehumanizing speech, military metaphors, and so on, should provide for significant ethical reflection in the wake of study of Holocaust atrocity. Solomon describes integrity as a synthesis of virtues that encompasses and represents many different traits of character. Integrity constitutes a wholeness of character: a sense of self-identity; an awareness of moral principles and social context; moral conviction; social openness; and a sense of connectedness with other human beings. From a philosophical perspective, study of the Holocaust and business provokes basic questions about the reasons and causes of moral action, especially with regard to actions derived from moral courage. If one lacks moral courage, one knows the right thing to do but does not do it because of conflicting desires and interests. Actions derived from moral courage, by contrast, admit of degrees. Weak moral courage entails doing the right thing in normal circumstances, in the face of ordinary conflicting desires and interests. Actions derived from strong moral courage are taken in opposition to strong desires and interests, and under duress. Solomon's account of integrity vividly depicts moral character that should be disposed to action derived from moral courage. But Solomon does not offer any discussion about how to develop and encourage integrity at the individual or organizational level or about how one achieves the depth of character that integrity signifies. Solomon's view of integrity is explicitly Aristotelian and calls for the wise moderation of emotions like compassion and empathy with victims. We might question whether Solomon's account of integrity captures the kinds of traits, feelings, and experiences necessary for acts of strong moral courage. Could Solomon's conception of integrity have provided adequate grounds for the courageous actions of, say, a manager at IG Farben? Study of the Holocaust should provoke an examination of Solomon's portrait of integrity, of the business professional, of the meaning of conscience, and of how conscience is present or absent in ourselves.

Two primary learning objectives for the module can be discerned: shifts in attitude, from self-interested motivation and perspectives to a stronger attachment to care and respect for persons; and development of strong commitment to and appreciation for moral conscience and a strong tendency to moral action. I leave to the instructor the development of additional learning objectives that are more directly related to class performance and evaluation. Weekly class and journal topics provide ample material with which to fashion such objectives. Instructors should be open to the possibility that journal entries, while they may exhibit progress in the kind of moral development desired, may still fail to exhibit corresponding progress in traditional academic performance.

The module may begin with a review of the topics in each phase and with the journal assignment. Suggested journal topics elicit reflections on how students relate to specific characters and experiences presented in the reading material. (Instructors, of course, may wish to use their own topics; topics concerning the history of the Holocaust have been left open.) In the introduction to the module, according to our assumptions, it is essential that the instructor act as a co-participant in the learning process when he or she presents the material. In keeping with the spirit of this commitment, I also keep a journal and share entries with the class.

Weeks 1–3

Topics for the first three weeks of the module include study of the historical background to the Holocaust up to 1936, study of the historical background to the Holocaust through 1945,[21] and study of the complicity of IG Farben in the Nazi war effort and in the Holocaust.[22]

The first three weeks of the module relate to the history of the Holocaust, IG Farben's involvement, and the decisions and participation of its managers. Journal assignments or tests during the first three weeks may range over a variety of historical topics that begin a process of association and identification between students, on the one hand, and Holocaust victims, perpetrators, and bystanders, on the other. These topics neglect many issues of historical knowledge, which can be treated at the discretion of the instructor:

> Who was Carl Bosch? Review Hayes's discussion of Bosch's actions and decisions.[23] Try to put yourself in Carl Bosch's shoes. Would you do anything different? Why? Be honest and frank in your answer.
>
> According to Hayes,[24] what was the driving force behind the complicity of German big business in the Holocaust? Briefly explain. Then explain why you desire to become a business professional. Compare your reasons for becoming a business professional with Hayes's account of why German business became involved with the Holocaust.
>
> On the basis of Hayes's analysis,[25] what do you see as the most troubling decision or practice at IG Farben during the war? Why? Offer your reflections.

Weeks 4–5

The topics for the next two weeks include study and/or discussion of the construction and operations of Auschwitz,[26] more historical background on Auschwitz and the Holocaust from 1943 to 1945,[27] selections from Charlotte Delbo's *Auschwitz and After,*[28] and selections from Elie Wiesel's *Night.*[29] Again, the topics focus on perceptions of association. Instructors may develop other assignments on the history of the Holocaust and Auschwitz:

> What does it mean to "see" the Holocaust? Reflect on Langer's discussion of "common memory" and "sense memory" in Delbo.[30] What does Delbo make you see as a reader? What does this do to you? Offer your own reflections.
>
> Select an excerpt or poem in Delbo or a passage from Wiesel that made a deep impact on you. Describe what is presented in the text. Why does this text affect you as it does?

What is dehumanization? Offer your reflections, making reference to passages in Wiesel and Delbo.

What is the importance of tears? Discuss Delbo's essay "Lulu" and Wiesel's frequent reference to lack of tears. Offer your reflections.

Are there any moral lessons to be gained from reading Delbo and Wiesel? Take a specific passage from Delbo and one from Wiesel and explain the moral lessons or lack thereof in those passages. Offer your own personal reflections on these passages.

Week 6

The topics of the final week are more nuanced:

Myths and metaphors about business[31]
The meaning of integrity and virtue in business[32]
Moral courage

Suggested journal topics help the students articulate sophisticated ethical issues:

Consider Solomon's discussion of the language of dehumanization and of "myths and metaphors" about business.[33] After your study of the Holocaust, what are your thoughts about these ways of looking at business? Offer your personal reflections.

What is integrity? Explain what Solomon says about integrity. What do you think integrity is? Can you think of any people in the writings of Delbo or Wiesel who exhibit integrity? Offer your reflections on what integrity means, in light of your study of the Holocaust.

What is moral courage? Can you think of any people in the writings of Delbo or Wiesel who exhibit moral courage? Does a person of integrity, in Solomon's sense, also have moral courage? Do you think you are capable of moral courage? Offer your reflections.

My journal is an example of how an instructor might get personally involved in class contributions. The topic is not directly related to business and the Holocaust but instead to the nature of moral courage as it relates to my intellectual development and experience:

> As late as 1965, in a famous interview in *Der Spiegel,* Martin Heidegger attempted to explain his early support of National Socialism and his close involvement with the Nazis without even once mentioning the Holocaust.[34] The interview stands as an ironic exclamation point to Heidegger's near-complete silence on the Holocaust for over thirty years. Heidegger's silence has prompted a swell of critical literature that began in the late 1970s and continues to grow.[35] Disturbing brute facts confront us: Heidegger directly supported National Socialism until at least 1934 and spoke favorably of the movement on occasions after 1934.[36] Heidegger was, of course, well aware of unimaginable atrocities of the Holocaust and was immersed in philosophical, ethical, and political issues directly relevant to the causes and effects of Nazi genocide. But we have no reason for believing that Heidegger held the suffering and murder of millions, at the hands of a movement he encouraged and supported, as matters of importance to his personal and intellectual life.

When I was a young graduate student, Heidegger's status as one of the most influential philosophers of the twentieth century commanded my attention. I developed a curious admiration for Heidegger and his work. In the early 1980s I heard about the controversy over Heidegger's involvement with the Nazis, but I didn't pay much attention. I would say to myself, "I don't see how it is relevant to his philosophy, his thought, and that is what interests me." Heidegger, in his very troubling interview with *Der Spiegel,* suffers from an absolute crisis of care. His relationships to the murdered millions are among the farthest things from his mind. And, when I was a student, such things mattered little to me as well. Heidegger appears most concerned with the status and legacy of his philosophical thought and intellectual standing, sharply expressed by his precondition for the interview: that it not be published until after his death. And I, the young philosophy student, in what I said to myself as I would brush aside talk of Heidegger and National Socialism, obviously cared for many of the same things. I have at least rearranged what I care about. I believe

I can say that. But my care is unoriginal and more bound to the threat of forgetfulness than to decisiveness. I do not easily forget children, especially little girls, shrieking wildly as they are torn from their mothers' arms on the rail platforms at Auschwitz. An image of children being carted off in the direction of the showers has been chiseled into my mind, as it would be in stone. I feel the light brush of ash settling on hair and arms and sense the horror of its origin. I have a three-year-old daughter of my own. I have trouble forgetting these things.

I think I have also learned something from Heidegger about the immeasurable distance between thought and care and about an even greater distance between thought and courage. Thought does not summon courage; courage is brought forth most powerfully in empathy and emotions that command action. Courage issues particular commands like "I can't do that!" or "Of course I will help. I must. How could I not?"[37] How I respond to those commands will reveal the unthinkable essence of my courage, if it exists. Courage does not find real strength in knowledge, not even if such knowledge reveals what is to be feared and not feared. The power of courage is nothing more than the depth of my concern and respect for others. Self-knowledge of that reality and power is not possible, I believe, but knowledge of what others do can make visible the reality and power of courage, and that is important to me.

Courage by its nature begs for hope and a belonging among others. So courage embraces a silent desire to be present with those who have shown what it is to be brave, but this desire will forever turn away from the painful self-knowledge of what courage is; the essence of courage does not want to be thought or known. It is easy to lament the tragedy of Heidegger's forgotten care and failed courage. I may turn away from him without any danger to myself, but I do not want to raise the painful question of my own self-knowledge. I would rather be silent and seek the company and comfort of others.

One cannot teach about the Holocaust and remain an objective bystander passing on knowledge and moral lessons. Teaching will necessarily involve us—who we are and what we do. This personal involvement manifests itself in a variety of ways in the proposed teaching module; but, prior to considering any plan for teaching about the Holocaust, we face an inescapable demand to examine our roles as teachers and why we do what we do. I teach the Holocaust in ethics courses because the nature of the subject personally delivers the formidable responsibility to commit oneself entirely to the loftiest ambitions of moral education. As far as business ethics pedagogy is concerned, these responsibilities provoke not simply admissions that analysis, case studies, and moral reasoning have limitations but also a profound inquiry into our own integrity as teachers as well as into the integrity and purposes of our institutions, our culture, and business education itself. I propose the teaching module and methods described here with those responsibilities in mind.

NOTES

I wish especially to acknowledge the contributions of John Roth and the other participants in his seminar on religious and philosophical implications of the Holocaust, held at the United States Holocaust Memorial Museum, Washington, D.C., in the summer of 2001.

1. See Hun-Joon Park, "Can Business Ethics Be Taught? A New Model of Business Ethics Education," *Journal of Business Ethics* 17 (1998), 965–977. Park identifies this common approach to teaching business ethics as simply "business ethics education."

2. See, for instance, Thomas W. Dunfee and Diana C. Robertson, "Integrating Ethics into the Business School Curriculum," *Journal of Business Ethics* 7 (1988), 847–59. Dunfee and Robertson outline methods for integrating the treatment of ethics into business courses at the Wharton School, University of Pennsylvania, that wholeheartedly accept the general approach to teaching business ethics described in this chapter. See also Thomas R. Piper, Mary C. Gentile, and Sharon D. Parks, eds., *Can Ethics Be Taught? Perspectives, Challenges, and Approaches at Harvard Business School* (Boston: Harvard Business School, 1993). The essays in *Can Ethics Be Taught?* that discuss the teaching of business ethics at Harvard show far more flexibility and ingenuity than do Dunfee and Robertson (and some ideas in the volume, like the importance of mentoring and of making institutional commitments to social responsibility, are closely akin to assumptions for the proposed teaching module on the Holocaust), but the volume's heavy reliance on the development of appropriate reasoning and cognitive skills in the teaching of business ethics is quite evident.

3. Emphasis on tangible results from business ethics courses is evident in

many ways. Stark, for example, turns this very demand against the traditional methods of teaching business ethics, arguing that the study of moral reasoning and theory provides no workable methods for solving the real moral dilemmas faced by managers; see Andrew Stark, "What's the Matter with Business Ethics?," *Harvard Business Review* (May–June 1993), 38–41, 44, 46, 48. Stark's appears to be a minority view, but the culture of focusing on the "bottom line" in ethics courses is not. The kind of creativity in pedagogy suggested in this chapter requires, I believe, rethinking this way of looking at business ethics.

4. See K. S. Froelich and J. L. Kotte, "Measuring Individual Beliefs about Organizational Ethics," *Educational and Psychological Measurement* 51 (1991), 377–83; James Weber, "Measuring the Impact of Teaching Ethics to Future Managers: A Review, Assessment, and Recommendation," *Journal of Business Ethics,* 9 (1990), 183–90; James Rest and Stephen J. Thoma, "Educational Programs and Interventions," in J. Rest, ed., *Moral Development* (New York: Praeger, 1986).

5. See James Rest, *Development in Judging Moral Issues* (Minneapolis: University of Minnesota Press, 1979).

6. See Park, "Can Business Ethics Be Taught?"; Jeanne Liedtka, "Wounded But Wiser: Reflections on Teaching Ethics to MBA Students," *Journal of Management Education* 16 (1992), 405–16. See also Thomas M. Jones, "Can Business Ethics Be Taught? Empirical Evidence," *Business & Professional Ethics Journal* 8 (1989), 73–94.

7. In this chapter, I will treat moral courage as a character trait prompting moral action that is contrary to desires and interests that would not be served, or that would be denied, by such action. We can, of course, speak of the exercise of moral courage in degrees.

8. See Betty Bardige, "Things So Finely Human: Moral Sensibilities at Risk in Adolescence," in Carol Gilligan, Janie Victoria Ward, Jill McLean Taylor, and Betty Bardige, eds., *Mapping the Moral Domain* (Cambridge, Mass.: Harvard University Press, 1988).

9. See Carol Gilligan, *In a Different Voice: Psychological Theory and Women's Development* (Cambridge, Mass.: Harvard University Press, 1982).

10. See James Rest, Darcía Narváez, Muriel J. Bebeau, and Stephen J. Thoma, *Postconventional Moral Thinking: A Neo-Kohlbergian Approach* (Minneapolis: Center for the Study of Ethical Development, University of Minnesota, 1999). Rest himself has called into question the relevance of Kohlberg's theory to what is dubbed "micromorality" (issues of care, empathy, sympathy, relationships, and the like), and he argues that the theory is best understood as an account of

the "macromoral" domain of rights, justice, and social norms and rules. Rest et al. point out that Kohlberg himself did not intend his theory to serve as a comprehensive account of the moral domain; see Lawrence Kohlberg, "A Current Statement on Some Theoretical Issues," in Sohan Modgil and Celia Modgil, eds., *Lawrence Kohlberg: Consensus and Controversy* (Philadelphia: Taylor & Francis/Palmer Press, 1986), 485–546.

11. In this chapter, I focus on pedagogy rather than moral theory; hence, I will discuss teaching method and theory as they are related to nurturing "moral development," that is, as they are related to improving moral character, fostering ways of thinking about moral problems, and encouraging a tendency to do what is right. But I will not discuss methods and theory aimed at determining and justifying the morally correct course of action in a given set of circumstances. In this chapter, the term "moral action" refers to doing or strongly intending to do the right thing according to common standards of decency and generally accepted norms of conduct. This descriptive definition does not, of course, provide a body of unambiguous rules for deciding what is right and wrong, nor do I intend the definition to articulate in any way the nature of what is good and right.

12. See Ervin Staub, "Values in a Motivational Perspective," in Nancy Eisenberg, Janusz Reykowski, and Ervin Staub, eds., *Social and Moral Values: Individual and Societal Perspectives* (Hillsdale, N.J.: Lawrence Erlbaum, 1989), 45–61.

13. Martin L. Hoffman, *Empathy and Moral Development* (Cambridge, England: Cambridge University Press, 2000).

14. This assumption stems from many sources, among them the Facing History and Ourselves National Foundation, the study of Betty Bardige on Holocaust study and moral learning in children, and the work of Martin Hoffman.

15. This is a common theme in the work of Philip Hallie. I am also indebted to John Roth and Lawrence Langer for this insight; see especially Lawrence L. Langer, *Preempting the Holocaust* (New Haven, Conn.: Yale University Press, 1998).

16. This assumption is generally consistent with observations made by Sharon Daloz Parks, "Is It Too Late? Young Adults and the Formation of Professional Ethics," in Thomas R. Piper, Mary C. Gentile, and Sharon D. Parks, eds., *Can Ethics Be Taught?* (Boston: Harvard Business School, 1993), 13–73, and especially 48–52, where Parks discusses mentoring. Nevertheless, there are aspects of mentoring presented in this chapter that are not discussed by Parks.

17. Charlotte Delbo, *Auschwitz and After,* trans. Rosette C. Lamont (New

Haven, Conn.: Yale University Press, 1995); Elie Wiesel, *Night,* trans. Stella Rodway (New York: Bantam Books, 1986).

18. See Peter Hayes, *Industry and Ideology: IG Farben in the Nazi Era,* 2nd ed. (Cambridge, England: Cambridge University Press, 2000). Also included in the first phase, as an addendum, is *Conspiracy,* directed by Frank Pierson (Los Angeles: HBO Films, 2001), which provides an interpretation of perpetrator psychology, the implementation of the Final Solution, and the bureaucratic debates surrounding the Wannsee Conference.

19. See *Conspiracy.* See also *Obedience,* a film dealing with the study of obedience by Stanley Milgram (University Park, Pa.: Audio-Visual Services, Pennsylvania State University, 1993).

20. Robert Solomon, *A Better Way to Think About Business: How Personal Integrity Leads to Corporate Success* (Oxford, England: Oxford University Press, 1999).

21. See Martin Gilbert, *The Holocaust: A History of the Jews of Europe During the Second World War* (New York: Henry Holt, 1985); Michael R. Marrus, *The Holocaust in History* (New York: Penguin, 1987).

22. Hayes, *Industry and Ideology,* 325–83. See also Peter Hayes, "Profits and Persecution: German Big Business and the Holocaust," J. B. and Maurice C. Shapiro Annual Lecture, presented at the United States Holocaust Memorial Museum, Washington, D.C., Feb. 17, 1998. Also consider using the film *Conspiracy* and the video *Obedience.*

23. See especially Hayes, *Industry and Ideology,* 2–4, 14–15, 20–21, 26, 29, 47–49, 65–67, 86–87, 91–94, 100, 110–11, 123.

24. Hayes, "Profits and Persecution."

25. Hayes, *Industry and Ideology,* 325–83.

26. Yisrael Gutman and Michael Berenbaum, eds., *Anatomy of the Auschwitz Death Camp* (Bloomington/Washington, D.C.: Indiana University Press in association with the United States Holocaust Memorial Museum, 1994), 5–49; Yehuda Bauer, *A History of the Holocaust* (New York: Franklin Watts, 1982), 193–226. See also the related articles on construction and maintenance of the Auschwitz concentration camp at the Web site of the Auschwitz Memorial and Museum, www.auschwitz-muzeum.oswiecim.pl/html/eng/historia_KL/index .html (accessed Feb. 2, 2006).

27. Gilbert, *The Holocaust,* 662–831.

28. See Charlotte Delbo, "None of Us Will Return," in *Auschwitz and After,* 2–114.

29. Wiesel, *Night,* 21–62, 99–109.

30. See Langer, *Preempting the Holocaust.*

31. Solomon, *A Better Way to Think About Business,* 1–34.

32. Ibid., 35–63.

33. Ibid., 1–34.

34. "Only a God Can Save Us: *Der Spiegel's* Interview [Sept. 23, 1966] with Martin Heidegger," trans. Maria P. Alter and John D. Caputo, published in English in *Philosophy Today* 20:4/4 (1976), 267–85 and reprinted in Richard Wolin, ed., *The Heidegger Controversy: A Critical Reader* (Cambridge, Mass.: MIT Press, 1993).

35. I present an incomplete list of some of the more important sources on this question: Jacques Derrida, "Heidegger's Silence," in Guenther Neske and Emil Kettering, eds., *Martin Heidegger and National Socialism: Questions and Answers,* trans. Lisa Harries (New York: Paragon House, 1990); Victor Farías, ed., *Heidegger and Nazism,* trans. Paul Burrell, Gabriel R. Ricci, et al. (Philadelphia: Temple University Press, 1989); Jürgen Habermas, "Work and Weltanschauung: The Heidegger Controversy from a German Perspective," in Hubert L. Dreyfus and Harrison Hall, eds., *Heidegger: A Critical Reader* (Cambridge, England: Basil Blackwell, 1992); Hugo Ott, *Martin Heidegger: A Political Life,* trans. Allan Blunden (New York: Basic Books, 1993); Thomas Sheehan, ed., *Heidegger the Man and the Thinker* (Chicago: Precedent Publishing, 1981); Jean-François Lyotard, *Heidegger and "the jews,"* trans. Andreas Michel and Mark S. Roberts (Minneapolis: University of Minnesota Press, 1990); Leslie Paul Thiele, *Timely Meditations: Martin Heidegger and Postmodern Politics* (Princeton: Princeton University Press, 1995), 142–43. Two books devoted solely to the issue of Heidegger's silence are Alan Milchman and Alan Rosenberg, eds., *Martin Heidegger and the Holocaust* (Atlantic Highlands, N.J.: Humanities Press, 1996) and Berel Lang, *Heidegger's Silence* (Ithaca, N.Y.: Cornell University Press, 1996), especially 101–11, where Lang includes recollections and diary entries by David Luban concerning discussions about Heidegger with Eduard Baumgarten in the 1970s, among the more revealing sources with respect to Heidegger's character.

36. Martin Heidegger, "The Self-Assertion of the German University," in Richard Wolin, ed., *The Heidegger Controversy: A Critical Reader* (Cambridge, Mass.: MIT Press, 1993), 29–39. See also Lang, *Heidegger's Silence;* Karl Lowith, "My Last Meeting with Heidegger," *New German Critique* 45 (Fall 1988), 115–16.

37. Bardige, "Things So Finely Human," notes these kinds of imperatives in the responses of children who are exposed to Holocaust materials. Hallie, in a moving essay, reports similar kinds of responses among the villagers of Le

Chambon sur Lignon, France, who sheltered Jews from the Nazis at considerable risk to themselves; see Philip Paul Hallie, *Lest Innocent Blood Be Shed: The Story of the Village of Le Chambon, and How Goodness Happened There* (New York: Harper & Row, 1979). Martin Hoffman's studies on empathy also indicate relationships between empathic reactions to the suffering of others and some of the most basic moral responses and concepts.

5

Teaching the Holocaust

The Ethics of "Witness" History

TAM K. PARKER

Teaching the Shoah and ethics in tandem can be an arduous task. In my experience, this is a landscape fraught with moral land mines for any student or scholar of the Holocaust. The question at hand is how one negotiates the relationship between the objects or subjects *of* study and the subject *who* studies. In particular, the question with which I struggle in teaching the Holocaust and ethics together is the nature of my role in helping students ethically negotiate the space between themselves and the historical record with which they are confronted. In asking this question, I suggest that the study of the Shoah in and of itself presents us, teachers and students, not only with the task of objective analysis but also with ethical dilemmas and challenges of our own.

The study of the Shoah lays upon its students the imperative of moral response. The pedagogical challenge lies in facilitating the possibility of that response. In particular, I want to address the issue of judgment in relation to the perpetrators. To many of us, this is a nonissue; of course, condemnation of genocide follows upon the study of the Holocaust. But I want to address the classroom situation in which the principles of moral relativism extend beyond the descriptive and into the prescriptive. In other words, what are the issues and pedagogical strategies involved in contending with what I call the "response of no response," that is, the student who abdicates the exercise of judgment on the grounds of a thoroughgoing relativism?

A descriptive relativism is commonsensical; every historical situation is unique and has to be queried on its own terms. But what I am calling a prescriptive relativism moves from the objectivity of observation to a refusal to make any judgment whatsoever regarding the moral values of the historical actors and actions observed. What may be considered the intellectual virtue of objectivity in the historical pursuit of—and the refusal to judge—the victims' actions or failure to act[1] translates into a moral vice when applied to the perpetrators. For example, historical and moral analysis of Jewish victims of the death camps (those "at the bottom"[2]), and of their capacity or incapacity as agents of resistance, is nuanced and made more decent by recognition of the unspeakable abjection and powerlessness of the "choiceless choices"[3] foisted upon them in the Nazi *umwelt*. In this case, historical analysis benefits from recognition of the inadequacy of "normal" moral categories and from refusal to pass judgment, on the basis of those categories, regarding the victims' actions or inaction. By contrast, the act of analyzing the perpetrators' participation in atrocities without also considering the categories of moral volition and personhood lends itself to a justificatory framework in which responsibility for torture and murder slides onto the back of the system and the "machine."[4] We could say that the meta-ethical dispositions of our students are irrelevant to the teaching of Holocaust studies; what they choose to do or not to do with the material presented is their business (to make a familiar argument). In a descriptive sense, this statement is true; but from the perspective of one who studies the intersection of the Shoah and ethics, the relativism- or indifference-driven "response of no response" resounds with the echoes of the innumerable private and public moral catastrophes of the period between 1933 and 1945. It is a prescription for human disaster, born of standing idly by.

Perhaps it is extreme to correlate the actions and failures to act of bystanders during the Third Reich with the ho-hum response of second- and third-generation after-the-fact hearers of the historical testimony. Yet the testimony is precisely that—testimony. It is written and oral accounts of, and witness to, the suffering of victims, the fear or apathy of bystanders, and the virulence of Nazi antisemitism and racial ideology put into mind-boggling and inhuman practice. The hearing of this testimony places us in a morally analogous position to that of witnesses. Going on sixty years after the fact, the reception of these accounts places us at the scene as secondary or even tertiary witnesses and asks us for a response. In addition to reflexive physiological and psychological shock, our encounters with this testimony can—and, some suggest, should— provoke a moral response in us.[5] If hearing and examining the testimony places us at any degree of temporal or spatial remove in the subject position of secondary witness, then what are the pedagogical issues and challenges of teaching Holocaust studies and ethics?[6]

I found myself faced with this question recently when I taught a course titled "The Holocaust and Morality." The best-written, most cogently argued paper I received in that course made a case for suspension of judgment in analyzing the behavior of the German perpetrators of the Holocaust. The writer, while abhorring the acts of torture and mass murder, argued that he did not deem it within legitimate bounds for him to cast judgment on the perpetrators of those acts. Specifically, we were examining Daniel Goldhagen's and Christopher Browning's respective and divergent analyses of the history, constituency, acts, and personalities of Reserve Police Battalion 101.[7] In class discussion, several students had responded with shock and openly expressed outrage at what amounted to nearly total freedom from legal consequences for the enlisted men as well as the officers of this particular section of the Order Police, who functioned as mobile killing squads. The student in question, on behalf of the right of perpetrators to be judged only by the standards of their own moral culture, responded in his paper with an impassioned argument advocating that moral judgment be withheld.

The student drew his arguments from his interpretation of the rhetoric and paradigms of communitarianism and virtue ethics. He argued that the values and mores of a culture derive from the concrete, historical particularities of that culture and not from universal standards of judgment that might be shared with different cultures. He reasoned that neither he nor any international tribunal, as outsiders forever unschooled in the experiential realities of Nazi Germany, had the right to judge the perpetrators and hold them legally accountable for their actions. He maintained that those actions had been born of twelve years of Nazi indoctrination in which definitions of right and wrong had been drawn in the formative light of virulent racial antisemitism and a pervasive and militaristic nationalism.

The student argued that *Wehrmacht* soldiers, ordered to participate in ghetto "mop-up" operations, and SS soldiers, who guarded slave-labor details or shot elderly Jews into mass graves, were simply doing right on behalf of the good, according to the dictates of National Socialism's moral culture. The predominant beliefs, values, and "moral" practices were what had formed and determined the ethical agency of the German citizen. Within the moral world of Nazism, the Aryan good was served, and the duty to the *Volk* fulfilled, by the expropriation of Jewish property and citizenship rights, by the quarantining of Jews, and, ultimately, the annihilation of the alleged Jewish viral threat to the body politic. Steeped in this ambience, my student argued, the person schooled in the Nazi worldview, and habituated to the cultural, familial, and social practices of antisemitism, could not be held accountable after the fact for crimes against humanity. These had been carried out prior to the establishment of international (read "universal") standards of behavior; hence the actor could not be held morally accountable. To state the issue as simply as possible, my student asked how a person could be charged with and punished for a crime that, by the definitions of his or her formative moral culture and legal system, was *not* a crime.[8]

Most other students will disagree with this student's position and will make reference to perceived codes of human decency that are or should be accessible to all, even to those awash in Goebbel's propaganda. Rarely do I hear articulated a position of supposedly principled moral relativism in which the speaker disputes the existence and legitimacy of universal or essentialist moral absolutes or imperatives. Yet a significant number of students, pressed on the issue of judgment, land in a position that I call "moral libertarianism." Although most of their arguments are not as sophisticated as those of the student whose paper has just been described, I hear variations on this theme every time I teach Holocaust studies in relation to ethics. Those students who do not call upon universal principles of right and wrong, whether in religious or philosophical garb, tend to resist the activity of judgment altogether. They may disagree with the atrocities themselves but are hesitant to condemn the actors who committed them. Their reasoning is that, however repugnant one may find the ideas and actions of the perpetrators, one does not or, presumably, cannot stand in their shoes. The subject positions of perpetrator and student of the Shoah are not perfectly reciprocal and reversible, and so the means and the right to condemn the perpetrator and his or her actions are therefore lost. This prescriptive relativism insists that we refuse the temptation to pass judgment illegitimately: because we cannot know what the individuals involved experienced, this argument goes, it is unfair of us to judge their acts, even when those acts were genocidal. From this perspective, to pass judgment is to impinge, from a safe spatial and temporal distance, on the integrity of another's personhood.

In this trajectory of moral reasoning, the fact that the Nazi mass murderers were "ordinary" people like you and me lends itself to a refusal to critique the perpetrators. Hence this commonality, instead of requiring judgment, precludes it. Ultimately, the argument goes, individual people have to decide for themselves if something feels right for them—even if that means participating in industrial-grade genocide. The reasoning here is Kantian in its appeal to the interior moral code and its respect for individuality. Yet the reasoning veers into libertarian territory, and into amoralism, when it is argued that the encroachment of *any* exterior or objective standard on the individual's domain of sovereignty threatens the integrity of all, even if that standard is a categorical imperative of human decency.

In outlining this position, I do not mean to imply that I am completely averse to postmodern arguments regarding the foibles and fantasies of claims to universality, nor do I mean that I am disinclined toward narrative constructions of human identity and moralities. What I find disturbing is not the theoretical substructure of moral libertarianism but its inherent refusal of reaction. The third-party onlooker, the student of the Shoah, is unwilling to subject the perpetrators and their cultures to moral analysis and discernment. Even the rabidity of Nazi antisemitism and its murderous enactment is ultimately off limits to judicial reproach. This approach abandons the capacity, right, or duty of judgment, regardless of how and from where the standards of judgment are derived and the extent to which they may be applied. The "response of no response" is perhaps, to put a benign spin on it, a defense mechanism reflecting an inability to hear and process the magnitude and facticity of the 1.5 million slaughtered Jewish children and the annihilation of millions of others who were deemed *untermenschen* (subhuman) by Nazi racial ideology. A less sanguine interpretation is that the "response of no response" is, as Emmanuel Levinas suggests, the temptation of disengaged knowledge that surveys the world from the privileged haven of indifference and the shelter of insensibility.[9]

My concern is that the refusal of judgment serves not to avoid judgmentalism but rather to evade the responsibility of ethical response. The hesitancy to condemn another is undoubtedly a virtue upon which many a humane act of merciful justice has been built. The disinclination to render another person an object of moral critique, to depersonalize another in the abstractions of judgment, is certainly an ethical impulse. But in the case of the Shoah and other organized and gratuitous barbarisms, it is clear that the proclivity to respond to atrocity with volitional detachment is in and of itself a moral failing. The reluctance to fix accountability engenders a form of distancing that surpasses the needs of academic objectivity. The encounter with genocide through historical study requires us to answer not simply the duty of description but also the prescriptive demand of critique and condemnation. Our reluctance to pass judgment on the perpetrators speaks not to our fairness as arbiters but to our refusal of the task placed before us, students and scholars alike, by our encounter with this testimony.

It is precisely the difficult and, often, pedagogically unchartable encounter with testimony that is the starting point for the possibility (and *only* the possibility, as the view expounded above suggests) of ethical response rather than indifference. All those who have taught the Holocaust have encountered in their students and themselves the gamut of responses that make up the phenomenology of shock, ranging from the dropped jaw of disbelief to the turmoil of ingesting the cognitively repulsive to the blank stares of emotional overload. At times, the nature and voluminous quantity of the material itself give rise to a shell-shocked shutdown of both empathy for the victim and indignation toward the perpetrator. The event of shocked silence in the classroom, when students become "secondary witnesses," has its source in the mental, emotional, spiritual, and physical annihilation attested to in the accounts of those who survived and of a few who did not. Many Holocaust testimonies, written and oral, articulate and sputtered, attempt to speak of the inexpressible horror and the absolute destruction of mind, body, and faith inflicted by the Nazis on their victims. The survivors' accounts attest not only to shocking cruelty but also to the unutterable shame and degradation of having one's very sense of self systematically obliterated by emotional terror and bodily vulnerability. For the student of survivor testimony, the subject of study includes the indescribable torture of being made an object, of dehumanization and "demolition,"[10] of an experience that, the survivors tell us over and over, cannot be translated. A central ethical concern in teaching victim testimony is that students encounter the material in ways that respect the theological, psychological, and ethical lacunae to which—to name but a few writers—Elie Wiesel's "silence," Jean Améry's refusal of healing, Levinas's "useless suffering," and Delbo's "useless knowledge" give testament.[11]

Survivors' accounts often present us with an act of witness to events, psychical and physical, that is painfully aware of its failure as witness. The narratives contain within them that which cannot be narratively contained. As writers, even the most literate and keenly lucid survivors adamantly insist to reader/witnesses on the depthless hell of their experience's incommunicability.[12] For example, Delbo's poetic work is shot through with the agony of the stammering failure of language to create a shared vista by which she might share the burden of her memory. As for oral narratives, they are disrupted in midsentence by silence, or by verbal expression of the inability to verbalize what was experienced in the past. As Lawrence Langer has pointed out, survivor testimony is often anguished not only by the memory of agony but also by the agony of memory that cannot be made "common" or shared with the contemporary hearer:

> Survival narratives are irruptions of the cognitively intolerable, for both teller and hearer; they give to us signs whose signification evades comprehension. For the hearer of these testimonies that so often testify to the impossibility of representing the unspeakable degradation and hideousness of suffering, the very human temptation is to fill in the gaps of the narrative with our own sense making ability. Our response to these narrative lacunae is to explain, to rationalize, and to grasp the ungraspable

by means of our own totalizing narrative. After the initial shock, unnerved
by these testimonies, we want to close the caesuras of total loss, meaninglessness, and pain wholly unrelieved they place before us. We have a
seemingly natural cognitive urge to make sense of the senseless, the horrific,
and the unbelievable. If these testimonies are to receive a fair hearing, this
urge must be resisted. If there is an ethical imperative to the secondary
witness in reading Holocaust testimony, it is to refuse the comforting cognitive reflex of narrative closure by which we grant ourselves the remediation of total loss and "useless suffering" denied to the victim.[13]

Part of the pedagogical dilemma lies in taking the unspeakable dark
witness spoken by those who survived (and those who did not) and trans-
lating it into cognitive acceptance of this "non-knowledge" by students.
I constantly seek to maintain—in my own scholarly analysis of the subject matter, and in my teaching on the basis of that analysis—the tension
between respect for the epistemological abyss presented by the testimony
and my own and my students' impulse to respond with some form of
analytical remediation. Part of what I do in the classroom is to model
my deep dis-ease with the material at hand. I frequently bring the students back to those places in the text where a survivor interrupts his or
her own (and hence our) narrative with the anguish of the inexpressible
(oral, videotaped testimonies exhibit these caesuras most powerfully).[14]
While engaging in analysis, I try to avoid overtalking in and around these
narrative and emotional breaks, in order to allow the students and myself
to sit in the discomfort of the moment and to heed the painful attesta-
tion of incommunicable disturbance.

In a classroom—presumably a locus of knowledge, and of the enactment of wisdom attained—the encounter with meaninglessness, useless
knowledge, and empty silence is exceedingly dissonant and uncomfortable. We so want the survivors to overcome their turmoil, to succeed in
the continuation of normal life, to heal themselves of their *Lager*-
inflicted dehumanization and attain a sense of closure (whatever that may
mean). Often when students compare different survivor accounts, they
express admiration for people who were able to reconstitute a sense of
existential hopefulness, whereas they express pity or even condemnation
for those who appear to have been more traumatized and haunted. The

understandable temptation to cast the survivor as a can-do hero who prevails against all odds is seemingly impossible to avoid, even as the survivor adamantly refuses this interpretation. That Primo Levi is of the "saved" is usually apparent to the reader; that he is also of the "drowned" is most often not so clear.[15] Améry's "bitterness" and "anger" almost never go over well in the classroom; hence he stays on my syllabus. I want my students to hear and respect the disruption and silence presented (often through absence) in these testimonies. Such a hearing has to be learned. It requires an intentional cessation of our impulse to completion and harmony. It also requires, in our examination—and, more important, in our analysis—that we practice epistemological humility and acknowledge the limits of our comprehension. Lastly, I argue, hearing these silences demands an engaged ethical response.

Herein lies my own logical conundrum and the very real possibility of my ethical hypocrisy in teaching the Shoah. Do I not instrumentalize the testimony of survivors and nonsurvivors, their "useless" revelations, in order to exemplify a moral agenda? Do not my written and classroom-spoken words transgress the horrific silence to which their testimony speaks? In outlining my judgment of perpetrators, do I not utilize the suffering of their victims as fodder for my self-appointed task of moral edification? Is not the very rhetoric of "task" a yoking of the suffering of the victims to the teleological structure of my project? The answer to all these questions is yes. In teaching ethics in relation to the Holocaust, I betray the testimony of survivors and nonsurvivors by determining these accounts' ethical "utility" and the pragmatic value of the moral imperatives that I perceive as proceeding from them. By the workings of my own reasoning on these issues, I transgress the noninstrumental acceptance of the testimony that I encourage in my classroom.

My dilemma lies in defining the proper response to a testimony that speaks of an unbearable and unanswerable impropriety. If we truly hear the testimony, then we must submit to its destruction of the possibilities of sensemaking, its destruction of the myths of modern intellectual and moral progress. In other words, the words and silence of the victims have leveled a devastating blow against the Western projects of philosophy, theology, and ethics. To speak constructively after the Shoah is to betray, to transgress, this ugly reality forced upon us by the presence of those who lived and the absence of those who did not. Our very acts of speaking, writing, and teaching betray and are an admission of their own failure. *And yet,* as John Roth suggests, we are compelled by ethical necessity to respond, even upon recognizing the utter inadequacy and futility of our response. It is in the tension of the *and yet* that the possibility of ethical response opens. As Roth suggests, "*and yet* we must say something."[16] And yet we must respond, where we are and how we can,[17] in a manner that forces us into embodied engagement with the real world, where genocides still rage. The hearing of the testimony, despite its destruction of word and action, impels us to work, in thought and deed, to prevent and intervene in the mass murder and dehumanization going on in our midst.

Teaching within the tension and moral ambiguity of this necessary and impossible imperative requires me to articulate my ethical anxieties and to ask students to be conscious of their own reception of this testimony. In teaching the Holocaust and ethics, I ask students to place themselves in dialogical relation to the course "material." Frequently students respond by openly discussing what they might or might not have done had history placed them in the subject position of perpetrator, witness, or victim. This is an interesting and sometimes painfully honest exercise, one that allows students to imagine the lived circumstances of those who were involved. Yet it is a hypothetical practice. What I ask of my students, and of myself, is that we hear the testimony in such a way as to be put, morally speaking, on the spot. Aside from our objective analysis of the behavior of actual perpetrators, witnesses, and victims, I ask students to place themselves in the position of contemporary witnesses to the historical testimony. In other words, I ask students to query themselves about the ethical import of their role as students of the Shoah. What does an ethical reception of and orientation to the testimony require of us? In what ways and in what arenas are we accountable to and for the survivors and nonsurvivors of the Shoah? What does our witnessing mean for our relationships to current and future victims of what Levinas calls the "hatred of the other man"?[18] How and why do we choose to act on behalf of others, and to what tasks does our hearing of the testimony direct us?

For me, teaching ethics in relation to the Holocaust is a task both academic and axiological. I want my students to grasp the sociological, psychological, political, and philosophical forces and conditions that gave rise to, and operated during, the events of 1933–1945 in Europe. I want my students to gain the analytical tools necessary for them to think critically about Holocaust history and a/morality. I also understand my job as an ethics/Holocaust studies teacher as that of one who facilitates the addressing of survivor and nonsurvivor testimony to new witnesses. My hope is that these secondary witnesses will see themselves as bystanders who cannot stand idly by, that they will refuse the apathy, indifference, and inactivity of the disengaged observer of someone else's history. I hope that the encounter will serve to cultivate righteous responders who, unlike the overwhelming majority of contemporary witnesses to the Shoah, will not demur from speaking out early on, and that, when the time comes, they will not shirk, individually or communally, from taking the measures necessary to prevent or stop another genocide.

If, as students of the Shoah, we are called upon to respond with decency, shame, and efficacy in the face of dehumanization, then we must nurture and exercise the faculty of what Aristotle called *phronesis,* or practical wisdom. *Phronesis* determines the appropriate course of action in any given situation and enacts the means to accomplish that course. I am not suggesting here the teleological or utilitarian position that our actions must attain their goal in order to be worthy. The history of resistance during the Shoah is rife with examples of the futility and failure of ethical action. Yet I think that Aristotle is right in his analysis of the roles played by habit and practice in what makes for phronetic action and, ultimately, virtue. In order for us, the inheritors of the testimony, to do right by its witness, we must hear and accept its imperative and take upon ourselves the burdens of analysis and judgment. In the face of genocide, relativism—even at its most benign, in the form of libertarian respect for the choices of others—is still mute and quiescent. The ethical and intellectual "response of no response" is a disavowal of my duty to respond humanely, an abandonment of my capacity and obligation to my neighbor who is in mortal danger at the hands of another neighbor.

In teaching the Shoah, I am concerned not to encourage an analytical orientation within which moral outrage is systematically abated by principled or habituated indifference to atrocity inflicted and suffered. The strength of my own and my students' ethical responses in the face of genocide requires practice. It requires minds and consciences attuned to the complexities of the world around us and to its grimmest realities. We must be versed in the activities of determining right from wrong—and we must be willing to speak and act and judge accordingly.

NOTES

1. Regarding the debate over moral analysis of the victims' actions and failure to act, see Raul Hilberg, *The Destruction of the European Jews* (New York: Holmes and Meier, 1985); Lucy Dawidowicz, *The War Against the Jews: 1933–1945* (New York: Holt, Rinehart and Winston, 1975).

2. Primo Levi, *Survival in Auschwitz: The Nazi Assault on Humanity,* trans. Stuart Woolf (New York: Collier Books, 1986).

3. Lawrence Langer, "The Dilemma of Choice in the Deathcamps," in John Roth and Michael Berenbaum, eds., *Holocaust: Religious and Philosophical Implications* (New York: Paragon House, 1989), 222.

4. See Hilberg, *The Destruction of the European Jews,* 161, for the author's analysis of the mechanized, bureaucratized characteristics of the "machinery of destruction." As indicated by Browning's analysis of *Einsatzgruppen* activities, and by Kaplan's examination of German citizens' abandonment of "neighbor relations" and their voluntary participation in antisemitic activities, individual choice was crucial in the execution of the so-called final solution. See Christopher Browning, *Ordinary Men: Reserve Police Battalion 101 and the Final Solution in Poland* (New York: HarperCollins, 1992); Marion Kaplan, *Between Dignity and Despair: Jewish Life in Nazi Germany* (New York: Oxford University Press, 1998).

5. Fackenheim has articulated this argument in ethical, philosophical, and theological depth; see Emil Fackenheim, *To Mend the World: Foundations of Post-Holocaust Jewish Thought* (Bloomington: Indiana University Press, 1994).

6. See Tamara Wright, *The Twilight of Jewish Philosophy: Emmanuel Levinas' Ethical Hermeneutics* (Amsterdam: Harwood Academic Publishers, 1999), 108, for the argument that the encounter with the "suffering of the other" functions, for Levinas, as a "negative revelation" that impels the recipient to respond actively to ameliorate this suffering or to preclude the possibility of further suffering on the part of others.

7. See Daniel Goldhagen, *Hitler's Willing Executioners: Ordinary Germans and the Holocaust* (New York: Knopf, 1996); Browning, *Ordinary Men.*

8. I gave the student an A on the paper—and vociferous talmudic marginalia rebutting the "morality" of abandoning judgment.

9. Emmanuel Levinas, "The Temptation of Temptation," in *Nine Talmudic Readings,* trans. Annette Aronowicz (Bloomington: Indiana University Press, 1990), 30–50.

10. Levi, *Survival in Auschwitz.*

11. See Emmanuel Levinas, "Useless Suffering," in *Entre Nous: Thinking of the Other,* trans. Michael B. Smith and Barbara Harshav (New York: Columbia University Press, 1998), 91–101; Jean Améry, *At the Mind's Limits: Contemplations by a Survivor on Auschwitz and its Realities,* trans. Sidney Rosenfeld and Stella P. Rosenfeld (Bloomington: Indiana University Press, 1980); Delbo, *Auschwitz and After;* Elie Wiesel, *Night,* trans. Marion Wiesel (New York: Hill and Wang, 2006), vii–xv.

12. See Levi, *Survival in Auschwitz.* See also Primo Levi, *The Drowned and the Saved,* trans. Raymond Rosenthal (New York: Vintage International, 1989); Delbo, *Auschwitz and After.*

13. Lawrence Langer, *Holocaust Testimonies: The Ruins of Memory* (New Haven: Yale University Press, 1991), 7–9. See also Levinas, "Useless Suffering."

14. Lawrence Langer's work on the irruptions of memory into oral testimonies, and on those irruptions' implications for narrative and psychological "completeness," has been helpful in negotiating students' encounters with survivor testimony; see Langer, *Holocaust Testimonies.*

15. Levi, *Survival in Auschwitz.*

16. For an analysis of the im/possibility and necessity of the post-Holocaust philosophical task, see John K. Roth, *Holocaust Politics* (Louisville, Ky.: Westminster John Knox Press, 2001). My citation on this subject stems from John Roth, "Ethics after the Holocaust: Key Issues for Philosophy and Religion," seminar presented at the Center for Advanced Holocaust Studies, United States Holocaust Memorial Museum, Washington, D.C., July 2001. This chapter and my thinking on this matter are deeply indebted to the participants of that seminar, and in particular to Roth's intellectual honesty and ethical commitment to do right by the testimony left us by the victims of the Third Reich.

17. See Fackenheim, *To Mend the World,* secs. IV and V, for an analysis of ethical imperatives derived from the actions of survivors and nonsurvivors.

18. Emmanuel Levinas, *Otherwise Than Being; or, Beyond Essence,* trans. Alphonso Lingis (Dordrecht: Kluwer Academic Publishers, 1991), epigraph.

6

From Archive to Classroom

Reflections on Teaching the History
of the Holocaust in Different Countries

PAUL A. LEVINE

More than a decade ago, Michael Marrus, one of the leading historians and teachers of Holocaust history, noted the intellectual and psychological impact of Holocaust studies on scholars and students:

> Researching and teaching the Holocaust, to point out the obvious, is not quite like researching and teaching everything else. . . . [It is] special in a way that is not commonly discussed: for a variety of reasons, among them the fact that this is an emotionally charged topic. . . . The questions historians put about it tend to become broad, rather than narrow, and require the making of distinctions frequently avoided in other fields of study. . . . Holocaust history has become exemplary in the demands that it makes upon researchers, teachers and students alike.[1]

What he asserted then is perhaps truer today than he imagined, for there can be no doubt that in Europe, and in much of the rest of the Western world, interest in studying and teaching the history of the Holocaust is at a level that few would have predicted ten years ago, let alone earlier. Moreover, there is broad agreement that a sense of the tragedy's moral gravity and its consequences should be taught in schools.[2] My essential argument is that this understanding can best be realized by teachers and students only after they have approached the event, at least initially, through its history, and not only or initially through the memory of the genocide of Europe's Jews. In fact, for the purposes of understanding, the approach to the Holocaust by way of its history should be not just initial but constant. Marrus is correct to assert that teaching and studying the Holocaust places great demands on the very willingness to teach and study, a statement echoed by the philosopher John Roth, who rightly states that "the Holocaust—its reality, history, politics—creates burdens. Those burdens are not abstract, nor are they impersonal. . . . The burdens of Holocaust history are immense because the Holocaust itself was immense."[3] I will support my argument by describing several aspects of the manner in which I have been teaching Holocaust history, in a number of countries, since the early 1990s. Before doing so, however, I will offer a few necessary comments about how I perceive some current problems.

THE HOLOCAUST VERSUS HOLOCAUST HISTORY

Is what is so often referred to as "the Holocaust" the same as what is more accurately labeled "the history of the Holocaust"? In at least a score of very different countries and cultures, frequent contact with teachers, students, and others interested in the background and narrative of the destruction of European Jewry has led me to conclude that these terms are not synonymous. In general, when nonspecialists refer to the Holocaust, they are much more likely to be referring to some aspect, some manifestation or representation, of the memory of the event—some social, political, or moral consequence of the genocide—than to any specific historical element of the Nazis' actual war against the Jews. It seems reasonable to assume, however, that those who use Auschwitz as a moral metaphor would know, in order to draw credible moral conclusions, something beyond the bare details of what actually happened and why, of what was done by whom and to whom, in that corner of southwestern Poland between 1940 and 1945. Logically, it seems impossible to understand the moral import, the "lessons of Auschwitz," without first understanding at least something of that time and place. The credibility of the teacher is at stake and, with it, the credibility of the moral message.

Particularly with the recent proliferation of interest in the subject, public and pedagogical discussion of the Holocaust has been character-

ized if not dominated by commentary on its vast and troubling consequences rather than by explications of its historical realities. Yet this rhetor-
ical discourse dominated by memory is far too often a move away from
historical context and into empirical inaccuracy, misconceptions, and even
mystifications.[4] In fact, the subject is too often taught in the wrong order:
memory first, then history, if history is taught at all. Again, it seems only
logical that if students and others in society are to make sense of the memory of the event, of its continuing impact on us today, its history must
first be grasped.

This tendency to relegate the history of the Holocaust to a secondary
place, rather than accord the event its necessary place of primacy, is a lam-
entable and growing problem in Europe and the United States alike, and
it does have consequences. One such problematic consequence of this
inversion has been addressed astutely by Michael Blumenthal in a short
essay titled "Of Rest and the Weary." Blumenthal made his observations
while teaching several years ago in Germany, a country with far more educational emphasis on the Holocaust than most. Blumenthal, visiting some
German friends, wrote that "there arose the subject of their adolescent
son's and his schoolmates' 'Holocaust fatigue'—their sense of having a
discussion of the event perpetually rammed down their throats by teachers and administrators at seemingly every turn. He was tired, the son said,
of hearing so much about the Holocaust."[5] Blumenthal then observed
that in his own class at a highly respected German university, few students (admittedly bright and intellectually engaged) could or would answer
simple questions about Holocaust history: "I was met by stares . . . blank
and unknowing. . . . On the other hand, those Germans . . . who actually know something about the Holocaust seem virtually immune from
Holocaust fatigue." His conclusion, one as relevant to Germany as to
Sweden, the United States, and anywhere else, is that "those prone to
Holocaust fatigue . . . tend to be those with a self-serving interest in being
tired rather than a moral stake in being curious—in other words, those
whose sense of fatigue has little to do with actual knowledge."[6]

As research on and teaching about the history and memory of the
Holocaust enter the twenty-first century, it must be emphasized that discussion, writing, and teaching in connection with the subject begin with
sound historical knowledge—a grasp of the *who, what, when, where,* and

how of the event's history. Only with sufficient comprehension of these fundamentals can anyone, teacher or student, even begin to approach the most important question of all: *Why?* As one philosopher of history correctly concludes in an important recent work, "There should [not] be any doubt that the historical center of the Holocaust will continue to have the last word in understanding not only the causal complexity of that event, *but also its moral darkness.*"[7] To put the issue simply, in order to teach lessons derived *from* the history of the Holocaust, a teacher must first know something *about* the history of the Holocaust. Lang is correct to conclude that the more one knows about the event, the more one senses, almost intuitively, its profound and disturbing moral darkness.

FROM THE ARCHIVE TO THE CLASSROOM

Scholarly efforts to reveal and reconstruct the history of the Holocaust in the many nations affected by the Nazi genocide have been under way for decades in Western Europe, North America, and Israel, and the results are impressive. The historiographic debates around many central questions have been intense and are likely to continue, but historians from many different countries have led us to a depth of understanding that was unthinkable in the immediate aftermath of World War II and even ten or fifteen years ago. Today, there are literally thousands of first-class academic publications that illuminate and analyze most of the important questions raised by any consideration of what happened in Europe from 1933 to 1945. And, for the most part, this work is based on either archival findings or survivor testimony; it is professionally critiqued and composed according to accepted methods of inquiry and (mostly nonideological) analysis. There is much catching up to do in Eastern Europe, where most of the slaughter took place, and where legitimate scholarship about what actually happened to the Jews was for so long discouraged, even politically impossible. Critical to continued progress is the fact that a growing number of historians in these countries, too, are now engaged in professional and methodologically sound research and publication.[8]

"Mastering the past" has been politically difficult and painful enough even in democratic countries (among which Germany itself, of course, is a special case), nor has teaching the subject well proved easy in free societies. Even in what used to be called the "free world," which is to say countries where scholars have been able to engage in methodologically sound inquiry, it has taken decades for societies and schools to accept the necessity of teaching this history. As for the former Soviet-bloc nations, they have only recently begun this task, and they do so with a double burden imposed by history: the Nazi occupation was infinitely more vicious and destructive in this region than in Western Europe, and teachers and students in these countries are now, even after a decade of independence, just beginning to crawl out from under the ideological burden of Soviet occupation and political dominance.[9] An acute if not insurmountable pedagogical challenge for teachers in these countries is the fact that for themselves as well as for their students (not to mention the students' grandparents) the Holocaust is "local history." It was mostly in those countries that the murder of millions took place, and, not least of all, here is where the burden of collaboration in genocide will continue to weigh heavily on political and pedagogical discourse for a long time to come.

In neither East nor West, however, will the fruits of recent scholarly progress be fully realized if the data and analyses published by historians are not effectively introduced into the classroom and, just as important, into general social debate. The historical complexity and moral weight of the Holocaust make it particularly important here. Yet, though our understanding of the fundamental questions may reach a satisfactory level even if our understanding is still incomplete, we remain far from any claim to understand the most important question: Why?[10] This unresolved and centrally important question will for years to come motivate the many scholars around the world to continue their explorations. Just as important, the continuing inability of scholars to adequately answer the question of why the Holocaust occurred is a clear motivation for teachers and students to commence their own explorations of Holocaust history.

Historians understand much more today than was the case ten or fifteen years ago about the details, decisions, and contours of Germany's relentless assault upon and destruction of Jewish life and culture between 1933 and 1945. But there is reason to question whether their understanding has been passed along to society at large, and to suspect that the failure to transmit their understanding is a problem for Holocaust education. Indeed, it is my experience that education based primarily on work in the archives fuels much of the continuing public interest in the event. If this inference is reasonable and acceptable, then the next step is to devise a method by which to move into the public domain the knowledge available and extant in the many archives (not least of all those opened to scholars in the wake of the collapse of the Soviet Union in 1989–90). The best and most efficient way to do so, it seems to me, is to use the classroom. As a historian who has written in depth about one episode of the Holocaust (the response of Sweden's government to the Nazi genocide), and as a teacher of a one-term university Holocaust course, I deem it increasingly important that historians and other scholars be sensitive and responsive to the necessity of comprehensively and coherently transmitting their research results—and those of other scholars—into the classroom.[11]

A collection of essays edited by the German historian Ulrich Herbert makes strikingly clear that it is no longer adequate to teach about "one Holocaust," and that it cannot be said, with any veracity, "*This* is how the Holocaust happened in Europe." We now understand that there wasn't a single decision by Hitler that brought about the murder of millions; rather, a complicated and relentless admixture of local initiatives and central directives was responsible. We now see clearly that the murder of Europe's Jews and Roma and Sinti happened differently in different countries (even different regions within one country), at different times and sometimes even for rather different reasons. All these initiatives and directives, of course, are connected to Hitler, Himmler, Heydrich, and others in Berlin, without whose authorization the genocide could never have happened, but it was not they who initiated much of the actual killing.[12] We now understand that chronologies, personalities, elements of local collaboration, and even methods of killing the Jews were different in Norway and Croatia. What happened to Jews in France at the hands of the collaborationist Vichy government, and why, is not the same as what happened, and why, in Italy, Germany's closest ally. Even countries as geographically close as Belgium and the Netherlands have different Holocaust histories. Indeed, Germany's own history of the Holocaust differs in important ways from the Holocaust history of the first country occupied by Hitler—his native Austria. Furthermore, since each country affected by Nazi Germany's genocidal policies has its own history of the event, each country inevitably has its own memory of the event—with all that this means for contemporary debate and understanding. If contemporary teaching about the event is to have its desired impact, these advances in understanding will need to be brought into the classroom.

Another such publication, a collection of essays edited by the historian Omer Bartov, reinforces the conclusion that it is both inappropriate and pedagogically incorrect to teach about the "aftermath" of the Holocaust without adequate comprehension of the event's origins and implementation, a hierarchy of understanding reflected in the book's title.[13] To generalize is to obfuscate, and surely no teacher would define his or her task in that way. Many documents suggest, as Primo Levi also does in his seminal essay "The Grey Zone," that the perpetrator-victim-bystander relationship is not always a matter of black and white, neither unambiguous nor morally cut and dried.[14] Some teachers may find it convenient not to acknowledge these complexities, but to do so is a teacher's responsibility.

But it must also be acknowledged that there are genuine difficulties in moving knowledge from the archive into the classroom. How can an educator, one who generally has little if any time for reading the latest literature, take advantage of the advances in historiography? How can he or she develop techniques that make it possible, within the always limited time available for the variety of subjects that must all be presented in the classroom, to effectively teach about the complexity that comprises the history of the Holocaust? I believe that the best way for the teacher to address these difficulties is to remain as close as possible to the history of the event as represented by the vast range of primary-source documents available in published and easily obtainable monographs, document collections, photo books, and survivor testimony.

TEACHING THE HISTORY OF THE HOLOCAUST IN DIFFERENT COUNTRIES

Many educators find that teaching the vast, complicated, violent, confusing, pancontinental, and multinational historical reality of the Holocaust is a daunting challenge. Doing pedagogical justice to its literally millions of stories, names, dates, places, ideologies, and explanatory concepts in a coherent and concise fashion is extremely difficult. Moreover, the teacher is often confronted by the emotional difficulty that many students (and teachers, for that matter) experience when encountering, usually for the first time, the extraordinarily violent, degrading, and upsetting details that make up the event and that are most clearly revealed in documents and testimonies.[15] Yet, here again, the available historical literature is helpful not only for these primary sources but also because it often contains judicious, clearly stated conclusions that are reached by the writer after he or she has had time to carefully consider the evidence and the story being told.

Another problem is that many teachers who want to teach the history and memory of the Holocaust did not study this subject as part of their training at the university level. That is changing in many countries, but it remains the case that many teachers never actually studied the Holocaust as part of their professional preparation. In Sweden, for instance—a democratic society for generations—only recently has any attention been paid to Holocaust history or Holocaust education. A noticeable change began to take place in the late 1990s, and interest in the subject continues to rise, but decades of neglect cannot be corrected overnight and much work will need to be done before Sweden's working teachers and student teachers can be considered properly prepared.[16] Encounters with teachers from countries as diverse as the United States, Germany, Latvia, and Russia suggest that the situation is much the same everywhere.

Anyone who has spent time in the classroom knows that teaching is a highly individualistic craft based as much on personality as on theoretically objective methods that can be taught and learned. The experienced teacher knows, even feels, what works and what doesn't, and the measure of success is hardly a matter of how students perform on tests.[17] Rather, success in teaching this subject comes from what the teacher senses from the responses of the students, in and out of the classroom. After more than a decade of teaching the history of the Holocaust, I believe that students and teachers generally respond in a positive, morally conscious, and ethically sensitive manner when what is taught and learned is details about who decided what, and when, and what happened to whom, and how. Those who study Holocaust history in this way are confronted by the enormities and particularities of the event, and I have rarely if ever encountered a serious student who failed to be drawn into further inquiry or became "fatigued" by the prospect of learning more.[18] Furthermore—and this is no small reward for the genuine emotional pain of engaging this horrible chapter of human history on a daily basis— the responses from students (and teachers) exposed to Holocaust history have been deeply gratifying, both professionally and morally. The majority of students sense that this is a vitally important subject, personally and for society at large, and they respond accordingly.

It was once feared that the Holocaust would be, in some sense, forgotten, even lost to history. This is not the case, of course, and where it was once feared that there was a deficit of interest in the subject, there are now those who complain about a surfeit of attention to the subject. This complaint is also an aspect of so-called Holocaust fatigue. But another problem, one related to this alleged fatigue, is that the ubiquity of "the Holocaust" in recent years has brought to classes in Holocaust history many students and teachers who are filled with misconceptions, myths, misleading national narratives, and, in general, a simplistic understanding of the event. As a historian and teacher who advocates critical examination of sources, preconceptions, and historical myths, whether personal or national, I often experience a certain intellectual pleasure in puncturing such myths, mistakes, and misconceptions. A related pedagogical problem that teachers may confront is that students who delve for the first time into the details of Holocaust history experience a certain cognitive disorientation. Having thought that they already knew a lot, most come to understand that they did not, and this realization can upset and confuse them. Out of this relative chaos there often emerges an expanded critical and creative desire to challenge previously held ideas, and a desire to know more is almost invariably expressed.

A deeply troubled look cannot be hidden after one has read, for instance, a German document detailing the construction and improvement of mobile gas vans, or one that describes the often voluntary participation of individual men (many of them fathers themselves) in the murder of thousands of people, including children and babies. Students can't stop shaking their heads in confusion and dismay when reading about Heinrich Himmler's plans for the radical demographic reordering of Eastern Europe. One significant aspect of my method is that I place equal if not greater emphasis on illuminating the ideas and experiences, however loathsome they may be, of the perpetrators. Most students and teachers have read about the victims before,[19] but they have never really encountered the "ordinary man" who so willingly murdered thousands, all in a day's work. The victims rarely if ever grasped what they had done to come to such an end—and part of the problem in teaching this subject is that the victims had not in fact done *anything* to come to that violent end. It was others who decided that their lives would end so gruesomely.

Two recent evaluations written by students illustrate the reactions to learning such details. One student wrote, "Your class has never ceased to shock me or send cold shivers down my spine or leave me speechless." Another student, after attending several lectures and feeling a shocking dismay, asked if it would be all right if her boyfriend sat in on the rest of the course. (He did). At the end of the course, I always ask students to reflect on what the Holocaust now means to them and to their world. Their answers are detailed, emotional, and often startlingly personal. One such response, written by a young American woman, is worth sharing at some length:

Although I feel the Holocaust has great meaning in our world today, I still feel it isn't enough. I find it quite surprising and unfortunate that there are still so many people who really haven't grasped what the Holocaust has done to us. . . . Many others don't even know what the hell it really encompassed, it's not just gas chambers and crematoria. . . . I looked at a book called *Photos in Auschwitz*. There was a picture of a nude woman covered in lesions, disease, infections. Her body was mutilated. I covered her body up with my hands and looked at her face and cried so hard. She was so beautiful. What was going on in her mind as she was told to smile so a Nazi doctor could take her picture? How sick . . . but my friends and so many others only know about Hitler. . . . I taught my roommates all I could about the Holocaust because to me it has become one of the most meaningful things in my life. . . . I needed this course. It gave me more than stress and bullshit. It taught me so much about the

meaning of life and death. Every day, I walked out of class sullen, but as
I went further I would realize I'm alive and . . . I can't give up on life.[20]

Indeed, one of the ironies of teaching about this area of human history
is that it is an extremely rewarding one to teach. The facts of the Holocaust
and manifestations of mostly awful but sometimes uplifting human behavior clearly affect the imaginations and consciences of those exposed to
them. Most rewarding, however, are the questions that students raise about
humankind, morality, democracy, and the nature of our civilization, for
it is from such questions that learning takes place.[21] Students, moreover,
aware of the dismal truth that the genocidal impulse seems to be part of
the human condition, often relate what they are learning about the
Holocaust to later genocides or to incidents of mass violence in Cambodia,
Rwanda, and the Balkans. They know genocide has happened and can
happen again, and they want to understand the human and structural
mechanisms that make it part of our culture.

But can the history of the event, as transmitted by the historians of
one country, reach across national and cultural boundaries? Don't the cultural, political, ethnic, economic, linguistic, and even racial differences
that define students make it impossible to teach this always controversial
history to all students in a similar manner, using similar methods and materials? And what about those nations without a tradition of democracy?
Can there possibly be one way of teaching Holocaust history that takes
into account the differences separating students from, say, Norway and
Hungary, or from Latvia and Spain, or from Argentina and Canada? The
answer, I think, is yes. If for no other reason than the multinational reality of the event, there seems ample cause to believe that students and
teachers from a wide variety of countries will respond positively to the
teaching of Holocaust history that is based on primary sources. Most of
the time, naturally enough, the student is first interested in the Holocaust
history of his or her own nation. But when he or she comes to realize the
empirical impossibility of studying only a single country's history of the
event, it is generally the case that the student quickly grasps that a uni-
lateral focus is also intellectually irresponsible. Further support for this
argument can be adduced from the following example.

In late 1997, the Swedish government commissioned Stéphane Bruchfeld and me to write a short, easily accessible book about the Holocaust. It was intended to be a pedagogical tool with which Swedish parents could engage their children in an informed discussion about the importance of democracy and human rights, a discussion that would take as its starting point the history of the Holocaust.[22] The book had been commissioned by Prime Minister Göran Persson because of what he understood to be the deplorable lack of knowledge about the event among Swedish youth, and as a response to an alarming rise in right-wing neo-Nazi activity, not least among Swedish youth. Interest in the subject hardly seemed to fit either his personal or Social Democratic political background, and yet Persson made the link between the teaching of Holocaust history and the defense of democracy.[23] The government's original goal—indeed, hope— had been that, after a mass mailing offering the book to 713,000 Swedish households with adolescent children, some tens of thousands might return the order form with a request for the book. It is important, in this context, to emphasize that the book was not simply distributed indiscriminately; rather, it was sent only after a parental request for it had been received. Much to the happy shock and surprise of those involved in the project, within weeks close to 500,000 copies had been requested, first by the originally targeted households and soon by school libraries, union educational groups, and tens of thousands of other Swedes. Today close to 1.5 million copies of the book have been requested, in a country with a population of slightly fewer than 9 million.

Since its original publication, in January 1998, this short summary of Holocaust history has been translated into German, French, Russian, Portuguese, Latvian (and, for Russian Latvians, Russian), Norwegian, Estonian, Japanese, and Finnish.[24] What is significant for my argument about our particular approach, about its capacity for successfully reaching across cultural and national boundaries, is the fact that most of these translated editions were commissioned or endorsed by the ministries of education or other political authorities of the countries in question. Each new translation has maintained the original content, format, and pictures, but a chapter has also been added to provide greater detail than the original could offer about the specific country's response to the genocide. What is it that explains this book's appeal across so many—and, often, such controversial—political, cultural, ethnic, economic, and linguistic borders? The answer can only be provisional, but there is no gainsaying the book's broad international appeal. At least part of the answer is that the book uses primarily historical sources, pictures, and representations, eschewing other approaches to the field.[25] It presents, in a clear and concise fashion, the brutally frank reality of what the Germans and their allies did to the Jews of Europe between 1933 and 1945. We believe that the book has international appeal because it is based on and inspired by the facts as understood by historians, and on virtually nothing but such documented facts.

DOES HOLOCAUST EDUCATION DO ANY GOOD?

Few dispute that the Holocaust represents a watershed in the history of Europe and of the world. It is sadly but indubitably true that, after Auschwitz and Rumbula, Drancy and Westerbork, Minsk and Babi Yar, the world would never be, could never be, the same. Surely there are lessons to be learned from this comprehensive tragedy, which still marks us today. Yet a fundamental question remains unanswered: What do students, teachers, and citizens learn from studying these years of persecution and murder? What social value is to be gained from reading about how hundreds of thousands of ordinary European citizens, from virtually every country (and not only those occupied by the Germans), participated in the plunder, in the persecution and murder of their neighbors and erstwhile friends? And what, indeed, is the moral lesson to be learned from studying in detail the shooting and gassing of some 95 percent of all Jewish children alive in Europe in 1939? What, if anything, is to be learned from this unprecedented violation of human life, spirit, and morality?

Even some who are not interested in shrouding the event in mystification have argued that there is perhaps nothing to be learned from the Holocaust. Bartov poses a challenging, even frightening, argument regarding the ostensible lessons of the Holocaust. He argues that its very nature prevents us from learning *anything* from the genocide; the Holocaust, Bartov says,

> is a tale that signifies nothing. Indeed, it is precisely the meaninglessness
> of the event, made all the clearer now with the benefit of hindsight, the

utter senselessness of it all, the total and complete emptiness in which this hell on earth unfolded, that leaves us breathless, bereft of the power of thought and imagination. And what is especially frightening is the impossibility of learning anything from the Holocaust, of drawing any lessons, of putting its facts to any use.[26]

If Bartov is correct, then we are wrong to argue that teaching the history of the Holocaust has social benefit. Though the urgency of Bartov's challenge cannot be ignored, teachers of Holocaust history can answer him in the positive. There are, it seems clear, valuable if still painful lessons for our common future to be drawn from the history of the Holocaust. However, these lessons are not to be drawn primarily from the responses of the victims, but rather from the motives and goals of the perpetrators and from the reactions of the bystanders. The victims were the engulfed minority, whereas those in the other two categories were the ones who had choices to make. It is mostly in their choices—almost always the wrong ones—that the lessons of the Holocaust (and other genocides) lie. There is ample evidence from those years that if fewer people had chosen, early in Hitler's rule, not simply to stand by, those seeking to perpetrate the crimes might well have been hindered and perhaps even stopped.

What, then, is the social value of teaching this subject? What, in fact, is the goal of Holocaust education? In a word: democracy. With the advent of the new century, the vital importance of liberal democracy has never been clearer. And for those of us engaged in teaching the history of the murder of the European Jews and their rich culture, there is little if any doubt about the value of passing on the details of this unprecedented failure of liberal, democratic, humane values. Indeed, this failure compels students to reflect on its irreplaceable importance for all our futures. There are lessons to be learned from this genocide that took place in the heart of Western civilization, lessons about how to strengthen democracy. The teaching of Holocaust history suggests that there is a need for all of us "to reflect upon issues that have direct relationships to the development of values and the fostering of behaviors emphasizing social responsibility."[27] There is in fact increasing reason to believe that the history of the Holocaust, properly taught, can be of direct and even profound intellectual, emotional, and existential interest for any thinking student or citizen. But to be effective, this kind of reflection must begin with the study of the history of this event. As Lang concludes, "Everything said or written about the Holocaust . . . turns [on] the facts revealed by historical analysis."[28]

The all too human motives that caused the Holocaust remain deeply embedded within the human condition, yet there is good reason to believe that among the strongest antidotes to the genocidal impulse are the social values inherent in a properly functioning liberal democracy, the humane values that suffuse the democratic mentality. "Democracy," Woodrow Wilson once said, "is more than a form of government. It is a form of character." If we teach our children about the worst failure of liberal democratic culture in world history, we at least give them a reasonable chance of recognizing another such failure on the horizon and possibly, just possibly, doing something about it. This hope alone is all we need to continue teaching the history of the Holocaust throughout the world.

NOTES

1. Michael Marrus, "Good History and Teaching the Holocaust," in *The Holocaust, Fifty Years After: Papers from the Conference of the Jewish Historical Institute of Warsaw* (Warsaw, Poland: Jewish Historical Institute of Warsaw, 1993), 52.

2. See Paul A. Levine, "Teaching the Holocaust in Different Countries: Problems and Possibilities," in *The Issues of the Holocaust Research in Latvia: Reports of an International Conference* (Riga, Latvia: Latvijas Universitates, Latvija vestures instituts, 2001), 153–68. Portions of this chapter were originally published in that volume.

3. John K. Roth, *Holocaust Politics* (Louisville, Ky.: Westminister John Knox Press, 2001), 38–39.

4. I leave out of this discussion the wholly different problem of the vicious, wildly inaccurate, and politically motivated "comparisons" of the genocide of the Jews with contemporary political problems.

5. Michael Blumenthal, "Of Rest and the Weary," *TIME Europe,* Feb. 28, 2000, 1. The article can be found at www.time.com/time/europe/magazine/2000/228/essay.html (accessed Feb. 9, 2006). In Sweden, too—a nation whose political and educational authorities scarcely paid any attention at all

before the mid-1990s to Holocaust history or memory—one already hears, both privately and in the media, about this growing phenomenon of "Holocaust fatigue."

6. Ibid., 2.

7. Berel Lang, *The Future of the Holocaust: Between History and Memory* (Ithaca, N.Y.: Cornell University Press, 1999), x–xii (emphasis added).

8. Where the Baltic countries are concerned, evidence of this progress can be seen in the existence of the national commissions of inquiry that have been mandated to explore this painful past. Although these commissions are not without problems and controversies of their own, they all include Holocaust scholars from the West, and the presence of these scholars makes a whitewash highly unlikely if not impossible. Also worthy of note is the growing number of conferences where historians from former Soviet-bloc countries present and discuss their research with their more established Western colleagues.

9. On the situation in the former Soviet Union, see Zvi Gitelman, ed., *Bitter Legacy: Confronting the Holocaust in the USSR* (Bloomington: Indiana University Press, 1997). Regarding Poland, an essential and brilliant work is Michael C. Steinlauf, *Bondage to the Dead: Poland and the Memory of the Holocaust* (Syracuse, N.Y.: Syracuse University Press, 1997) is essential. The more recent controversy about Jedwabne is usefully discussed in *Yad Vashem Studies* XXX .

10. The most knowledgeable historians in the field remain modest, even humble, before this question. A recent and, indeed, poignant example of such intellectual modesty is the landmark study by Saul Friedländer, *Nazi Germany and the Jews: The Years of Persecution, 1933–1939* (New York: HarperCollins, 1997).

11. See Paul A. Levine, *From Indifference to Activism: Swedish Diplomacy and the Holocaust, 1938–1944*, 2nd ed. (Uppsala, Sweden: Acta Universitatis Upsaliensis, 1998).

12. See Ulrich Herbert, ed., *National Socialist Extermination Policies: Contemporary German Perspectives and Controversies* (New York: Berghan Books, 2000). Translated from the German, this book contains groundbreaking research on such questions as the murder of Jews in the general government; anti-Jewish policy and the murder of the Jews in the district of Galicia in 1941–42; the extermination of the Jews in Serbia; German economic interests, occupation policy, and the murder of the Jews in Belorussia in 1941–43; and the murder of the Jews of East Upper Silesia.

13. Omer Bartov, ed, *Holocaust: Origins, Implementation, Aftermath* (London: Routledge, 2000).

14. This essential meditation about and from the "grey zone" can be found

in Bartov, ed., *Holocaust,* but it comes, of course, from Levi's *The Drowned and the Saved.*

15. As noted earlier, I have taught primarily university-level classes that are of many weeks' duration. For teachers who have far more limited time, the challenge is even greater. Nevertheless, experience shows that considerable impact can be achieved by means of a focus on certain themes, ideas, and concepts central to the Holocaust.

16. On why Swedish historians have all but ignored the study of the Holocaust, see Paul A. Levine, "Förintelsens historiografi I Sverige idag—nytt hopp efter många år av bristande intresse?," in R. Fjällstedt & S. Fruitman, eds, *Sidor av Förintelsen* (Lund, Sweden: Studentlitteratur, 2000), 69–95.

17. Indeed, how one "tests" knowledge "learned" about, for instance, Sobibor or Belzec, this deportation or that, *Einsatgruppe* A or *Einsatzkommando* 1B, remains a real and heretofore unsolved dilemma for the teacher of Holocaust history.

18. This is not to argue that other forms of representation are inherently inadequate. Rather, time strengthens my conviction that obtaining some grasp of the concrete history of the event must come first. Then and only then can other disciplines and forms of representation have the desired impact.

19. Indeed, it seems that one of the "causes" of so-called Holocaust fatigue is that students in Europe believe, however incorrectly, that they have heard enough about the experiences of the victims, about "Jewish victimization."

20. K. Braun, final examination, spring 1996; used with permission.

21. There nevertheless remains a genuine need for more serious and quantifiable evaluation of the impact of Holocaust education, to be conducted in the many countries where teachers are engaged in the field.

22. The original Swedish version of our book, titled *Om detta må ni berätta: en bok om Förintelsen i Europa, 1933–1945,* was published in Stockholm in January 1998. As part of the original campaign, the book was also translated into the languages of the largest immigrant groups in Sweden. Thus the original Swedish was translated into Finnish, Arabic, Persian, Turkish, Spanish, Serbo-Croatian, and English.

23. The background and details of the campaign cannot be analyzed here. Suffice it to say that the response to it in Sweden—and, literally, around the world—has surprised even the most cynical observers. Its fascinating story remains to be analyzed and told by some enterprising journalist.

24. Inquiries have also been received from publishers and educational authorities in Holland, Belgium, Denmark, Italy, Spain (and Catalán), Kurdistan, Poland, Japan, Australia, and the United States.

25. Conceptually, the book mirrors my university course on Holocaust history and historiography.

26. Omer Bartov, "An Idiot's Tale: Memories and Histories of the Holocaust," in *Murder in Our Midst: The Holocaust, Industrial Killing, and Representation* (New York: Oxford University Press, 1996), 89.

27. W. Fernekes, "Developing Reflective Citizens: The Role of Holocaust Education," paper presented for the panel titled "Pedagogy: Theories, Tools, and Results" at the Stockholm International Forum on Holocaust Education, Remembrance, and Research, Jan. 27, 2000. The full text is in the files of the First Stockholm International Forum, which in turn can be found at the Riksarkivert (national archives), in Stockholm.

28. Lang, *The Future of the Holocaust,* x.

7

Teaching as Testimony

Pedagogical Peculiarities of Teaching the Holocaust

DAVID PATTERSON

"I wanted to come back to Sighet," explains Moshe the Beadle in Elie Wiesel's *Night*, "to tell you the story of my death. So that you could prepare yourselves while there was still time. . . . And see how it is, no one will listen to me."[1] In these few words, we have a paradigm for the dilemma of the survivor. He comes to us from the depths of a mass grave known as the Kingdom of Night, in which millions lie buried—not in the earth, mind you, but in a sky transformed into a cemetery. He comes to us and he speaks to us, with the muted voices of the six million resonating in his voice. He tries to warn us of the collapse of meaning and the mutilation of the human and divine image taking place all around us, both then and now. Most of us, however, do not listen. Those who listen cannot understand. For, unlike the survivor, we have not seen the inside of our own grave or the visage of a corpse staring back at us from a mirror. We have not held in our arms the broken remains of a *Muselmann* and there "caressed the head of the Twentieth Century."[2]

And yet, when we do have the courage to listen to those voices, there is something in the soul of each of us, something in our very flesh and blood, that cries out in the midst of their outcry. Suddenly we realize that the tales of terror we receive are not only about them—they are about us. In graphic and literal ways, we are connected to this thing that we cannot understand. For the ashes that ascended on high have rained down to cover the face of the earth. "These ashes," says a character created by the survivor and author Arnošt Lustig,

> will be contained in the breath and expression of every one of us, and the next time anybody asks what the air he breathes is made of, he will have to think about these ashes; they will be contained in books which haven't yet been written and will be found in the remotest regions of the earth where no human foot has ever trod; no one will be able to get rid of them, for they will be the fond, nagging ashes of the dead who died in innocence.[3]

When a single cloud of radiation rose from Chernobyl in 1986, within days radiation levels in Montana were up. We can measure the amount of air pollution for a given year by taking a plug of ice and snow from Antarctica. Thus the winds tie each person to every event on the planet. How deeply, then, are we bound to the event called the Holocaust, when dozens of clouds of ashes bellowed into the air for a thousand days, twenty-four hours each day! Those ashes sleep in the bread we harvest from the earth and place in our mouths. They stir in our bodies that are made from that bread, and they disturb our souls in a transformation of matter into spirit. For it is their voices—the voice of the ones who collided with the thing itself—that reverberate in the voices of the survivors.

Therefore, even if we cannot understand the survivors' accounts of the Shoah, their tales cut us to the quick. For the stories they tell are part of our own stories; deciding something about this matter, we decide something about ourselves, about why we live and die, what we hold dear, and where we go from here. When the survivors bear witness to what few eyes have seen, they entrust us with a message that we must struggle to deliver and a testimony that we must attempt to bear. Thus transformed into messengers and witnesses, we are transformed into teachers. But, similar to the survivors who must deliver a message that cannot be delivered, we are faced with teaching something that cannot be taught. This matter that comes to us from the antiworld cannot be accommodated by the categories of the world. Therefore, "the Holocaust" is not just one subject among many others that a student may elect to take, or that a teacher may decide to teach; you do not go from Spanish I to

Accounting II to Holocaust to Botany III. Indeed, the problem of which department to put Holocaust studies into is tied to a deeper reason that has to do with why it frustrates our thinking and our teaching.

There is more than the disciplinary issue at work here, and that "more" makes the Holocaust disturbing to the point of denial. And this "more" about the Holocaust is something that other subjects do not demand so directly or so insistently: you cannot teach the Holocaust without teaching something about life and meaning, about human being and divine being, about home and family—all the things that came under assault in the concentrationary universe and that continue to be targeted in academia. For the Holocaust does not lend itself to such intellectual fads as postmodernism, the new historicism, radical subjectivism, and moral relativism or to certain forms of gender studies, ethnic studies, and multiculturalism. (Indeed, inasmuch as they take power to be the sole reality, such "-isms" rest on premises that are in no way inconsistent with Nazism.) Efforts to isolate Holocaust studies within departmental contexts amount to efforts to insulate ourselves from the event. What, then, is pedagogically appropriate to teaching the Holocaust? What does one talk about? What "discipline" does Holocaust studies belong to? And what materials are most useful?

THE HOLOCAUST AS SUBJECT MATTER, AND THE ISSUE OF SINGULARITY

When teaching the Holocaust, we must be as clear as possible about what we are teaching—and on what we are not teaching. The term "Holocaust" is not a synonym for atrocity, catastrophe, racism, ethnic cleansing, or even genocide. It does not lend itself to these categories any more than to the categories by which we divide up the areas of academic inquiry. For the Holocaust is steeped in historical, epistemological, and metaphysical singularity. Therefore, the pedagogical difficulties surrounding it are singular as well.

In *The Holocaust in Historical Contexts,* Steven Katz argues quite convincingly that the historical singularity of the Holocaust lies "primarily in the premeditated Nazi plan to murder all Jews."[4] While he is correct in this claim, he is only partly correct. Concerned exclusively with the

Holocaust as a historical phenomenon, Katz overlooks the epistemological uniqueness of the event. This uniqueness lies not only in the fact that Auschwitz is beyond the methods and categories of our "-ologies" but also in the fact that those who passed through its gates came to know what reason might suggest they could not know: they came to know more than the dictionary meaning of *Arbeit macht frei*. Does this mean that Auschwitz cannot be studied? No. Does it mean that the survivors' testimonies cannot be trusted? Certainly not. But it does mean that we must take seriously the refrain from the Majdanek anthem, as recalled by Paul Trepman:

> There has never been,
> Nor will there ever be,
> Anywhere on earth,
> A sun like that which shines
> Upon our Majdanek.[5]

It means that in addition to posing the epistemological question "What is Auschwitz?" we must also ask, "What does Auschwitz command?"

This point is eloquently and thoroughly made by Emil Fackenheim in *To Mend the World*. There he cites numerous examples of prayer even though the gates of heaven were closed, resistance even though the only outcome could be death, and determination to live even though life had lost its value. One key to his argument is a passage from Pelagia Lewinska's memoir *Twenty Months at Auschwitz*, where she writes, "From the instant I grasped the motivating principle [at Auschwitz], it was as if I had been awakened from a dream. . . . I felt under orders to live."[6] And Fackenheim asks, "Whose orders? Why did she wish to obey? And—this above all—where did she get the strength?"[7] For Auschwitz is a realm where there is no voice from on high or from humanity, no affirmation of life's sanctity or meaning, no reason or rational principle for living. And yet Lewinska hears a commanding voice above the roar of the deafening silence that shrouds the concentrationary universe; she arrives at an understanding that thought cannot deduce. Therefore, Fackenheim argues, her grasp of the motivating principle of Auschwitz—a principle that determined the destruction not only of people but also of the very concept of person—is "epistemologically ultimate."[8] Why? Because there is nothing to be known on Planet Auschwitz that might impel her to live or enable her to hear such a command.

This epistemological singularity is related to the event's metaphysical singularity. For in its essence, like no other event, the Holocaust entails an undermining not only of what we know and how we know but also of any meaning that might be derived from our knowledge. In the Jewish tradition, the ground of all meaning is God; the Holocaust, as an assault on God's Chosen, is above all an assault on God. That is why it is not reducible to a case of genocide but is also a case of deicide. To be sure, Rashi, the great sage of the eleventh century, stated the principle at work here: "Whoever attacks Israel is as though he attacks the Holy One, blessed be He."[9] And it is echoed in the *Vittel Diary* of Yitzhak Katznelson: "It is against the great Beth Hamedrash, the spirit and soul of East European Jewry, that the nations have set this Horror."[10] This attack upon the Holy Spirit of Israel manifests itself in the calculated destruction of Jewish cemeteries and synagogues, of Jewish souls and prayers, of Jewish texts and traditions, of Jewish homes and families—all of which was planned according to the Jewish calendar of holy days.

If we recall a teaching articulated by the Koretzer Rebbe, a disciple of the Baal Shem Tov (the founder of Chassidism), this point will become even clearer: "God and Prayer are One. God and Torah are One. God, Israel, and Torah are One."[11] Jews who were rounded up and placed in ghettos to await deportation to death were forbidden to pray. Rabbi Shimon Huberband, who was murdered at Treblinka in 1942, points out that wherever Jews were found with Torah scrolls, they were either tortured or killed and the scrolls were burned or desecrated.[12] This assault on Torah is an assault on the teaching of Torah that each human being bears a trace of the divine image and is therefore morally and existentially connected to every other human being—a Jewish teaching that cannot live in the same universe with Nazi ideology. Therefore, Emmanuel Ringelblum notes, the Nazis ordered pregnant Jewish women to undergo abortions and made pregnancy a capital crime.[13] And therefore, Rabbi Huberband notes, the Nazis destroyed or desecrated ritual baths, the key to laws of family purity, which affirm the sanctity of the human being by sanctifying the process of creating a human being.[14] There must be no Jews because there must be no Torah; there must be no Torah because there must be no teaching or testimony contrary to the Nazi worldview, especially a teaching that comes from God.

There is no precedent in history for this assault on the holy, which, according to the light that comes unto the nations through the Jewish people, is the basis of all meaning and value in life. And without this metaphysical dimension of the assault, the Holocaust would not be the Holocaust. If we are to teach the Holocaust, then we must address this assault on the Jews and Judaism that takes us beyond all disciplinary boundaries. For this assault undermines the principles that define those boundaries. To situate the event within the conventional contexts of history, sociology, political science, literature, philosophy, and so on, is to avoid the event and ignore the Jews. If, as Elie Wiesel has said, at Auschwitz not only human beings died but also the very idea of a human being,[15] it is the idea of a human being that comes to the world through the Jews. And yet that is precisely what most Holocaust study, teaching, and scholarship ignores: the Jews. If the Jews are not to be eclipsed by the academic endeavor, then the endeavor must transcend the disciplines.

THE METADISCIPLINARY ASPECTS
OF TEACHING THE HOLOCAUST

"A novel about Treblinka," Elie Wiesel has said, "is either not a novel or not about Treblinka. A novel about Majdanek is about blasphemy. *Is* blasphemy."[16] In *A Jew Today,* he elaborates:

> There is no such thing as Holocaust literature—there cannot be. Auschwitz negates all literature as it negates all theories and doctrines; to lock it into a philosophy means to restrict it. To substitute words, any words, for it is to distort it. A Holocaust literature? The very term is a contradiction.[17]

The point he makes here is not that nobody can say anything about the Holocaust but that the Holocaust, as the object of academic inquiry, cannot be accommodated by the categories of literature, philosophy, or history, for these are the disciplines that constitute a way of understanding the world, whereas the Holocaust unfolds in an antiworld that is opposed to such understanding or intelligence.

What is an antiworld? It is a world without children, a world where children are old and old men are as helpless as children. It is a world, as Elie Wiesel was told, without mothers, fathers, sisters, or brothers.[18] It is a world, as Primo Levi points out, without criminals or madmen.[19] It is a world where men are called dogs, dogs are named "Man," and people feed on the scraps left by animals. It is world in which Jewish infants are destroyed to save mothers, and no Jew dies of natural causes. It is a world in which every Jew is homeless, "living" in a camp, in a ghetto, or in a hiding place.

The difficulty is not that the concentrationary universe cannot be imagined; indeed, it consisted of everything imaginable. The problem, rather, is that it cannot be *thought*. Recall in this connection Jean Améry's observation on the function of the intellect in the murder camps. "It was not the case," he says, "that the intellectual—if he had not already been destroyed physically—had now become unintellectual or incapable of thinking. On the contrary, only rarely did thinking grant itself a respite. But it nullified itself when at almost every step it ran into its uncrossable borders. The axes of its traditional frames of reference then shattered."[20] Although we are light years from Planet Auschwitz, those of us who try to "teach" the Holocaust or situate it within a curriculum are faced with similar difficulties. Here, too, we are operating within traditional frames of reference—frames of thought and intelligence that have been in place since the time of Plato. And the difficulty we have in categorizing the Holocaust reveals the shattering that Améry invokes.

Franklin Littell has rightly argued that the study of the Holocaust should not be confined to one department or discipline but should be part of what is taught across the disciplines. But this is not to say that Holocaust studies should be interdisciplinary or cross-disciplinary. In this connection, I have chosen the term "metadisciplinary" because the study of the Holocaust goes *beyond* the parameters of any given discipline or combination of disciplines. And this is so because the Holocaust is distinguished by a metaphysical assault on the premises of meaning and truth that define any discipline. A Holocaust memoir, for example, cannot be studied according to the codes and conventions of the memoir genre. It is not the composed recollection of one's life story; it is the impassioned testimony of one's own death in an effort to reconstitute a life that might have a story. Similarly, a Holocaust diary is not a gathering of the remains of the day in a moment of introspection; it is a cry unto a silent heaven for the sake of a community, written in clandestine desperation. A Holocaust history does not relate the account of an event; it bears witness in such a way as to transform its listener into a witness. Therefore, the reason to refrain from filing the Holocaust into one academic department or another is not just that it involves other disciplines but also that it challenges the epistemological foundations of disciplinary study.

"Under Hitler," says Emmanuel Levinas, "the Jews endured an ordeal that is without name, and cannot be placed in any sociological category. It is a lie to locate it within the series of natural causes and effects or to defer to 'human sciences' and seek to explain it by examining the thoughts and 'readings' of an Eichmann, the 'inner crises' of a Goebbels or the 'structures' of European society between the wars."[21] The statistics that social scientists invoke, the analyses that historians and psychologists apply, the methods that shape literary and philosophical investigations—all of these do not merely pervert the event into something that it is not, something more harmless, more comfortable, and more distant from us; worse than that, they betray the Jewish mothers and fathers and children whose outcry continues to haunt heaven and earth. As Levinas says, it is a lie to file the Holocaust into an academic category because to study the Holocaust is to be implicated in it. That is one reason behind the phenomenon of Holocaust denial. It is also why we often flee from the event while pretending to study it, leveling its history into one more tragedy among tragedies, or its literature into one more challenge to textual convention.

Where, then, should the study of the Holocaust be situated within the educational structure? For the sake of the blood spilled, and not just to attain some understanding, the study of the Holocaust should not be filed into one area of "knowledge" or another; rather, it should address the whole point of seeking any knowledge. Ideally, perhaps, Holocaust studies should consist of a series of courses that are either in a "category" of their own or are a significant part of a general education curriculum. In some cases, it could be made into an area-studies program. All these attempts at a solution to this problem are themselves problematic. And, short of restructuring the entire educational system, they will remain problematic. We can, however, maintain an awareness of the metadisciplinary aspect of what we are up to. Part of that endeavor entails a consideration of what materials to study when we engage in Holocaust studies.

WHAT TO STUDY IN HOLOCAUST STUDIES

For the last sixteen years, I have used a variety of texts and materials in my course on the Holocaust. To capture the interest and imagination of students, I have found it best to start with a short work and a film. In my experience, the best short text for this purpose is Elie Wiesel's *Night*. While it is written in a very simple, accessible style, it is laden with allusions and implications that are essential to any examination of the Holocaust. But in order to "get" these allusions and implications, a teacher must be familiar with certain things. A background in Judaism, for example, is crucial not only to understanding Wiesel but to any approach to the Holocaust that does not ignore the Jews. The Nazis certainly had such a background, and they used it. In reading *Night* it is important to know, for example, that in the Jewish tradition the Messiah appears either as a child or as an old man. Likewise, it is essential to know about the link between children and the *Shekhinah* as well as to know about the significance of the *Kaddish* and the holy days, not to mention the kabbalistic allusions in the opening pages of the text. Those of us who would teach the Holocaust, then, must have a background in Jewish teachings and traditions if our teaching is to be part of a resistance to what the Nazis set out to accomplish in the annihilation of the Jews.

There are numerous good documentary films that one can use to establish some groundwork for a course on the Holocaust; the "Genocide" episode from the series *The World at War* and a similar episode from Abba Eban's *Heritage* series are both good. An excellent documentary film that offers a concise history of antisemitism is *The Longest Hatred*. I do not like to use documentaries that are too graphic; I have used such films and have seen students slip into a perverse voyeurism.

A good drama is *Schindler's List,* but, like fire, this film has to be handled with caution. Any sense of a "happy ending" (Land of Israel), for instance, or the idea that "not all the Nazis were so bad" (Schindler) or that they were "a bunch of lunatics" (Goeth) must be dispelled. As with *Night,* the teaching and discussion of *Schindler's List* must include a great deal of background on Jews and Judaism if it is to be effective. For example, when considering this black-and-white film that is framed by color scenes of Sabbath observance, one should discuss the profound significance of the Sabbath and the implication that everything it stands for was slated for destruction. A knowledge of Hebrew is helpful, too, since one may then note that when Schindler sees the little girl in *red* he beholds the *humanity* of the other, for in Hebrew "red" is *adom* and "human being" is *adam,* both spelled alef-dalet-mem. In approaching this film in which names are so prominent, there is value in knowing the Jewish teachings on the relationship between the name and the soul.[22] And in teaching and discussing this film about responsibility, it is helpful to know something of the Talmud and its saying that "he who saves a single life saves the world entire" (*Sanhedrin* 37a).

Once the interest of the students has been stimulated, the next step is to provide them with some historical background. Some good texts in this regard are the histories written by Yehuda Bauer, Lucy Dawidowicz, Raul Hilberg, and Martin Gilbert. These histories can be used to direct interested students toward other texts that deal with more specific topics, such as Righteous Gentiles, war-crimes trials, ghettos, camps, resistance, bystanders, music, literature, art, medicine, and other broad areas of study. From this general overview, students may be guided into the lives of individuals through the study of diaries, memoirs, and literary texts. While these materials may be difficult to come by, among the best are the diaries of Chaim Kaplan, Emmanuel Ringelblum, Adam Czerniakow, Avraham Tory, Yitskhok Rudashevski, Yitzhak Katznelson, and Moshe Flinker. From the ghettos examined in the diaries, one may then go into the memoirs on the camps. Among the best authors of these works are Primo Levi, Isabella Leitner, Sara Nomberg-Przytyk, Fania Fénelon, Gerda Klein, and Simon Wiesenthal. Some of the literary figures who have responded most eloquently to the event are Elie Wiesel, Ka-tzetnik 135633, Arnošt Lustig, Aharon Appelfeld, Paul Celan, and André Schwarz-Bart.

I believe that it is essential to include accounts written by women, not in the name of equal time, or to make a point about how women are nurturing and men are not, but in the interest of a deeper understanding of the scope of the event. According to Jewish teaching, for example, it is through women that Torah enters the world, that blessing falls on a home, and that creation comes into being.[23] Women also face, in unique ways, the dilemma of killing one person to save another—that is, killing infants to save mothers so that both the infant and the mother lose their essence.[24] The accounts written by women open up these depths in ways that those written by men cannot.

Once students have been taken into the event (inasmuch as that is possible), the next step is to explore its ramifications from a variety of standpoints. To take one example, Jean Améry, in *At the Mind's Limits*, does an excellent job of examining the implications of the Shoah for intellectual understanding. Because the Holocaust arises in the heart of Christendom, it harbors serious implications for Christian thought and understanding. Effective books along these lines are *The Crucifixion of the Jews,* by Franklin Littell; *Long Night's Journey into Day,* by A. Roy and Alice Eckardt; and *Reflections of a Post-Auschwitz Christian,* by Harry James Cargas. One of the foremost thinkers to examine the implications of the Holocaust for Jewish thought is Emil Fackenheim. Among the best of his works for this purpose are *To Mend the World, God's Presence in History,* and *The Jewish Return into History.* Moreover, the event has implications not only for Christian doctrine and Jewish thought but also for the Western intellectual tradition, particularly as it has unfolded since the Enlightenment. While few scholars have thoroughly examined this issue, one good text is *Ethics after the Holocaust,* edited by John K. Roth.[25]

Other methods and materials should be incorporated whenever possible. In the spring semester, for example, students can be involved in the observance of Holocaust Remembrance Day and can be alerted, as the day approaches, to relevant television programming. In some communities, there are museums to be visited and survivors who may be willing to visit a class. To be sure, no teacher is as effective, no voice as eloquent, as the flesh-and-blood voice of the survivor. Survivors and others in the community may have artifacts—such as ghetto currency, camp outfits, or yellow stars—that can also bring this history to life. All these methods—the use of films, texts, exhibits, observances, artifacts, and people—should be geared to bringing out the metaphysical dimensions of the event, the metadisciplinary nature of studying the event, and the implications of the event for those who study it.

Finally, a word of caution: in venturing into the antiworld, the point is not to get lost in it and succumb to despair, even though that is a risk that we take, for the Holocaust can become a prison to those who would engage it. No, the point is to acquire a deeper capacity for response—a deeper responsibility—to and for the other human being. The point is to realize that what is most essential is most quickly forgotten, and that what is most precious is most fragile. The point, therefore, in teaching the Holocaust is not to cash in on the "Holocaust industry" but to introduce a dimension of true height to higher learning—something that in our time is dangerously lacking. Therefore, one will encounter a certain tension between prevailing intellectual fashions and the seriousness of moral or metaphysical engagement with the Holocaust. But the stakes are too high to try to avoid this tension.

In teaching the Holocaust, more than anywhere else in the educational endeavor, teaching is testimony, for teaching the Holocaust is a way of resisting it, of refusing the Nazis a posthumous victory. During the days of that darkness, the world was divided into those who resisted evil and those who became parties to it, and that division remains in force. Therefore, teaching the Holocaust has implications for every other aspect of an educational endeavor aimed not only at informing human beings about the facts of the world but also at affirming the sanctity of the human being as it is revealed through the texts and traditions of Jews and Judaism. That sanctity was under assault then; it must be affirmed now.

NOTES

1. Elie Wiesel, *Night*, trans. Stella Rodway (New York: Bantam, 1982), 5.

2. Ka-tzetnik 135633, *Sunrise over Hell*, trans. Nine De-Nur (London: Allen, 1977), 111.

3. Arnošt Lustig, *A Prayer for Katerina Horovitzova*, trans. Jeanne Nemcova (New York: Harper, 1973), 50–51.

4. Steven Katz, *The Holocaust in Historical Context*, vol. 1: *The Holocaust and Mass Death before the Modern Age* (New York: Oxford University Press, 1994), 60.

5. Paul Trepman, *Among Men and Beasts,* trans. Shoshana Perla and Gertrude Hirschler (New York: Bergen Belsen Memorial Press, 1978), 137.

6. Pelagia Lewinska, *Twenty Months at Auschwitz,* trans. A. Teichner (New York: Lyle Stuart, 1968), 150.

7. Emil L. Fackenheim, *To Mend the World: Foundations of Post-Holocaust Jewish Thought* (New York: Schocken, 1989), 218.

8. Ibid., 248.

9. Rashi, *Commentary on the Torah,* vol. 4, trans. M. Rosenbaum and N. M. Silbermann (Jerusalem: Silbermann Family, 1972), 146.

10. Yitzhak Katznelson, *Vittel Diary,* 2nd ed., trans. Myer Cohn (Tel-Aviv: Hakibbutz Hameuchad, 1972), 202–3.

11. See Louis I. Newman, *The Hasidic Anthology* (New York: Schocken, 1963), 147.

12. Shimon Huberband, *Kiddush Hashem: Jewish Religious and Cultural Life in Poland during the Holocaust,* ed. Jeffrey S. Gurock and Robert S. Hirt, trans. David E. Fishman (Hoboken, N.J.: Ktav and Yeshiva University Press, 1987), 44.

13. Emmanuel Ringelblum, *Notes from the Warsaw Ghetto,* ed. and trans. Jacob Sloan (New York: Schocken, 1974), 230.

14. Huberband, *Kiddush Hashem,* 61.

15. Elie Wiesel, *Legends of Our Time* (New York: Avon, 1968), 230.

16. Elie Wiesel, *Dimensions of the Holocaust* (Evanston, Ill.: Northwestern University Press, 1977), 7.

17. Elie Wiesel, *A Jew Today,* trans. Marion Wiesel (New York: Random House, 1978), 197.

18. Wiesel, *Night,* 105.

19. Primo Levi, *Survival in Auschwitz: The Nazi Assault on Humanity,* trans. Stuart Woolf (New York: Simon & Schuster, 1996), 98.

20. Jean Améry, *At the Mind's Limits: Contemplations by a Survivor on Auschwitz and Its Realities,* trans. Sidney Rosenfeld and Stella P. Rosenfeld (Bloomington: Indiana University Press, 1980), 19.

21. Emmanuel Levinas, *Difficult Freedom: Essays on Judaism,* trans. Sean Hand (Baltimore: Johns Hopkins University Press, 1990), 129.

22. For example, according to Jewish legend, when we die and lie in the grave, the Angel of Death comes to us so that he might bring us into the presence of the Holy One, blessed be He. There is, of course, a catch: in order to draw nigh unto the Divine Presence, we must correctly answer a certain question. The question is the same for all, but for each the answer is different. And so, with his

thousand eyes gazing upon us, the Angel poses the fearsome question: "What is your name?"

23. For a discussion of the Jewish teachings on the women and the classical sources, see David Patterson, "The Assault on the Feminine," in *Along the Edge of Annihilation: The Collapse and Recovery of Life in the Holocaust Diary* (Seattle: University of Washington Press, 1999), 176–91.

24. Sara Nomberg-Przytyk and Isabella Leitner relate very powerful accounts of this dilemma unique to women. See Sara Nomberg-Przytyk, *Auschwitz: True Tales from a Grotesque Land,* trans. Roslyn Hirsch (Chapel Hill: University of North Carolina Press, 1985), 67–71; Isabella Leitner, *Fragments of Isabella,* ed. Irving Leitner (New York: Thomas Y. Crowell, 1978), 31–32. See also David Patterson, "The Moral Dilemma of Motherhood in the Nazi Death Camps," in Harry James Cargas, ed., *Problems Unique to the Holocaust* (Lexington: University Press of Kentucky, 1999), 7–24.

25. My essay in that volume, "Nazis, Philosophers, and the Response to the Scandal of Heidegger," particularly examines this issue. See John K. Roth, ed., *Ethics after the Holocaust: Perspectives, Critiques, and Responses* (St. Paul, Minn.: Paragon House, 1999), 148–211.

8

Histories

Betrayed and Unfulfilled

TIMOTHY A. BENNETT AND ROCHELLE L. MILLEN

> In many instances it must appear as mockery to look
> to tradition when we want to be sure of our origins. It
> may be that it is not we who have traditions but that
> the traditions have us, but often in the same way that
> a devastated city has denizens or in the way that the
> vicious circle traps players who run toward their own
> ruin along its circumference.—Peter Sloterdijk,
> "Poetics of Beginning," in *Zur Welt kommen—*
> *Zur Sprache kommen. Frankfurter Vorlesungen*
> (Frankfurt: Suhrkamp, 1988), 45

Peter Sloterdijk's statement suggests the peril of discussing traditions in the post-Shoah era, for in the twentieth century, as he reminds his German audience, traditions may no longer embody the noble aspirations and humane ideals of a people. Instead, in a nightmarish inversion, traditions may perhaps imprison a people as a bombed-out city holds its denizens captive. More recently, George Steiner has described our century as a "time out of hell":

> The collapse of humaneness in the twentieth century has specific enigmas.
> It arises not from riders on the distant steppe or barbarians at the gates.

National Socialism, Fascism, Stalinism (though, in this latter instance, more opaquely) spring from within the context, the locale, the administrative social instruments of the high places of civilization, of education, of scientific progress and humanizing deployment, be it Christian or Enlightened.[1]

For us—one a student of Judaism and Jewish thought, the other a student of German literature and culture—these statements capture tensions that we have worked to mold into the very fabric of a course titled "Germans and Jews: Culture, Identity, and Difference." In our course, we endeavor to confront the troublesome and schizophrenic question of tradition, both as a hallmark of the "high places of civilization" and as a scene of catastrophic devastation. In fact, rather than arguing that tensions arise in the context of our course on the Holocaust, we contend that an honest encounter with these tensions—the tensions between the emancipatory and destructive forces embedded in Western traditions—is necessary to help students begin to cope with the overwhelming tragedy that characterizes the Shoah.

Indeed, in its very focus, "Germans and Jews" points to the integration of tensions into the learning process. The class is and is not a Holocaust course. It is true that students enroll because the title clearly suggests the Shoah—indeed, any reference to Germans and Jews in the postmodern era immediately invokes images of death camps and Nazi atrocities—and yet, though our approach may seem paradoxical, we do not introduce the Holocaust and its events before the latter portion of the course. Instead, we require students to begin their studies with a survey of German history since the Reformation. Too often, we fear, students leave a course on the Holocaust having learned to see Germans and Jews as perpetrators and victims and thus persist in thinking in stereotypes. We wondered whether it was possible to construct a course that would introduce students to the horror of the Holocaust without leading them to believe that atrocity is inevitable, and morality ineffective. Similarly, we asked ourselves if it was possible to structure a course that would help students avoid a facile moralizing about the Holocaust that failed to wrestle with the complexity of its history.

These questions arose for us as we worked together with colleagues at Wittenberg University to plan an international conference titled "Teaching the Holocaust: Issues and Dilemmas." In the course of our planning, we found ourselves confronting a dilemma: aside from one course on the literature of the Holocaust, Wittenberg—a small liberal arts college of about 2,100 students affiliated with the Evangelical Lutheran Church in America—had no course devoted to the Holocaust. Furthermore, the Evangelical Lutheran Church had extended a declaration of regret concerning the influence of Martin Luther's antisemitism on the church's teachings and actions (and inaction).[2] Therefore, we discerned the possibility of constructing a course that would reside in the interstices of several tensions: drawing on the fields of religion and German studies, it would be interdisciplinary; it would model interfaith dialogue as well as interdisciplinary dialogue; and it would ask students to conduct a critical interrogation of their own beliefs about history and difference as they considered what became the essential question of the course: Was the Holocaust inevitable?[3]

Bringing these issues to the classroom proved both exciting and risky. In *The Courage to Teach,* Parker J. Palmer lists some core paradoxes about teaching: "My inward and invisible sense of identity becomes known, even to me, only as it manifests itself in encounters with external and visible 'otherness.' . . . Teaching always take place at the crossroad of the personal and the public, and if I want to teach well, I must learn to stand where these opposites intersect. Intellect works in concert with feeling, so if I hope to open my students' minds, I must open their emotions as well."[4] Thus, although our course had originated in the context of our developing an interdisciplinary class on the Holocaust, we soon discovered that professional and personal identities intersect and inform one another. Rochelle Millen is the daughter of Polish Jews who escaped to the United States in 1936, and for her the study of the Holocaust can never be purely academic; the Shoah is a palpable presence in her sense of family, in her personal history, and for her co-religionists. Timothy Bennett, a Lutheran, has played an active role in exploring the significance of Wittenberg's relationship to the church and the nature of the liberal arts in a church-related setting. We found that effective teaching meant foregrounding our professional (public) and personal identities. By doing so, we hoped to help our students learn to integrate what they were learning about the past, as historical knowledge, with how they acted in the present to make ethical determinations. Clearly, intellectual pursuit and what psychologists call the affective domain—spiritual and emotional insight—need to work in productive tension for students and teachers alike.

Palmer's teaching-related paradoxes translated into our learning goals for the course:

> Students can learn to examine critically their sense of identity by engaging "otherness" and entering into a process of dialogue both with others and with otherness.
>
> Students can learn to study history so as to make more informed ethical decisions in their lives.
>
> Students can learn to regard history as a scene of tension—between conflicting interests, motives, and forces—that requires ethical response by individuals.

To achieve these goals, we structured a course that examines the history of the Jewish experience in Germany, without presupposing the inevitability of the Holocaust. In taking this approach, we followed Jacob Katz's admonition to consider each historical period as a scene of open possibilities rather than historical inevitabilities:

> A historian who wants to describe a specific historical period also possesses knowledge of later periods that are the results of countless subsequent decisions. If, however, he wants to discover the choices open to and the difficulties encountered by people acting in the earlier period, then he must exclude his own knowledge [of subsequent developments]. It requires, as the great Dutch historian Johan Huizinga put it, that "one imagine the past as though it were just now present."[5]

Katz's insight is fundamental to the course: we structure the syllabus and presentations so that students begin to appreciate that at any given moment other histories were possible, but that the aggregate force of decisions made by reasoning, civilized human beings— either acting in accord with the inherited wisdom of their traditions or claiming the authority of those traditions (sometimes falsely)—had resulted instead in the institution of death camps. This fateful tension—between, on the one hand, the hope and promise of emancipation and mutual respect that characterized some Enlightenment thinkers and, on the other, the eventual rise of genocidal fascism—determined the outline of the class, the selection of texts, and the shape of the dialogue between instructors and students.

OUTLINE OF THE CLASS AND SELECTION OF TEXTS

Because interdisciplinary experiences require a conversation between disciplines and areas of expertise, we chose to set the course up as two intersecting yet distinct classes. Millen's section focuses primarily on intellectual history and examines a series of original and secondary sources that reflect the public controversy on the civil status of German Jews, focusing on the period from the Reformation on. Bennett's section investigates primarily imaginative literature and essays, in an effort to help students understand how images of cultural identity and difference both reflect and shape social reality in the same period. Students meet in separate sections approximately two-thirds of the semester. In the remaining time, joint sessions provide an opportunity for students in each section to bring their work and insights into a larger forum.

Millen's section, for example, works primarily with *The Jew in the Modern World: A Documentary History,* an anthology of original sources collected and edited by Paul Mendes-Flohr and Jehuda Reinharz. She selects secondary sources that augment these texts and further explore the issues that the documentary history raises. Bennett has students read works that either bear directly on the issue of Jewish emancipation or reflect the Jewish contribution to German culture.

Some examples of how the two sections work together will best illustrate how we endeavor to nurture dialogue on several levels. The introduction to the course is a joint session that requires students to begin grappling with the complexity of the issues the course raises. We begin by showing students slides of the Marienkirche, a church in Wittenberg, Germany, the place for which Wittenberg University is named. After reminding students that Luther taught at the original Wittenberg University in Germany and preached at the church they now see, we show them a close-up of the exterior choir wall. The Marienkirche displays a

Judensau there—a medieval antisemitic motif (the word means, literally, "Jewish pig")—which commemorates the expulsion of Jews from the city in the fourteenth century. We then ask students to consider what might explain why such a vile memorial has been incorporated into a sacred building. Of fundamental importance here is the need to let students explore ideas and work at trying to understand the mentality of an era that would view the expulsion of the Jewish community and the defamation of Jews as a tribute to God. As students overcome their initial revulsion, they begin to formulate concepts that help them understand doctrines of supersessionism. Luther's own antisemitic writings are introduced (and studied later in individual sections). Fundamentally, however, we urge students to consider the force of the belief that the expulsion was a holy act, and we impress upon them the need to understand the motivation for that sentiment. While we share their need to condemn that sentiment, we contend that they cannot hope to understand how hate arises and functions unless they can see how a hateful action, in this instance, derives from a firm belief that the action is pleasing to God. As students struggle with this concept, they begin, of course, to try to understand the past as a "present" moment, without seeing past events strictly in terms of later events. Students begin to appreciate how much their knowledge of the Holocaust, however limited it might be, has become a lens through which they view the past; and they also begin to appreciate how difficult it is to understand an era in its own terms.[6]

The complex interaction of past and present becomes more compelling when we focus students' attention on another memorial, this one in the ground directly below the *Judensau*. Erected in 1988, this memorial commemorates the victims of the Shoah and acknowledges the role that Christian supersessionism played in the cataclysm. The inscription for that monument reads as follows:

Gottes eigentlicher Name, der geschmähte Schem Ha-Mphoras, den die Juden vor den Christen fast unsagbar heilig hielten, starb in sechs Millionen Juden unter einem Kreuzeszeichen.

God's true name, the name Schem Ha-Mphoras reviled [in the motif described above], which the Jews held so holy as to be unutterable in the presence of Christians, died beneath the sign of a cross in the deaths of six million Jews.

The reference in the inscription to a cross is darkly ambiguous: it evokes images both of the Christian cross and of the swastika—in German a *Hakenkreuz,* or hooked cross. The Wittenberg congregation initially had considered removing the *Judensau* but was advised by the Jewish community of neighboring Halle that Germany had to confront its history, not bury it. This moment, then, becomes emblematic of the dialogue that shapes the course.

The introduction of these themes is rather more perilous than the preceding brief description suggests. After all, we hope that students will leave the course having wrestled with ethical questions and in possession of a moral compass. Yet we are aware, as Sloterdijk and Steiner eloquently argue, that blind reliance on the achievements of humane cultures is not possible. How, then, can we guide students to ask difficult and critical questions about their traditions—religious, cultural, political—without leading them to abandon faith altogether in the possibility of humane action? Even as we ask them to undertake a critical interrogation of the history that leads inexorably to the Holocaust, we also try to acquaint them with other historical forces opposing the trends that emerge triumphant in periods of incredible brutality and violence.

Early in the course, for example, we discuss the eighteenth-century distinction between natural and positive religion and its significance in the emancipation debate. Natural religion was, for German thinkers during the Enlightenment, the set of reasonable, rational truths underlying all religions, regardless of tradition and creed. By contrast, positive religion proclaimed the unique and exclusive truth of the particular revelation upon which Christianity or Judaism or Islam is based. Many thinkers sought to reconcile reason and revelation by referring to religious traditions as sentimental legacies, which insured that people would integrate the reasonable truths of a tradition into their actions and live responsibly and ethically. Tradition itself was venerable yet relative—only the underlying reasonable truths were eternal and did not vary from one faith to the next, though these truths might be expressed through different symbols.

The friendship between the Lutheran dramatist, theologian, and librarian Gotthold Ephraim Lessing and the Jewish philosopher Moses Mendelssohn exemplifies this moment in German-Jewish history. Mendelssohn's efforts to eliminate the barriers that hindered the full participation of Jews in German civil society coincided with Lessing's battles against Lutheran orthodoxy and his efforts to secure the support of the German bourgeoisie and aristocracy for the emancipation of the Jews. Students in Millen's section of the course read several documents surrounding the emancipation debate and analyze in greater depth Mendelssohn's longer tract, *Jerusalem.* Students in Bennett's section read two plays by Lessing, *The Jews* and *Nathan the Wise,* as well as Lessing's controversial critique of Christianity, *The Education of the Human Race.* Indeed, this portion of the course provides one of the more challenging (and, possibly, more charming) moments for us as instructors: we introduce this portion through a dramatic dialogue of our own as we impersonate Lessing and Mendelssohn. The discussion of the texts and our dramatization of the exemplary friendship between Mendelssohn and Lessing permit us to introduce students to a utopian moment in German history. Indeed, in a sense, we regard this brief episode in the history of Christianity and Judaism in Germany as one of those *messianische Splitter,* messianic fragments, that figure prominently in Walter Benjamin's philosophy of history.[7] For Benjamin, himself a victim of Nazi persecution, the past held brief utopian or emancipatory episodes that looked toward a future when greater freedom and equality would govern human affairs. There were, he stated, in his own distinctive heterodox Marxist and theological terms, messianic fragments scattered throughout history. By introducing students to German Enlightenment thought, we hope to indicate to them that at any given moment, and in any particular present, other possible histories are present and can develop.

But we do not want to inculcate a naive view of events, of course. As we and our students probe the Enlightenment-era tension between reason and revelation, we also explore the slow decline in the influence of religion and the rise in importance of scientific explanation. As we do so, we examine the concomitant rise of the modern bureaucratic nation-state in Germany. In essence, our earlier inquiry into the tension between reason and revelation yields to an examination of religion's diminished role in the modern era (the era following Nietzsche's proclamation of God's death), and of what Richard Rubenstein describes as two fundamental factors contributing to the Holocaust: "the triumph of value-neutral, functional rationality as the predominant mode of problem solving in advanced technological societies such as Germany" and "the impulse to centralization, homogenization, and leveling that we find so frequently as a feature of modernization and bureaucratization."[8] These considerations inform our study of the Shoah proper as we examine the modern era. While Enlightenment ideals ushered in an era of greater religious tolerance, this tolerance was made possible in part by a decline in the role of religion in cultural life. As religion becomes less relevant to cultural life and loses its power to define absolutely a culture's understanding of itself and the natural world, a society may find it more difficult to reach moral and ethical consensus.

Of course, students readily recognize this modern world as one they inhabit. Undergraduates, it seems, come to courses looking for answers. We prefer, however, to provide them with difficult questions. Steiner, in *In Bluebeard's Castle,* seeks at least in part to locate the origin of the death camps in the decay of religion: "It is to the ambiguous afterlife of religious feeling in Western culture that we must look, to the malignant energies released by the decay of natural religious forms."[9] Steiner's statement focuses our attention on the paradox that anchors our course and thus on the fundamental tension that shapes our inquiry: the Enlightenment's utopian dream is transformed by the early part of the twentieth century into its very opposite—the hellish nightmare of Auschwitz. The hope promised by the messianic traditions of Judaism and Christianity, whose ideals form the deeper structures of Enlightenment philosophies of progress and perfectibility in human affairs, has failed to materialize. Students encounter that failure through documentaries on the Holocaust, memoirs of survivors, and imaginative literature that tackles issues of conscience and responsibility.

RESIDING IN THE TENSION

Finally, then, we encourage students to recognize the ambiguity in which they live. Unable to discover black-and-white answers to the question of what made the Holocaust possible or to the enigma of anti-Judaism's enduring legacy in the Christian world or to Christianity's failure to prevent the Holocaust, we work to help students develop habits of mind that enable them to begin negotiating the difficult questions and passages they confront in modern pluralist culture. For example, since the vast majority of our students come from Christian backgrounds (recall that Wittenberg University is affiliated with the Lutheran Church), we find that they leave the course having learned to see the Holocaust as a matter of central importance for Christian belief. Recent discussions on the role of the Vatican in World War II have rendered this aspect of the course more relevant to students as they wrestle both with the historical debate and with dramas such as Rolf Hochhuth's *The Deputy*. In concluding, however, we cite here George Steiner's references to Good Friday, to suggest the lesson we endeavor to communicate in "Germans and Jews":

> There is one particular day in Western history about which neither historical record nor myth nor Scripture make report. It is a Saturday. And it has become the longest of days. We know of that Good Friday which Christianity holds to have been that of the Cross. But the non-Christian, the atheist, knows of it as well. This is to say that he knows of the injustice, of the interminable suffering, of the waste, of the brute enigma of ending, which so largely make up not only the historical dimension of the human condition, but the everyday fabric of our personal lives. . . . We know also about Sunday. To the Christian, that day signifies an intimation, both assured and precarious, both evident and beyond comprehension of resurrection, of a justice and a love that have conquered death. If we are non-Christians or non-believers, we know of that Sunday in precisely analogous terms. We conceive of it as the day of liberation from inhumanity and servitude. We look to resolutions, be they therapeutic or political, be they social or messianic. . . . But ours is the long day's journey of the Saturday. Between suffering, aloneness, unutterable waste on the one hand and the dream of liberation, of rebirth on the other.[10]

By the conclusion of the course, if we have lived up to our intentions, students have learned to live in that Saturday. They have learned not only to remember the history that was, and that culminated in, the Holocaust, in that dark night whose tragic consequences are beyond imagining, but also, perhaps, to discern that other history that awaits fulfillment but informs, to borrow from Steiner's vocabulary, the Sabbatarian hopes and ideals of a Lessing and Mendelssohn. They have navigated this intersection of histories in an exploration—of historical documents, memoirs, imaginative literature, and the arts—that constitutes a probing of the interstices of ethics and aesthetics, hope and despair. If we have done our job well, we have helped students begin to negotiate the difficulty of living in the shadow of Auschwitz while suggesting to them that ethical, conscientious living and decisions, even if these fail to bear fruit immediately or to avert catastrophe in their own lives, may well contribute to a greater light that illuminates the path toward a just future for all humanity.[11]

NOTES

The translation of Sloterdijk is our own. The original reads: "In vielen Fällen muß es wie ein Hohn erscheinen, uns an die Tradition to verweisen, wenn uns unserer Anfänge vergewissern wollen. Es mag sein, daß nicht wir die Tradition haben, sondern die Tradition uns, aber oft hat sie uns so, wie eine zerstörte Stadt ihre Einwohner hat oder wie der vitiöse Zirkel seine Spieler festhält, die in ihm dem Ruin entgegenrennen."

1. George Steiner, *Grammars of Creation* (New Haven: Yale University Press, 2001), 4.

2. The Declaration of the Evangelical Lutheran Church in America to the Jewish Community was adopted by the Church Council on April 18, 1994. It is available at http://www.elca.org/ecumenical/interfaithrelations/jewish/declaration.html (accessed Feb. 8, 2006).

3. This is similar to the question asked in Jacob Katz, "Was the Holocaust Predictable?," *Commentary*, May 1975, 41–48.

4. Parker J. Palmer, *The Courage to Teach: Exploring the Inner Landscape of a Teacher's Life* (San Francisco: Jossey-Bass, 1998), 63.

5. Jacob Katz, "War der Holocaust vorhersehbar," in *Zwischen Messianismus und Zionismus: Zur jüdischen* Sozialgeschichte (Frankfurt Jüdischer Verlag, 1993), 208. This is our translation of a passage from the German version of Katz, "Was the Holocaust Predictable?" The German translation, authorized by Katz, differs from the earlier version published in English. Apparently Katz revised

the essay for publication in Germany. The German "original" reads as follows: "Ein Historiker, der einen bestimmten Abschnitt der Vergangenheit beschreiben will, besitzt auch Kenntnisse über die späteren Abschnitte, das Ergebnis unzähliger nachfolgender Entscheidungen. Will er aber die Optionen und Schwierigkeiten der in der ersten Etappe handelnden Menschen aufzeigen, dann muß er sein eigenes Wissen ausklammern. . . . Es kommt darauf an, wie es der große niederländische Historiker Johan Huizinga formulierte, 'sich die Vergangenheit so vorzustellen, als wäre sie dennoch erst Gegenwart.'"

6. To guide the students through this fundamental ambivalence, we rely on Rubenstein's application of the theories of cognitive dissonance and dissonance reduction. See Richard Rubenstein, *After Auschwitz: History, Theology, and Contemporary Judaism,* 2nd ed. (Baltimore: Johns Hopkins University Press, 1992), 84–87.

7. Walter Benjamin, "Über den Begriff der Geschichte," in *Illuminationen: Ausgewählte Schriften* (Frankfurt: Suhrkamp, 1980), 251–61.

8. Rubenstein, *After Auschwitz,* 122.

9. George Steiner, "A Season in Hell," in *In Bluebeard's Castle: Some Notes Towards the Redefinition of Culture* (New Haven: Yale University Press, 1971), 53.

10. George Steiner, *Real Presences* (Chicago: University of Chicago Press, 1989), 231–32.

11. See Harry James Cargas, *Shadows of Auschwitz* (New York: Crossroad, 1990), 1. Cargas poses a question that illustrates how apt the Good Friday and Saturday analogies employed by Steiner are. We ask students to wrestle with this question in the course, even as we ourselves wrestle with its implications: "The Holocaust is, in my judgment, the greatest tragedy for Christians since the crucifixion. In the first instance, Jesus died; in the latter Christianity may be said to have died. In the case of Christ, the Christian believes in a resurrection. Will there be, can there be, a resurrection for Christianity? That is the question that haunts me."

9

Cross-Disciplinary Notes

Four Questions for Teaching the Shoah

DAVID R. BLUMENTHAL

Many years ago, I was teaching a course on the Shoah,[1] and a woman student suddenly raised her hand and asked, "Professor Blumenthal, why are you barking at us?" I was, to be sure, taken aback, but I realized immediately that she was correct: I had been unpleasantly sharp with my students. I stopped the class to explain that at the next session we were to see *Night and Fog,* and that, although I had seen it several times, I was upset at the coming film. This disclosure led to a long discussion about how all of us, including professionals, find the material of the Shoah so difficult to deal with. The very facts offend our sense of humanity. They fragment, mercilessly, our concept of who we are as people. For Jews, dealing with the Shoah is brutal, since we know it was directed against us, against our bodies and souls. The Shoah assaults our sense of the value of Jewish being. It brings us to rage. Sometimes, it brings us to despair.

Is the Shoah unique? Or, to put the question perhaps more accurately, in what sense is the Shoah unique? This issue has been a source of contention among scholars for many years. Sometimes "unique" means "inexpressible"; but then how can one teach the Shoah at all? Sometimes "unique" means "different"; but then what is unique about the Shoah, since all moments in history are, by definition, different? Sometimes "unique" describes a deeply intense emotion that one experiences when one studies and teaches the Shoah. In this sense, "unique" means that the Jew hatred, or the inhumanity, or some other aspect of the Shoah is experienced by us as very intense. But how does one teach this intensity without either diluting it or making it so central that nothing else can be taught or learned except this intensity? Finally, "unique" sometimes means that the subject is alien to the structures of perception, thought, and affect that we usually use in examining and responding to human situations. Does this mean that the Shoah cannot be taught because it just doesn't fit into our usual categories of analysis and response? On the contrary, "nothing human is alien to me"—even at its ugliest—should be our motto. The question is, how do we teach that which is alien, indeed repulsive, to us as human beings?

The first step is to admit our own humanity. We must begin by confessing, to ourselves and our students, that the Shoah upsets us, that the material assaults, indeed abuses, our sense of humanity and, if one is Jewish, our sense of Jewishness. Only through forthright confrontation with our own hurt in connection with the Shoah can we appreciate how hard it is for others to learn. Only through honest self-examination can we come to the realization that the facts of the Shoah preclude—and perhaps *should* preclude—an "objective," "ethically neutral" examination. We are who we are, and we must admit that.

Notwithstanding the bruising quality of our engagement with the Shoah, it seems to me that four questions beg to be answered, and four conclusions demand to be drawn. Any one of them might constitute a course of study unto itself; but, equally, any one of them could be a part of any course of study or any extended thought on the subject of the Shoah. One need not teach a class on the Shoah to confront these questions, and one need not be an expert in any of the disciplines suggested to confront the problematic that these fundamental questions raise, for each question is part of *la condition humaine* after the Shoah.

THE QUESTION OF HISTORY

The first question deals with the accuracy of what we know. Historians must go over and over the material, checking and cross-checking for truth. There is still so much to be uncovered. For instance, is it true that American oil companies were shipping oil to the German war machine through Spain almost until the end of the war? Is it true that American banks helped finance the Nazi war effort and provided cover for the saving of Nazi wealth after the war? What is the exact evidence? Does such action make such companies guilty of treason? And why were no trials held of Americans who acted this way after the war?[2] Can scholars decide whether the genocide of the Jews was part of Hitler's vision from the beginning or was instead a later improvisation?[3] What of the received numbers of six million Jews and twenty million total dead? How accurate are they? How could we know? How accurate are the stories of survivors? How accurate do they need to be?[4] And so on. Especially in view of the rewriting of history by the revisionists, the work of checking and uncovering the truth is very important. Research and seminars on this topic must be held continuously.

THE QUESTION OF THEODICY

The second question, which is of more interest to me as a theologian, is *Where was God?* I am asked this question in every class I teach, whether it is Psalms, modern Jewish theology, the prayer book, Jewish mysticism, the sociology of evil, or Judaism and Hinduism. I get this question from children, students, and adults; from Jews, Christians, Muslims, Hindus, and atheists. The question of God's responsibility in the Shoah is a perfectly reasonable one to ask, even for secularists. The question jumps out at anyone who tries to think religion and the Shoah in the same sentence.

In addressing this question, it is my custom to label the problem, present the usual answers, and show why I feel they are inadequate. Then I present my own answer. Briefly, in classical theological thinking, the problem of the good God Who does unjustified evil, or allows it to occur, is called "theodicy," or the problem of theodicy. It is a hoary issue in religious thinking, and the roots go back to God's punishment of Cain. God has not told Cain not to murder, and in a certain sense Cain's action is a reaction to God's favoring his brother. So is God's punishment of Cain just? From there the issue runs like a thread through the Bible. Why does God kill the animals in the flood of Noah? How can God destroy the whole population of Sodom and Gomorrah? And so on, all the way through to Job, who asks how God can punish him when he has committed no sin. The same question surfaces after the destruction of the First Temple and then the Second, and again after the massacres of the crusades and, to be sure, after the Shoah.

One classical answer to the question of theodicy is that those who were killed were really guilty, and hence what happened to them is not evil but justified punishment. Their innocence, and hence the injustice of what happened, are illusions. This is one of the answers of the so-called friends of Job. It is also the theology embodied in the Book of Lamentations and developed in rabbinic liturgy with such formulas as *u-mipnei hata'einu,* "because of our sins." It became the classical rabbinic response to catastrophe: no matter how grave the catastrophe, the Jews deserved it, and there follows a list of sins that justify the destruction. In the case of the Shoah, this classical biblical/rabbinic argument for theodicy has been made: that the Jews of the nineteenth and twentieth centuries had indeed deserted God and God's Torah, and hence God chose to punish them. I know people who accept this theodicy; I cannot. I just cannot agree that any sin (or sins) of the people justified the extermination of one and one-half million children, or that it justified the cruelty and inhumanity of the way Jews died during the Shoah.

Another classical answer to the question of theodicy is that we humans, finite as we are, can never know why God, infinite as God is, did what God did. This answer proposes that the gap between God and humans is so great, in every sense, that we simply cannot know why God does anything. The very transcendence of God argues against our comprehending the reason behind God's actions. This understanding of theodicy, too, is rooted in the biblical and rabbinic sources. It is embodied in the phrase *hester panim,* "God hides God's Face." Sometimes the biblical authors hear God say that God will hide God's Face, and sometimes they poignantly express their own sense of being cut off from the presence of God. The rabbis, too, use this answer. Even as modern and nonrabbinic a thinker as Martin Buber used it when he called God's presence in the Shoah an "eclipse" of God.[5] It is also another of the answers of the so-called friends of Job. This answer to the problem of theodicy is the easiest for contemporary Jews. It enables them to escape from the question of where God was in the Shoah. Affirming the utter transcendence of God, and hence God's *noninvolvement* in the Shoah, enables contemporary people to keep God clean of responsibility. They can have their God, for whatever reason, and they do not have to pose the uncomfortable question of God's involvement in history: they can have their cake and eat it, too, so to speak. They do not realize that this answer, even though it is classical, denies God's role in history and is precisely contrary to the other Jewish view: that God is deeply involved, directly and indirectly, in the history of the world and especially of God's people. Providence is denied because, if affirmed, it raises a question that is just too cruel to ask: *Where was God in the Shoah?*

Another classical answer to the question of theodicy is that we humans did it. God gives humans free will, and it is we who act wholly on our own, for better or for worse. Therefore, it is we humans who bear sole responsibility for the Shoah, not God. This answer, too, is a hoary one, deeply embedded in biblical and rabbinic thought. The whole theology of commandment, sin, reward, and punishment hinges on it. So does the theology of revelation and of redemption. It seems like a good answer and, indeed, can serve as such at first glance. However, neither biblical nor rabbinic Judaism allowed itself to be drawn into an assertion of human moral responsibility that would clearly deny God's action in history. The doctrine of free will never takes precedence over the doctrine of providence except in the matter of *individual* responsibility. On the matter of rational action, Judaism frankly asserts both doctrines even though they are contradictory. Hence humans are free, but God also acts, and *both* are responsible.[6] Again, contemporary people like this answer to the problem of theodicy. The idea that God leaves us free to act is very precious to contemporary sensibility. We would rather be free, if guilty, than under God's continuing influence and presence. In the matter of the Shoah, this leaves the Nazis guilty, together with the collaborators, but it lets God off the hook. Such a God is abstract, remote—and contemporary people like their God that way. An active, intimate God would be harder to deal with. Therefore, many prefer a remote God, even if this means that one cannot pose the question of theodicy.

Another classical answer to the question of theodicy is that God was active but suffers with us. God goes into exile with us and suffers our pain with us. The rabbis in particular developed this theology.[7] According to this answer, God may have acted unjustly, but God's suffering is somehow expected to mitigate that injustice. If God is infinite, then so is God's suffering, which then becomes a kind of repentance for God. Contemporary Jews do not like this answer, though Christians, working with the crucifixion as a model, are fond of it. Rather, we respond: "So what if God suffers? Why would suffering justify an unjust action, especially for God?"

It seems to me that none of the four answers just listed are really any good. The first and the last make no sense to most contemporary people, and the second and the third are evasive and unsatisfactory because they do not really answer the question; they defer it. There are other classical answers, but none are any better. Is there, then, a "better" answer—one that would, on the one hand, affirm God's presence in history and hence God's responsibility and, on the other hand, hold God to account for what is clearly an unjust action: causing, or allowing, the Shoah?

The Bible itself provides another—and, to my mind, more satisfactory—answer to the question of where God was in the Shoah. When God announces to Abraham that God is about to destroy Sodom and Gomorrah, Abraham realizes that this action involves an injustice, and he protests. In the end, Abraham loses the argument, but his reaction is the correct one: not to deny God, not to deny God's power or right to act, but to protest God's *judgment*. Similarly, when God announces to Moses God's intention to destroy the Jewish people, Moses responds with protest. In the several cases in which he does so, Moses is more successful than Abraham in stopping an unjust act on the part of God. Similarly, though on a personal scale, when God decides to punish Job unjustly, Job responds with protest. From the beginning of the Book of Job to the very end, Job maintains that he is innocent and that God is just plain wrong. Job does not maintain that there is no God, or that God has no power or right to act, or that God has hidden God's Face, or that God's ways are by definition unknowable. These are the arguments of Job's so-called friends, whose "support" for God is specifically rejected by God at the end of the book. Rather, Job maintains that God is God, that Job is innocent, and hence that God is wrong. This theme of protest, which is occasionally renewed by the rabbis but in much attenuated form, resurfaces in Jewish civilization after the Shoah, in secular Jewish poetry.[8]

As a contemporary theologian, I favor the answer of protest to the question of theodicy. Protest allows me to affirm that there is a God, that God is active in Jewish history, and hence that God was indeed present in the Shoah. Protest also allows me to affirm that God was wrong—that, as a matter of moral judgment, God's permitting the Shoah was an unjust, immoral step. This answer itself raises several uncomfortable questions— *What kind of God would do such things? Why would one worship or even have a relationship with such a God? How does one protest?*—but there are reasonable, satisfactory answers to be considered.[9]

THE QUESTION OF SOCIOLOGY

Another question—again, one that I find interesting and important, and that demands an answer—is *Where was humanity in the Shoah?* Put differently, *How were so many otherwise quite normal people persuaded to go along with the Shoah? How did they let it happen?* My interest in this subject was aroused when I realized that the statement "I did nothing special; I was just doing what was expected of me" is reportedly offered by perpetrators and rescuers alike.[10] How, I asked, can those who murdered Jews *and* those who rescued them contextualize their actions by saying that they did not do anything extraordinary but just followed instructions given explicitly or implicitly by those whom they respected? It seemed too paradoxical to be true, so I checked sources and found that the statement is indeed accurate as reported. Perpetrators almost always insist that they were not themselves demonic or pathological, and psychological tests show that this is true. They almost always say that they were just following orders, no matter how horrible the acts they committed. Similarly, rescuers—as much as Jews and some Christians would like to see them as heroes—almost always deny having done anything heroic. And, almost always, they insist that they were only doing the normal, natural thing that anybody would do, though they know that the evidence against that generalization is compelling.

Fascinating and relevant data are to be found in the studies on obedience and altruism. The obedience studies conducted by Stanley Milgram[11] at Yale are the best known in a series of such studies, though there are many others. In Milgram's electroshock-based experiment, each of the subjects was asked to administer shocks of increasing intensity to another human being. The final range of the shocks was clearly desig-nated as lethal. When the subjects objected, the only pressure put on them came from the experimenter, who firmly instructed them to continue and included the assurance that he assumed all responsibility. Between 65 and 85 percent of the subjects (the variance depended on the subject group) went on to administer what they believed to be lethal levels of electroshock. The film that accompanies the book on this experiment is particularly disturbing.[12] Other experiments on obedience have shown the same phe-nomenon: the overwhelming majority of people will do what they are told to do. If an order conflicts with their moral instincts, they will show signs of nervousness, but they will indeed do as instructed.

Studies of altruism have shown the same results. In a study conducted by Ervin Staub,[13] himself a Shoah survivor, subjects were assigned tasks to keep them busy and were divided into three groups. Subjects in the first group were told that they were allowed to leave the room. Subjects in the second group were told that they were not allowed to leave the room. Subjects in the third group were given no instructions at all about leaving or remaining in the room. Then a cry of distress was simulated as coming from an adjacent room. Almost no one left the room who had been prohibited from doing so. Almost everyone left the room who had been explicitly permitted to do so. Results varied for those who had been given no instructions. Again, the evidence was clear: most people will do what they are told, and if they are given permission to do good, they will do so.

A particularly interesting study[14] has shown that theology students who had just spent time studying the parable of the Good Samaritan (a bib-lical personage who acted with spontaneous goodness toward an outcast while acknowledged religious leaders passed by) walked right past an osten-sibly suffering person if they were told to hurry to an appointment. That is, the study showed that the theology students followed instructions per-ceived as legitimate even if doing so meant ignoring the ethical lesson of a text they had just studied.

The implications of these data are enormous: if we wish to have people do good (even rescue others), we must give them instructions to do so. Indeed, fully 67 percent of the rescuers in Staub's study did not rescue anyone until asked to do so by someone in authority. One might say that the most important factor in creating people who do good is not *what* we teach them, though that of course does count, but *how* we teach them. It may not be the content of our classes that is so important but rather what we give permission for and what we choose to proscribe. For example, is the excuse "I was with a sick friend and couldn't do my homework," if true, an excuse we would accept in a classroom? Are we assigning so much work that people feel obligated to do the work and do not have permission to perform spontaneous acts of kindness? If we want people to do good spontaneously, we need to give them permission. Should doing good, then, be an actual course requirement—and not only in ethics, philosophy, and religion classes?

Family and institutional discipline is a second factor relevant to the analysis and teaching of good and evil in the Shoah. Samuel and Pearl Oliner have shown that almost all the rescuers in the Shoah came from homes where discipline was fair.[15] The criterion of fairness was that any particular act of discipline was commensurate with the wrongdoing and could be appealed if it was too strict. The background of a rescuer is formed by his or her growing up in an environment where reasonable punishment is expected, but unreasonable punishment is wrong. Children and young adults growing up in environments where punishment is reasonable, and where unreasonable punishment can be questioned, grow up to be fair and reasonable authorities, and they expect all authority— civic, political, religious, legal, and so on—to be fair and reasonable. Hence rescue, for them, is normal behavior. Fully 52 percent of the rescuers in the Oliners' studies acted out of "normocentric" motivations.

Studies on abused children show the opposite:[16] growing up in a home or school environment where unreasonable punishment is the rule, and where no unreasonable punishment can be questioned, most often produces children and then adults who learn to accept unreasonable authority. They expect all authorities to be unreasonable, or least arbitrary, and as adults they often wield authority themselves in unreasonable and arbitrary ways. Since they have no choice, such people also become very obedient. Studies of perpetrators show them to have come from homes that were authoritarian.

Again, the implications of these data are enormous: if we want people to do good and not to do evil, we need to pay attention not so much to what we are teaching them as to how fair the rules are by which we are asking them to live. One might say that the most important factor in creating people who do good is to make sure that they think we are fair with them. For instance, do we always ask our students if the exam we are about to give is fair? Do students have the right to question our integrity, and how do we react to that kind of challenge? Do we encourage students to challenge the university administration? Do we do it ourselves?

THE QUESTION OF SOCIAL ACTION

The fourth question is perhaps the most pressing: *What does one* do *with all the knowledge and feelings one acquires when one studies the Shoah?* Given what the Shoah was, and still is, to us as human beings, it is not enough to study the facts or to analyze their theological and sociological implications. It is not even enough to take the theological next step of active protest to God, or to take the sociological next step of intelligent pedagogy at home and in our social institutions. The issue here is injustice and apathy, and the proper response is to reject apathy and become active in issues involving social justice. It does not make much difference which oppression one works against. It might be other genocides. It might be child abuse or issues related to the treatment of immigrants or to women's health or to land mines. Whatever it is, one must choose at least one injustice and try to help correct it. And one must help others make similar choices.

One year I led the departmental senior seminar, in which students form groups, pick a problem on campus, and try to remedy it. Out of that seminar came action on rejection of labor pools that exploit illegal workers, recognition for the janitorial and food-service employees, and other projects. For many years I led the departmental internship program in social ethics and community service, in which each student had to choose an agency, set up a supervised internship, and then accomplish the goals for which he or she had contracted with the agency. Projects included working with gangs in Denver, working for peace in Northern Ireland, working with Betselem (the Israeli-Palestinian human rights organization), serving in the local juvenile courts, conducting a prison ministry, working with immigrants, promoting the voting rights of homeless people, fostering AIDS-related awareness, and many others. Over the years, I have solicited and received funds to send students for summer and year-long internships in social ethics and community service. In addition, I have broadened the program from the department to the entire university.

Not all political and social protest is Shoah-related, in the strict sense of the word; but, in a broader sense, social action is part of the legacy of the Shoah, and, in my opinion, it is an integral response to the Shoah.[17] I only regret that my own personal involvement in these issues has not been more intense.

NOTES

1. I prefer "shoah" to "Shoah" and both to "Holocaust" because the latter has the connotations of a sacrifice, which the victims were not, and because the use of a Hebrew term to describe the destruction of Jewry appears to me more appropriate. It is my custom, for ethical reasons, not to capitalize words referring to the destruction of the Jews; hence "nazi," "shoah," "final solution," and so on. Ethics must prevail in scholarly writing; this is one of the ways in which consciousness of the shoah must penetrate the lives of those who live after it. However, in order to comply with editorial custom, I submit to the request of this volume's editors and publishers to capitalize these words.

2. See John Loftus and Mark Aarons, *The Secret War Against the Jews: How Western Espionage Betrayed the Jewish People* (New York: St. Martin's Press, 1994).

3. This is the *Historikerstreit* question.

4. As the editor of one such autobiography, I am very aware of this problem; see Alex Gross, *Yankele: A Holocaust Survivor's Bittersweet Memoir* (Lanham, Md.: University Press of America, 2001).

5. Martin Buber, *The Eclipse of God: Studies in the Relation between Religion and Philosophy* (New York: Harper, 1952).

6. The most classical statement of this doctrine is Maimonides, *Code of Jewish Law,* Hilkhot Teshuva, chap. 5. I usually give the following example as an illustration: If I give the keys to my car to my teenage son, and he does damage to another with my car, am I responsible? I may or may not be legally responsible—that depends on local statutes—but surely I am morally responsible and feel

myself to be morally responsible. My son acts and is responsible, but I have also acted and am responsible.

7. See, for example, E. Urbach, *The Sages* (Jerusalem: Magness Press, 1975), chap. 3.

8. See David Blumenthal, *Facing the Abusing God: A Theology of Protest* (Louisville, Ky.: Westminster John Knox Press, 1993), 251–53.

9. See ibid. for a full discussion of these issues.

10. For the presentation of this problem, and for the data on the experiments and studies listed below, see David Blumenthal, *The Banality of Good and Evil: Moral Lessons from the Shoah and Jewish Tradition* (Washington, D.C.: Georgetown University Press, 1999). My Web site also contains articles on this subject as well as a syllabus for teaching the material; see http://www.emory.edu/UDR/ BLUMENTHAL (accessed Feb. 20, 2006; note that the link is case-sensitive).

11. Stanley Milgram, *Obedience to Authority: An Experimental View* (New York: Harper and Row, 1974).

12. *Obedience,* a film dealing with the study of obedience by Stanley Milgram (University Park, Pa.: Audio-Visual Services, Pennsylvania State University, 1993).

13. Ervin Staub, "Helping a Distressed Person," in L. Berkowitz, *Advances in Experimental Social Psychology,* vol. 7 (New York: Academic Press, 1974), 293–341.

14. See John M. Darley and C. Daniel Batson, "From Jerusalem to Jericho: A Study of Situational and Dispositional Variables in Helping Behavior," *Journal of Personality and Social Psychology* 27:1 (1973), 100–108.

15. Samuel and Pearl Oliner, *The Altruistic Personality* (New York: Free Press: 1988); see also the review of this book by David R. Blumenthal, *Critical Review of Books in Religion* 3 (1990), 409–11.

16. See, for instance, Alice Miller, *For Your Own Good: Hidden Cruelty in Child-Rearing and the Roots of Violence,* trans. Hildegarde and Hunter Hannum (New York: Farrar, Straus and Giroux, 1983).

17. See Blumenthal, *The Banality of Good and Evil,* for a good list of methods of protest (appendix) and a list of prosocial causes (index). For prosocial causes, see also http://www.emory.edu/UDR/BLUMENTHAL (accessed Feb. 20, 2006; note that the link is case-sensitive).

IO

Developing Criteria for Religious
and Ethical Teaching of the Holocaust

DIDIER POLLEFEYT

> And if any of you would punish in the
> name of righteousness and lay the axe unto
> the evil tree, let him see to its roots;
> And verily he will find the roots of the
> good and the bad,
> the fruitful and the fruit-less,
> all entwined together in the silent heart of the earth.
> —Kahlil Gibran, *The Prophet*

Christian theology and Christian religious education as such are no guar-
antees against genocide; on the contrary, the Christian religion and
Christian religious education (catechetics) were themselves involved in
the genesis of the Holocaust.

It is not correct, as the Vatican's statement *We Remember* does, to separate radical (Christian) anti-Judaism from (racist) antisemitism.[1] The
Christian theology of substitution and supersessionism and especially the
Christian teaching of contempt (in catechetics, preaching, and liturgy)
are necessary conditions for understanding the Holocaust. Substitution
theology assumes that, thanks to belief in Jesus as the Messiah, the election of the Jewish people was definitively and exclusively transferred to
Christians, and that Christianity and the church took the place of Judaism,

172

for all time and completely. The implication of this theology is that there is no longer any place for Israel in God's plan of salvation, and that Israel no longer has a role to play in the history of revelation and redemption. It is claimed that the Jewish "no" to Jesus, the Messiah, meant the end of God's involvement with Israel. Consequently, Christian education developed a teaching of contempt: the Jewish people had been, at one time, the beloved of God, but after missing its invitation with the coming of Christ, it lost its election and thus its right to existence—it is now a cursed or, at best, an anachronistic people. It is true, as *We Remember* asserts, that Nazi ideology was directed against the Jews as a race (antisemitism), not as a religious group (anti-Judaism). Nevertheless, without this theology of substitution and the religious teaching of contempt, the Holocaust cannot be explained. This is why Western (Christian) ethics and the teaching of Western ethics (Christian religious education) are not proof against genocide.

Nor is it correct to understand the Holocaust simply as a diabolical revolt against ethics, as some educators so easily do. Nazism used modern ethical arguments and theories that were acceptable, or at least debatable, in light of Western ethics. The Holocaust is not so much a question of immorality as a question of the vulnerability of ethics. An extreme example is so-called Nazi ethic.[2] According to Peter Haas, the Nazis were neither diabolical[3] nor banal[4] but instead, throughout the war, considered themselves ethical beings. Thus, for Haas, the Nazi ethic can be seen as a new construction, but one erected from the old building blocks of Western ethics. And this explains, at least in part, the success of the Nazi ethic, both within and outside Germany. For Haas, the ethical framework of Nazism stood in continuity with the formal framework of Western ethical discourse. Of course, Nazism was a perversion of morality, but, according to Haas, it is important to see how ethics and ethical education itself became involved in this process of perversion.

Obviously, teaching ethics and religion is no guarantee that genocide will be prevented in the future. This is true even when the Holocaust itself is taught. During the Holocaust, in fact, classes and university auditoriums were filled with students taking courses on ethics and religion. Religion and ethics should start by recognizing their limits, their responsibility, and even their guilt with respect to the Holocaust.

The teaching of the Holocaust in courses on religion and ethics is always influenced by certain ethical and religious interpretations. There is no neutral way to present the Holocaust within an ethical and/or religious perspective. That this is true is not a problem as such, but all Holocaust educators should be aware of their presuppositions when teaching the subject. They should understand the tensions within the hermeneutical complexity of the Holocaust, the particularity of their own positions, and the specificity of their pedagogical goals.

Indeed, Christian educators can misuse the Holocaust for religious goals of their own. They can select only those facts or stories that correlate well with their own religious faith. An example of the misuse of the Holocaust by Christian theologians involves Elie Wiesel's *Night* and the religious and pedagogical misappropriation of that work's famous story about the hanging of an angel-faced little boy. At the hanging, someone asks, "Where is God now?" Wiesel's inner voice answers: "Where is He? Here He is—He is hanging here on this gallows."[5] The Christian identification of this scene with the scene of the suffering Christ on the Cross is problematic for many reasons, and from moral, pedagogical, and theological perspectives. The boy hanging on the gallows is not an adult who has freely chosen to die for a good cause; his suffering is not redemptive, nor is his death answered by divine redemption. Comparing the boy to Jesus puts Christians on the side of the victims, not on the side of the perpetrators and bystanders. Two instances of suffering are compared rather than recognized in their uniqueness and historicity.

Educators teaching Western ethics can also misuse the Holocaust for pedagogical goals of their own. They, too, can select only those facts or stories that best match their own anthropological and ethical presuppositions. For example, teachers who want to demonstrate the evil of human nature can focus primarily on stories of extreme and terrible atrocity and violence, whereas teachers who want to develop a more optimistic view of human nature can focus primarily on heroic examples of solidarity or rescue. The moral lessons one draws from the Holocaust are primarily determined by the selections one makes from the history of the Holocaust. For example, a famous sentence from Anne Frank's diary—"In spite of everything, I still believe that people are really good at heart"—is used to support very general and optimistic conclusions about humanity after the Holocaust.[6]

To (mis)use the Holocaust for one's own pedagogical goals is to commit an injustice toward the victims. It is also to carry out an a priori elimination of the radical challenge of the Holocaust for every kind of ethics and religion.

CRITERIA FOR TEACHING THE HOLOCAUST

There is an increasingly critical attitude toward the possibly ideological character of Holocaust teaching, and not just on the extreme right. It is evident, of course, that extreme-right neo-Nazi movements do not want to be confronted with the historical consequences of their ideologies. But questions are being asked from moderate political and educational perspectives as well—about Holocaust education, its assumptions, its goals, and its consequences for international politics, nationalism, and contemporary moral positions on such topics as abortion, euthanasia, homosexuality, and so on. The only adequate reply to these questions is the development of criteria for Holocaust education. We are in urgent need of an instrument for analyzing existing Holocaust curricula according to scholarly standards. This chapter proposes the following central criterion: *In Holocaust education, students should learn to deal, in a critical and open way, with the basic dilemmas and problems entailed in ethical and religious Holocaust education and, consequently, in their own understanding of human evil and religious convictions as influenced by the Holocaust.* Consideration must be given to the aspects described in the sections that follow; indeed, they constitute a virtual checklist that can be used to evaluate existing Holocaust curricula and to develop new pedagogical tools for teaching the Holocaust.

Universal and Unique Aspects of the Holocaust

When all the emphasis is on the universal elements of the Holocaust, the event loses its historicity, and the unique suffering of the victims is reduced to a metaphor for suffering in general. When all the emphasis is on the unique aspects of the Holocaust, the event becomes not only "extraterrestrial" but also (pedagogically) noncommunicable and, finally, irrelevant to contemporary society.

Perspectives of Victims, Perpetrators, Bystanders, and Rescuers

Holocaust education should allow and stimulate multidirectional partiality. The Holocaust itself was a consequence of the impossibility of understanding the perspective of the Other. When one studies the Holocaust only from the perspective of the victims, one risks not coming to a broader and more analytical understanding of the Holocaust, an understanding necessary to the prevention of future such events. When one studies the Holocaust only from the perspective of the perpetrators and bystanders, one risks becoming insensitive to the concrete suffering of the victims and to the ultimately unexplainable character of this enormous moral evil, and one falls into the danger of confusing an understanding of the mechanisms that led to the Holocaust with acceptance and even legitimization of them.

Continuities and Discontinuities between Western History and the Holocaust

Students need to learn that the Holocaust did not come from nowhere but was a logical consequence of certain developments in Western history. Nevertheless, the Holocaust must not be presented as an unavoidable "effect" of this history because that kind of presentation denies the free agency of human beings and groups, nor must the Holocaust be presented as just a logical next step in this history, since that kind of presentation denies the novelty and the absolutely unexpected immoral nature of the event.

Small-Scale and Large-Scale Events

A focus on small-scale events helps students understand the immense tragedy of the Holocaust for concrete human beings, the daily moral evil of the perpetrators and bystanders, and the human courage of the rescuers. It reveals the Holocaust in a narrative form that can touch the student's mind, heart, and body. A focus on the large-scale events helps students see the social and political factors involved in the Nazi genocide. Showing the link between small-scale and large-scale events is crucial to helping students discover their moral, political, and religious responsibilities in preventing future genocides.

Emotion and Rationality

It is not enough to explain the Holocaust rationally, using the human sciences. Holocaust education should aim at cognitive, emotional, psychomotor, and social goals. Nevertheless, teaching about the Holocaust must not end in emotionalism, in touching students' feelings alone. Failure to acknowledge the cognitive dimension, even that of emotions, puts one in danger of becoming manipulative and can render the results of Holocaust education temporary, even evanescent.

The Science of History (Statistics) and the Pain of History (Anedcotes)

Holocaust education requires balance between an objective approach and a subjective approach to the facts. Objectivity without a subjective element leads to indifference. Subjectivity without an objective element leads to irrationality and blindness.

The Normality and the Abnormality of the Event

Students should be made aware of the extraordinary character of the Holocaust, in quantitative as well as qualitative terms. The debate on the Holocaust's "uniqueness" must be reflected in every Holocaust curriculum. The danger in emphasizing only the abnormality of the event, however, lies in feeding students' sensationalism and creating an absolute discontinuity between the Holocaust and Western civilization. When the Holocaust is isolated from the rest of Western history, it risks becoming an abnormal, exceptional curiosity rather than an event that is relevant to today's society.

The Humanity and the Inhumanity of the Perpetrators

Holocaust education should show how normal human beings can do morally inhuman things. The greatest challenge for Holocaust education is to show that the perpetrators were not monsters but human beings. If the Holocaust had simply been the work of monsters, then explaining why and how inhuman beings did inhuman things would be tautological. It should also be shown, however, that inhuman acts can affect a person's humanity to such an extent that the person excludes himself or herself from the human realm. It is important to help students reflect, in a nuanced way, on the relationship between the person and that person's acts.

Jews as Holocaust Victims, and Jews in Other Contexts

It is important to show how religious and racial prejudices made the Jews victims of history. It is just as important to show that, historically, Jews were not only and always victims but also a strong people who created an immensely rich moral and religious tradition, contributed to the arts and sciences, and also resisted the evils of the world, both physically (for example, in the revolt of the Warsaw Ghetto) and politically (for example, in the state of Israel).

Jewish and Non-Jewish Victims

"Not all the victims of the Holocaust were Jews, but all Jews were victims," asserts Elie Wiesel, aptly summarizing the balance that has to be established in Holocaust curricula between the Jewish perspective and the perspective of non-Jewish victims. The exercise of this kind of balance will also bring up the question of the role of antisemitism in Nazi ideology. Was antisemitism the dominant motive of the Nazis, or should the extermination of the Jews be situated in the broader eugenic program of Nazism?

Pessimistic and Optimistic Aspects of the Holocaust

Holocaust education and study should be careful not to formulate general conclusions about human nature that are too optimistic or too pessimistic. Sometimes Holocaust education falls into the trap of essentialism, or using the Holocaust to make pronouncements about the essence of human beings (for example, that human beings are intrinsically evil, or always free to do good). Holocaust education should make students aware of the very contextual character of the Holocaust. It is impossible to say things about human nature as such on the basis of the Holocaust because human beings are not made to live in such extreme circumstances.

Revisionist Denial and Ideological Misuse of the Holocaust

No history is simply a recitation of facts. It is also a reconstruction of the facts, one that reflects the hand and the mind of whoever does the reconstructing. Therefore, *it is impossible to create a neutral reconstruction of the history of the Holocaust.* Students should be made aware of this fact, especially when they are confronted with extreme products of this reconstruction process: denial of the Holocaust, on the one hand, and ideological misuse of the Holocaust, on the other. It is especially important that students learn to understand the connection between both forms of extremism. For example, in ideological misuse of the Holocaust, historical facts are selected in a one-sided way so as to construct a version of the Holocaust that does not reflect the totality of the Nazi system; this very one-sidedness is then often used by revisionists to call the reconstruction into question and to label it, and the Holocaust itself, a hoax. Therefore, a necessary element of Holocaust education is the science of historical critique, used to examine and exclude certain ideological presentations of Holocaust history. In other words, Holocaust education should also be education in scientific historical critique.

Clichéd and Less Known Stories and Pictures

Holocaust education should introduce students to the basic facts of Holocaust history and to the "classics" of Holocaust literature. Since the Holocaust is mostly treated as a topic in courses offered over time within separate disciplines (history, religion, moral education), it is important to incorporate enough differentiation into didactic tools (histories, testimonies, poems and other texts; artworks; videotapes; multimedia technologies) and course content (history, philosophical analysis). In this way, one can avoid Holocaust "saturation," mostly the consequence of a too limited arsenal of didactic tools and content in Holocaust curricula, by which Holocaust education becomes too predictable, preprogrammed, and repetitive.

Didier Pollefeyt

Theodicy and Anthropodicy

The questions "Where was God in Auschwitz?" and "Where was man in Auschwitz?" should be raised in post-Holocaust education. The Holocaust poses questions both to religion and to secular humanism. Religious education should develop, in this context, the relationship between human ethics and authentic religiosity, along the lines of Levinas's idea of God entering our existing through the face of the vulnerable Other. Secular moral education can show how religion as such is neither good nor bad but has good and evil potentialities, as the Holocaust also demonstrates.

The Role of Modernity and the Role of Christianity

Christianity and modernity have been analyzed as two main perspectives through which to understand the Holocaust. In the first case, the Holocaust is understood as the logical outcome of centuries of furious Christian anti-Judaism. In the second case, the Holocaust is seen as possible only when modern society had produced the technology to kill Jews in a rationalistic manner and on a large scale. In the first case, the Holocaust is understood as a relapse into primitive, premodern barbarity. In the second case, the Holocaust is understood as the end point of modern society. A third interpretative perspective is often forgotten: that the Holocaust is neither a relapse into premodern barbarity nor the end point of modernity but rather the anticipation of postmodern society, in which emotionalism, the lack of universal values and norms, and relativism are main features. The advent of postmodernity, at the end of the twentieth century, can then be understood because of the possible association between postmodernity and Nazism.

Demonic and Banal Aspects of the Genocidal System

A danger of Holocaust education is the temptation to select only those historical facts that emphasize the demonic aspects of the Holocaust and to condense these into a single picture that is then offered as representative of the Holocaust in all places and at all times during World War II. The opposite danger of Holocaust education is the temptation to concentrate only on the large-scale, industrial-grade, rationalistic aspects of the Holocaust so that students become inured to concrete suffering, and the Holocaust is studied in the same way as the Industrial Revolution.

Analyzing and Moralizing

A moralistic approach to the Holocaust can do harm to correct, nonselective historical presentation, but a purely historical approach can be so objective and neutral that the Holocaust's meaning for ethics is lost. Moralizing can create resistance in students because they may feel that they are being associated too much with the perpetrators, but too much analysis can render students morally indifferent to the subject.

Determinism and Human Freedom

In Holocaust education, it is necessary to strike a delicate balance between notions of determinism and notions of human freedom. Students often use determinism to excuse the perpetrators of the Holocaust, and human freedom to criticize the victims for their perceived lack of resistance. The opposite line of reasoning should also be developed. The perpetrators' behavior was not completely determined by the system; they could always have made use of remaining sites of freedom within the totalitarian system to slow down or undermine the processes of extermination and to help individuals or groups. As for the victims, they had very limited resources for acting freely within the Nazi system (even if they sometimes did so); their survival depended much more on external factors than on the exercise of human freedom.

Human Evil and Human Holiness

In Holocaust education, students should discover that human evil is a possibility, but so is human holiness. Narratives describing acts of terrible atrocity that illustrate the depths of human evil should be combined with stories about extraordinary and sometimes paradoxical moral and religious behavior (for example, stories about people who gave their lives for others). Moreover, such extraordinary goodness should not be presented only in the form of heroic stories; it should also be presented in the form of more modest stories illustrating such ordinary or "daily" virtues[7] as human dignity, caring, and creativity in the midst of evil and catastrophe.

Remembrance of the Past and Hope for the Future

The central idea of post-Holocaust education should be that the Holocaust happened and can therefore happen again. Thus it is necessary to remember for the sake of the future. Remembrance is the only acceptable graveyard for the victims of the Holocaust. Remembrance is more than just sterile repetition of past events. Remembrance should not be reproductive but instead productive, creating a new future out of respect for and as a tribute to the victims of the Holocaust.

Holocaust education should always be aware of its context. The Holocaust can be taught in a Jewish, a Christian, a humanistic, or a pluralistic setting in Israel, the United States, or Europe (with its different national contexts: German, Belgian, Dutch, and so on) and in the first, the second, or the third world. In order for Holocaust education not to be(come) ideological, each setting should integrate those particular aspects of the Holocaust that most challenge its own ideological presuppositions. Thus descendants of Holocaust victims should be open to the universal aspects of the Holocaust and attentive to the perspective of the perpetrators. Descendants of the perpetrators should be open to the unique aspects of the Holocaust and especially to the perspective of the victims. Believers should be attentive to the challenges of "death of God" theology (theodicy). In a humanistic setting, the crisis of Western ethics (anthropodicy) should be analyzed. Jews should be careful about "victimism"; Christians, about apologetically refusing guilt (*We Remember*).

MORAL AND RELIGIOUS EDUCATION
FOR THE FUTURE: THREE DANGERS

A New Ethical Absolutism

Nazism can be seen as a (pseudo-)ethical movement. It (mis)used ethical categories. It was the outcome of a certain Manichaean ethics, which used the dual categories of good and evil. In Nazism, the complexity of good and evil was reduced to a simple confrontation between absolute good and absolute evil, God and the devil, the Übermensch and the Untermensch.

Nazism can also be seen as a (pseudo)religious movement. It was the outcome of a certain exclusivist theology, which used a concept of God's being with us (*Gott mit uns*). For Nazism, man was not created in the image of God; rather, God was created in the image of the collective identity of (Aryan) man.

In response to the Holocaust, post-Shoah ethics and moral education should make clear the complexity of good and evil. Even if Manichaeism is an interesting pedagogical and ethical tool for teaching the Holocaust, a Manichaean presentation of the Holocaust reproduces and imitates the logic of Nazi evil itself. Nazi ideology did not allow ethical complexity, and post-Shoah ethical education is not necessarily a good thing in and of itself; if it feeds Manichaean ideology, it can even establish the mentality for a new genocide. Thus the first challenge for post-Shoah education is to avoid the danger of a new ethical absolutism by recognizing that, in the name of the Holocaust, one can become so fanatical in searching for the good that one commits new evils. If ethics excludes any degree of doubt, dialogue, discussion, attention to gray zones, balancing pros and cons, and so on, post-Shoah education can itself become the source of new violence, perpetrated in the name of the good.

A New Religious Absolutism

In response to the Holocaust, post-Shoah Christian religion and religious education should find ways to transcend exclusivist theology—and, specifically in relation to Judaism, to transcend supersessionism. The central question of religious education after Auschwitz should be "How can we affirm the truth of our own faith tradition without denying the religious claims of the Other?" Post-Shoah religious education, like post-Shoah ethical education, is not necessarily a good thing in and of itself; if it feeds exclusivist theology and new theologies of substitution, it, too, can even promote the mentality for a new genocide. Thus the second challenge for post-Shoah education is to avoid the danger of a new religious absolutism by recognizing that, in the name of the Holocaust, one can so absolutely affirm one's own religious truth, one's (imagined) support by a particular God, that post-Shoah education can itself become the source of new violence, perpetrated in the name of a God who is "with us." If any degree of otherness, challenge, questioning, heteronomy, or pluralism is excluded from our post-Shoah discussions of religion, we can again commit evil in the name of religion.

Ethical and Religious Relativism

The third challenge for post-Shoah education is to avoid the danger of ethical and religious relativism. After Auschwitz, it is just as dangerous to say that all ways are the same (ethical and theological relativism) as to say that there is only one way (ethical and religious absolutism, or Manichaeism). Ethical and religious teaching should be oriented toward the discovery of a basic moral norm or standard according to which all ethical values, cultures, ideologies, and religions can be tested and criticized, and through which individual human beings and whole societies can be oriented toward the good and/or the Good. Therefore, Western civilization must turn to its Jewish roots because Judaism brought and still brings the perspective of Other(ness) into the picture. And Auschwitz is an adequate starting point because no matter how people differ in their ethical views, they will almost unanimously condemn the Holocaust as a most brutal denial of the "face of the Other."[8] Indeed, those who do not condemn the Holocaust place themselves automatically outside the sphere of humanity. The confrontation with the Holocaust can teach students that morality is not just a matter of personal preference and that not every moral claim can be deconstructed, but that there are basic moral norms and values, which are not matters of individual choice and taste but which have categorical meanings.

Post-Holocaust education should not reduce religion to ethics; that is, it should not present Judaism and Christianity only in ethical terms. Everything is ethical; but, even after Auschwitz, ethics is not everything! Ethics and religion alike have their own interrelated, complementary, but distinctive meanings. Moral education after Auschwitz should embrace and move beyond both the moral emotion of pure horror and the moral rationality of pure cool analysis. To be sure, the shocking confrontation with the cruel facts of the Shoah is not automatically frightening or guaranteed to educate people. But the opposite is also true: rational analysis can kill empathy and moral feelings (such as anger, indignation, helplessness, despair, fear, engagement, and hope) as well as moral identification with the victims, and it can open the way to moral relativism. Narratives are appropriate pedagogical tools for creating adequate moral attitudes because they engage both emotion and reason and because they are unique instruments for bridging the gap between the general and the abstract, and between more pessimistic and more optimistic perspectives. They can be chosen carefully, in light of the students' particular stage of growth. Stories should be given preference over pictures of the Holocaust. Moral education in particular should be very careful with the use of well-known photographs showing extreme aspects of the Holocaust (piles of corpses, sadistic acts, lamps made from human skin, and so forth) because such photos quickly reduce the Holocaust to a cliché, and they risk replacing long-term moral imagination with endless and, in the long term, "tiresome" repetitions of what is always the same. As Roland Barthes argues, "In confrontation with such pictures, our own evaluation is taken away. Someone has already been horrified, thought, and judged in our place: the photographer has left nothing for us but our duty of moral accord."[9] Showing crimes against humanity is not in itself a weapon against those crimes. Moreover, it is important to speak not only about genocide in general and the Holocaust in particular but also about more moderate forms of evil, which do not lead to genocide, and of which Jews are not the only victims. Otherwise, we risk damaging students' sense of proportion. When students are exposed too frequently and too exclusively to the most extreme examples of evil, they run the risk of becoming relativistic toward more "ordinary" forms of evil, and even of becoming, in the long run, insensitive to extremes that have become "ordinary." Constant exposure to extreme forms of evil can destroy sensitivity to degrees of immorality in daily forms of subtle evil. It is also important to try to bridge the gap between the Holocaust, on the one hand, and contemporary society and daily life, on the other—for example, by identifying Manichaeism in television programs or supersessionism in contemporary religious-political conflicts. The Holocaust was not the work of devils, monsters, or animals but of human beings. We should warn

not only about the final steps in extreme genocidal evil but also and especially about the first steps leading in that direction. Otherwise, we risk
the possibility that students will be horrified, will not understand, and
will turn back home, but with nothing having changed in their moral
attitudes—or in political life within democracy.

Religion cannot be reduced to ethics after Auschwitz. Religion in particular is challenged by the Holocaust, but it can also make its own positive contribution to post-Shoah education. Religion and ethics are deeply
interrelated, but they are not identical. Auschwitz made clear how religion without ethical concern, and ethics without a transcendent point
of reference outside one's own community, can contribute to extreme
forms of immorality. Today there is sometimes a tendency to replace
Jewish and Christian religion, centered on the biblical God, with a kind
of alternative civil religion of the Holocaust that is centered on the commandment "Never again!" But Judaism and Christianity alike have a much
richer and longer tradition, which cannot be transmitted exclusively by
reference to the Holocaust. The Holocaust as a cult or creed is not a substitute for traditional religion. In Judaism and Christianity, centrality is
not given to evil but to Go(o)d; not only to repentance and remembrance
but also to healing and forgiveness; not only to immorality but also to
reconciliation; not only to despair but also to hope. Each religion possesses a rich legacy of and expertise in stories, metaphors, symbols, and
rituals to help people and cultures repent, remember, confess, mourn,
forgive, and reconcile— to open a perspective "beyond Auschwitz" without denying the "after Auschwitz."

NOTES

1. Holy See, *We Remember: A Reflection on the Shoah* (Vatican City:
Commission for Religious Relations with the Jews, 1998), available at http://www
.vatican.va/roman_curia/pontifical_councils/chrstuni/documents/rc_pc_chrstu
ni_doc_16031998_shoah_en.html (accessed Feb. 22, 2006).

2. Peter J. Haas, *Morality after Auschwitz: The Radical Challenge of the Nazi
Ethic* (Philadelphia: Fortress Press, 1988), 1–9, 175–77.

3. George Steiner, *In Bluebeard's Castle: Some Notes towards the Re-Definition of Culture* (London: Faber & Faber, 1971).

4. Hannah Arendt, *Eichmann in Jerusalem: A Report on the Banality of Evil* (Harmondsworth, England: Penguin, 1984).

5. Elie Wiesel, *Night,* trans. Stella Rodway (New York: Bantam Books, 1982), 62.

6. Anne Frank, *The Diary of a Young Girl* (New York: Pocket Books, 1953), 237.

7. Tzvetan Todorov, *Facing the Extreme: Moral Life in the Concentration Camps* (New York: Henry Holt/Metropolitan Books, 1996), 64.

8. Emanuel Levinas, *Totalité et infini: Essai sur l'extériorité* (Nijhoff: Den Haag, 1971), 173.

9. Roland Barthes, *Eloge de la désobéissance* (Paris: Le Pommier, 1999).

T eaching the Holocaust imposes a sensitivity toward students that also carries a responsibility to them. The subject itself poses confrontations to students' cognitive and emotional stasis. As the writers in this section explain, Christian students are likely to experience dissonance; they are constrained to question assumptions about the influence that Christianity exercised in preparing the context for and assisting in the perpetration of the Holocaust. They face the facts about a long tradition of Christian antisemitism and are compelled to reconcile that history with genocide, and with the teachings of their particular Christian churches. To be sure, the subject evokes emotional responses for which the instructor must be prepared. Marla Morris's judgment bears repeating—"representations of the Holocaust should not be made comfortable" and "consoling."[1] In a similar vein, Henry Friedlander argues that the Holocaust is not "sacred history; it is a public event" that demands our intellectual acuity and analytical skills, and he enjoins us to teach the Holocaust in order to help our students understand the milieu that "made genocide possible" and allowed "leaders to motivate followers to commit acts of inhumanity on a vast scale."[2]

Amy Shapiro, in chapter 11, describes having structured her course on the Holocaust so that students would feel safe and personally connected to the material. She provides a classroom environment that diminishes the possibility that her students will feel hopeless about the future. She selects memoirs that will facilitate her students' understanding of their reading about Holocaust experiences. Shapiro has also designed an interview process that provides each of her students with a compassionate ear—that of another student, who is trained to listen to responses to the course. In Shapiro's experience, students take responsibility for learning the course content as they also learn to accept their affective responses to the material.

Mary Todd, the author of chapter 12, believes that someone who studies the Holocaust loses "the option of being a bystander." Todd found that students at the conservative Lutheran university where she taught were deeply disturbed by the history of Christian antisemitism. She explains that because her students were reluctant to acknowledge the relationship of Christianity to the Holocaust, she provided narratives of rescuers as well as narratives of victims. Because a class on the Holocaust is, in her words, a "journey into darkness," she made it a point to "keep hope before the class" by involving its members in a liturgy to observe Yom Hashoah and by having her students develop a culminating activity that was shared with the rest of the university community. The students' projects ultimately helped them come to terms with the subject and to articulate their impressions and some aspect of what they had learned.

In chapter 13, Juergen Manemann, a Catholic teaching theology at a German university, describes a course that he strove to design in such a way that his students would understand the idea that theology can never be the same after Auschwitz. Compassion, cultural memory, facing the Other, and tolerance of ambiguity are among the obligations of post-Auschwitz Christianity. Manemann's students are coached to learn to ask questions and to value memory—including the memory of suffering—as a tool against oppression. He also hosts extra, informal sessions so that his students can learn to communicate the questions that the subject of the Holocaust inevitably evokes.

For the contributors to this book, it is inconceivable to ignore the impact of the content of Holocaust courses on our students. We approach our classes with tentativeness and, perhaps, hesitation and humility because we know that what we teach will affect our students profoundly.

Clearly, we need to step cautiously in a society where, in living memory, "gas chambers for human beings [were] considered normal."[3] The three chapters in this section are aids in guiding us through the landscape of a course that is fraught with such cognitive and emotional land mines.

NOTES

1. Marla Morris, *Curriculum and the Holocaust: Competing Sites of Memory and Representation* (Mahwah, N.J.: Lawrence Erlbaum, 2001), 10, 18.

2. Henry Friedlander, "Postscript: Toward a Methodology of Teaching about the Holocaust," in Henry Friedlander and Sybil Milton, eds., *The Holocaust: Ideology, Bureaucracy, and Genocide* (Millwood, N.Y.: Kraus International Publications, 1980), 328, 329–45.

3. Friedlander, 329.

Students' Affective Responses
to Studying the Holocaust

Pedagogical Issues and an Interview Process

AMY H. SHAPIRO

This chapter is about the role of the affective dimension in students' learning about the Holocaust—as an expression of the ways in which students give value to and take responsibility for their knowledge and understanding, and as a means for instructors to help students toward better integration of the knowledge they have gained through study of the Holocaust.

Student populations are changing, and in any one classroom there is a widening range of diverse perspectives. These changes in turn have raised pedagogical issues that indicate how important it is for students to learn in contexts where they not only feel safe but can also find their own means of connecting with the course material. When these pedagogical issues are considered in the design of classroom learning, what is studied becomes more personally valuable to students and is more freely transformed into lessons and knowledge learned for life. If this is true for students generally, it is doubly so for those who choose to study the Holocaust.

The teaching of the Holocaust presents unique pedagogical challenges. One of those challenges has to do with the affective dimensions of learning. Holocaust study, genocide studies, the study of evil, and the like, conducted as part of a general liberal arts curriculum, all raise the question of how much of the learning needs to involve individual responses from students. For instance, too much information, graphic details, and endless lists of facts can allow students to "know" without thinking or genuinely connecting with the material, and yet too little information can support superficial and banal understanding. As teachers, we must determine the parameters of what we teach so that we can limit the topic and thus make it accessible to our students. In teaching about the Holocaust, we are also confronted with the potential for extensive emotional and psychological responses to such material. This chapter demonstrates how I have used students' affective responses to advance their learning.

The intellectual connections that some students make between themselves and the material of the Holocaust are often found in the affective dimension of their learning, though these connections are difficult to assess. This affective dimension of learning is expressed through emotional responses, metaphorical understanding, and psychological insights rather than, for example, in papers that theorize about causes or historical connections. It is true that employing students' affective responses can often deepen their learning and lead them to produce well-crafted research papers, but the affective dimension is often where students actually take responsibility for what they have learned.

There is too much at stake in students' learning for educators not to be clear about what they see happening. Regardless of whether courses on the Holocaust allow students to articulate personal connections to the material, students taking such courses often experience a dramatic loss of hope for humanity, along with confusion about what it means to live and act in a world that created the Holocaust. Often the more knowledge students acquire, and the more abilities they develop as a result of the intellectual pursuit of understanding, the greater their emotional responses to the study of the Holocaust. Though I haven't done any research studies to establish a direct correlation between the amount students have learned about the Holocaust and the strength of their emotional responses, I would venture to say that students' emotional responses are deepened as a result of the extent of their research into the material. I have found that it is not unusual for students to experience a kind of emotional paralysis partway through the semester, once they have become immersed in the material. And such paralysis is not necessarily negative. It can be a symptom of latent intellectual or psychological insight.

In a final assessment in one of my courses on the Holocaust, a student reflected on a choice she had confronted as a result of studying the material: to "curse the darkness" of ignorance or to "light a candle" and illuminate the world. In order to light a candle and illuminate the world, she claimed, one had to encounter the darkness of ignorance. The idea of cursing the darkness held, for her, a pessimistic approach to living in the world; she needed to find a way to live in the world after having learned about the Holocaust. To illuminate the world meant to reveal the evil and then to act from her awareness of it. Even the language that this student used to express the options she perceived indicates that there can be powerful affective dimensions of learning, and that these affective dimensions have significance for the integration of knowledge into a student's life. We can see how this student felt, and how her feelings led her to a sense of connection with and responsibility to the world. What is also significant is the student's choice of language to describe her emotional response and the way in which it reflected her intellectual understanding of the material. She was responding to a poem that relied on the Jewish practice of the *Yahrzeit*. She had incorporated the imagery of the poem and the concept of the memorial candle into her understanding of the choice she felt she was making. Though she herself was not Jewish, her affective response found voice in the use of imagery specific to Jewish experience, and it demonstrated the use of intellectual understanding as a means of articulating both an affective and an ethical grasp of the issues important to her.

I want to emphasize this affective component of the study of the Holocaust, not only because it actually concerns our students but also because it is linked to the idea of students becoming responsible for their learning. There are many diverse styles of teaching, and educators may have a need to conduct the teaching of the Holocaust in as emotionally antiseptic an atmosphere as possible. (Whether this is appropriate is a matter for another discussion.) It has been my experience that no matter how I teach the Holocaust, the majority of my students, regardless of my intentions, will respond emotionally to their study of the event. Moreover, sometimes when emotion is lacking, I find correlated with this flat response some gross deficiency in intellectual understanding. One might also point out that when students' emotional reactions are extremely strong, to the

point of displacing the search for understanding through adequate exploration of the material, it becomes extremely difficult to teach such students. Interestingly, I have not experienced this kind of superficial response
in my students, though on occasion I have seen students use their study
of the Holocaust for the purpose of advancing and privileging their own
emotional displays. Class dynamics often preclude the privileging of emotional expression, partly because everyone in the class is involved in the
pursuit of the same learning. But this can be a problem when affective
responses either are not acknowledged or are overacknowledged at the
expense of real intellectual pursuit. It is a pedagogical responsibility to
explore what one should do with students' affect, but it is also important
not to allow affect to take the place of real learning.

As a consequence of exploring the pedagogical issues involved in students' emotional and psychological responses to the study of the
Holocaust, I am obliged to safeguard their learning and help them treat
emotions as a means to deeper understanding and greater knowledge.
To safeguard students' learning means to acknowledge their emotional
and psychological responses to the material. We acknowledge not only
the emotions that arise in the context of Holocaust study but also the
psychology that arises in the context of the individual who is studying
the material. In this regard, safeguarding students' learning involves
respecting individual students' responses and their need to express (or
not to express) the emotions they experience.

In looking for ways to safeguard students' learning and tap their
affective responses, I've tried to find methods of directing their emotional
responses into places where students can apply their knowledge without
falling into either false hope for the future or crippling despair born of
what their knowledge signifies to them about the world. To this end, I
use an interview process that, I believe, helps students continue their learning and employs their affective responses to further their understanding
and intellectual development. As I describe the interview process, I will
also explain part of the educational rationale behind its use, the results
I see in my students, and the implications that this particular process has
for our understanding of the role played by affective learning in study
of the Holocaust. I am not recommending this interview process for use
in other classes. I offer it to illustrate the role of affect in promoting stu-

dents' learning. The process was designed for a particular student population and a particular course, and it works in those conditions.

To understand the context of the interview process, it is important for the reader to know that I teach at a women's college and that the great majority of my students are women. Those who take my course on the Holocaust are upper-level students who have demonstrated four developmental levels of each of the eight abilities identified by the college as defining a liberal arts education.[1] The students have been prepared for advanced work in the humanities, and I can expect them to be grounded in the frameworks of a variety of disciplines and to be independently and creatively able to explore a range of disciplinary frameworks in approaching a field of study.

THE INTERVIEW PROCESS

In my course on the Holocaust, I am responsible for work on four advanced-level abilities: communication, analysis, valuing, and aesthetic engagement. The interview process is meant to advance students' understanding and demonstration of all four of these abilities. Focus on the development of these abilities has aided both the design of the interview and the articulation of its outcomes. Thus the process itself is adapted to meet the objectives of the course. There are three parts to the interview process: written responses to a set of readings, the ninety-minute interview itself, and a written self-reflection.

My course on the Holocaust is part of our weekend college program and is given every other weekend, in seven four-hour sessions. Because of the time frame, many of the course's experiences have been created for independent learning. Class assignments are designed to facilitate intellectual integration both in class and afterward. I have learned that students benefit less from contact with a teacher and more from well-designed independent learning experiences that help them integrate course material. There are times when I relinquish my love of class discussion and instead honor the need of students to work in pairs, small groups, or individually. I find that our discussions, though fewer, are that much richer and more informed, and that students are better prepared to ask and answer complex and integrating questions.

By the fourth class session, students have done extensive reading on the history of the Holocaust, have considered the need to establish their own right of entry into the material, have explored the concentrationary universe by reading Terence Des Pres's *The Survivor,*[2] and have reflected on frameworks for interpreting the accounts of survivors. The fourth class begins the interview process, and students are assigned seven specified chapters in a volume edited by Carol Rittner and John K. Roth, *Different Voices.*[3]

I have found that accounts by women can help female students relate to the material and bring them face to face with moral issues that they might otherwise keep at a psychological distance. My consideration of who my students are influences my choice of materials. In this instance, I consider that the experience of being female is significant for my students' learning. I don't shy away from teaching difficult materials, nor do I fail to provide materials that come from experiences that are dramatically different from the students' own. The course content by its very nature provides that level of difference; and, since very few of my students are Jewish, and many are of German or Polish heritage, they are confronted with a host of challenges to their understanding.

Giving students a way "in" through identification or recognition of shared experience is often the catalyst to deeper understanding. The women who take the course discover how much they have in common, as women, with the women who wrote the narratives. (Men in general, and my occasional male students, have other narratives and other means of making such connections, and they also find their own ways to identify with women's narratives.) This recognition allows my students both to identify and to look beyond superficial similarities, because identification often motivates their desire to understand more.

One issue that often arises, for instance, is a question about menstruation. When my students read narratives by women, they think about themselves. Many of these women have or someday hope to have children. Questions emerge for them about what it might mean to suddenly stop menstruating, and how that would affect their futures and their sense of themselves in the future. This identification leads students to question the camp experiences of women who were in their childbearing years. Why did women in the camps stop menstruating? What were the influences of the environment on their bodies? How did they come to think about themselves, and what was the effect on women in the camps if they believed that they had lost the ability to have children? These questions lead to significant insights into the camp experience and how it was articulated by women of different ages. These questions also lead to others: about how women in the camps interacted with and perceived each other, about the consequences that the loss of their children had for their own survival, and about some of the differences between religious and secular Jewish women in terms of how they responded to their experience of the camps. Cessation of menstruation is only one example among many of how women use their identification with other women to raise significant questions about women's experiences in the camps. This example allows them a way into the material that is based on issues that speak to them, but their exploration does not stop there. Their reflections on the cessation of menstruation merely give them a starting point of their own choosing.

Of the seven selections I assign from *Different Voices,* students are asked to choose two on which to reflect after having completed the reading. I use the framework of aesthetic engagement to teach students to identify narrative voices and consider the perspectives expressed in the writings. Students must choose two selections (an assignment that implies a valuing process, one of the advanced abilities). If the students do nothing else, they make a commitment to the selections by virtue of choosing them. And they are asserting that, in some way or another, the chosen pieces have value or meaning. By giving students a choice, I both allow for differences in how students relate to the selections and create a forum for personal expression.

As a way to have students explore their responses to the readings and reflect on their chosen selections, I ask them to write responses to the following six items:

1. Compare and contrast the styles of writing in the two selections you chose (considering narrative voice, use of imagery, perspective, sense of audience, tone, and so on).
2. Write a reflection on how each of the two selections affected you (for example, emotionally, psychologically, politically, philosophically, and so on).

3. Discuss how the style of writing in each of the two selections influenced the way you were affected by it.
4. How would you describe the different approaches and perspectives of the writers of the two selections?
5. Given what you have learned so far about the concentrationary universe, how do you account for the differences between the two writers? How do you account for the similarities?
6. What did you learn about yourself in writing this reflection and/or in the process of reading?

These items attempt to elicit articulated emotional responses from students. They have to use their formal critical-thinking ability in order to perform the assignment. But the items are also meant to avert the tendency to use information as a way of distancing themselves from the material and thus avoiding feeling.

When students come to the fourth class session, they are expected to have completed this writing for use in the interview. At the beginning of the class, I show them the documentary *One Survivor Remembers,* Gerda Klein's testimony of her experiences in concentration camps and on a death march.[4] If there is time, I also show them *Diamonds in the Snow,*[5] a documentary made by a former child survivor recounting her own and two other child survivors' stories through interviews, old film footage, and her return to the town in which she was born and, later, hidden. Thus these two films provide additional media to which students can respond. They also give faces to survivors. Students have to encounter personal testimony through the faces of those who have stories to tell and whose experiences took place within living memory.

I invite a few comments on these documentaries but do not give students a chance to engage in extended discussion of them. I then ask each student to pair up with someone else in class with whom she is not on familiar terms. I want students to confront their feelings, but to do it formally so that they have an opportunity to realize what things they do and do not share with others who are also having the experience of learning about the material.

Asking students to work with others with whom they are not well acquainted is a way to ensure that they don't rely on already shared discussions or on the comfort of being easily understood. At this juncture, I am aware of how raw and exposed students feel. They want to hide. And so some of them, despite my instructions, do find friends in class with whom to pair up so that they can protect their feelings. My instructions are given, but those who have a need not to follow them do not. One of the things I want students to learn is the significance of who is listening and who is speaking, and how that plays a role in what is told and experienced.

In the context of this four-hour class session, the paired students are instructed to take forty-five minutes each. While one acts as the interviewer, the other acts as the interviewee. The students are asked not to engage in discussion but to help each other reflect on the six items that were previously assigned and to probe more deeply into the meaning of each one's written responses.

It should be evident that in this process I am enlisting the students' ability to communicate. The student acting as the interviewer needs to be an active listener. She is expected not to interrupt, to record the essentials of what the interviewee says in order to document them, and to prompt the interviewee to give more complete answers. The interviewer also needs to be sensitive to the emotions of the interviewee, and to the limits of what the interviewee is able to give. And when it is this student's turn to be the interviewee, she has the challenge of speaking clearly and succinctly, conveying her thoughts, and integrating the work she did to prepare for the interview into her communication with the interviewer.

The interview process has many purposes. Because study of the Holocaust can have an extremely isolating effect on some students, the interview process allows those who have had no one with whom to speak the opportunity to speak with someone. In addition to helping students move forward in their understanding, it is also designed to help them understand their responses and share those responses with others. Before introducing the interview process, I found that too many students were reaching a point during the semester when they believed that they were the only ones to feel devastated by the material and hopeless about the world. As much as we may have discussed issues in class, students needed more opportunities to voice their responses and to reflect on the significance of what they had come to know and think. Moreover, some students infer from others' involvement in class discussions that they themselves are somehow deficient for not participating as much. A student's conclusion that there is something wrong with her for not participating in class discussions can also be accompanied by the specious belief that others do not feel the same powerful emotions in the face of the material, for if they did, they would not be able to discuss the issues as calmly and coherently as they do. The interview prompts students to verbalize such responses and to say out loud much of what they couldn't share or did not have time to articulate and reflect on, either in the class setting or, perhaps, outside the class. (Students often report having tried to share what they are learning with colleagues, family members, or friends, only to meet with disdain, or with disbelief that anyone would want to study such a subject.) The interview gives students time to talk, as a way of sharing what they think and feel with someone who is trying to be open to hearing them.

The design of the interview is straightforward. It provides the student with information about herself and one other person. On the basis of this information, she will write a self-reflection. The following questions elicit the interviewee's feelings and information:

1. Without reading to the interviewer, share how the comparison of two of the readings from Rittner and Roth affected your response to those selections. How did the writer's choice of form affect the way she conveyed content? How did it affect your response and your understanding of circumstances? What new insights did you have?

2. Describe your experience of studying the Holocaust so far this semester. How does it make you feel? What does it make you think about yourself? About others?

3. When you imagine yourself in the camps, what experiences do you think might be hardest for you? Why?

4. Which of your own values do you imagine might play a part in your response to such conditions?

5. What concerns might you have about yourself, your behavior, and your beliefs when you imagine yourself in the camps? How are your concerns affected now?

6. Have you had the experience of someone suggesting that studying

the Holocaust is stupid or idiotic? What did or would you say to such a person?

7. How does Des Pres's *The Survivor* help you understand the selections in Rittner and Roth (give examples), and what have you learned from reading the selections assigned for today?

The dominant principle, which underlies my approach to the interview, is the idea that students often make emotional connections to material, but that such emotions, if there is no opportunity to express them, rarely contribute to further learning. Without expression, they may even present an obstacle to further learning.

It will not have escaped the reader's notice that the interview process is something that I, as instructor, cannot observe at close range. If I have between ten and fifteen pairs of students interviewing each other, it will be impossible for me to watch all of them unless I have them videotape the process. Although this would be quite possible, I don't believe it is necessary. I would rather emphasize the results of the interview—how a student reflects on her experiences, and the ways in which that reflection increases her knowledge. It is quite possible for the interview experience itself to be unsuccessful without detracting from the benefits of the process, as long as the student is adequately directed to reflect on the experience. As one student wrote in her self-reflection, "During our interview process, I discovered that I simply did not have or was unable to convey [any] depth of feeling because I did not know words that were strong enough." Another student wrote, "I did not probe deeply because I felt that [the interviewee] was having a hard enough time expressing herself. . . . I did not have revelations during the interview itself. However, upon reflection, I found that I missed the more intense interaction I [might have had] if I [had] probed as deep[ly] as I wanted to and responded as strongly as I wanted to. I regret that reservations got in the way." The second student went on to talk about what a more experienced interviewer would have done, and she described the interviewer's responsibility in terms of the duty to convey to the interviewee that she will not be judged harshly.

One student talked with me after class about how angry she was that I had made her respond to the material with a student whom she did not know. She related how she had come to realize that her response held within it a responsibility to convey her own perceptions and share with another what she was feeling. She was aware that she had had trouble listening, and that made her more cognizant of her need to listen harder to what others had to say. But she was still angry and unsettled. Upon further reflection, she became aware that she was angry about the course. She didn't want to learn the material. It upset her too much. And she realized how easy it was to bring her anger into a situation from which she could have learned much more if she had been a less angry listener. This was a wonderful lesson to her in becoming aware of obstacles to her own learning. In the next three classes, she showed dramatic improvement in her ability to grasp concepts analytically and explore ideas. She eventually employed theoretical frameworks from her history major to write a complex analysis of methodological issues regarding women's writings about the Holocaust.[6]

THE WRITTEN SELF-REFLECTION

In addition to class discussion following the interview, I learn about the interview experience through students' written self-reflections. It is through the student's self-reflection that I can identify misperceptions in her thinking or any difficulties she may be having with the material. But the self-reflection is meant to carry the student's affective learning further, into the realm of an articulated written response that must be handed in and assessed by the instructor.

Students are asked to reflect on the following questions:

How have you been affected by your study of the Holocaust? Using this question as an organizing principle, write a narrative self-assessment in which you answer the following questions, making sure to spell out and give examples to illustrate your meaning:

What did you learn through the interviewing process about the material? About yourself?

What new insights did you have, or what assumptions did you uncover?

What new questions do you have?

What kind of listener are you? *How* did you listen?

What influenced your ability to hear the other? What got in the way?

How did you influence the person to whom you were listening? (What verbal and nonverbal cues did you use that helped her articulate her ideas or that may have hindered her?)

How did your listening affect your learning? How did your being listened to affect your learning?

Is there anything special about this material that warrants using any special responses as an interviewer?

What Alverno College abilities did you use in the process, and how did you use them?

The responses that students give in their self-reflections are wide-ranging and offer a powerful view of the kinds of approaches and ways of thinking they employ in relation to their study of the Holocaust. Most students use the questions as prompts to think further instead of answering each of the questions separately. Like most student writers, some are more eloquent than others. Nevertheless, one student who struggles to write and speak clearly was very eloquent in her self-reflection:

> When I purchased my ticket to embark on a journey to learn about what happened during the Holocaust, I knew that I was about to experience something like never before. What I didn't realize was that I had purchased a one-way ticket to a place that would penetrate my soul and leave me immobilized with astonishment. . . . At times the many shocking, thought-provoking and gut-wrenching details become too much for my mind to process before my brain overload[ed]. While I try to analyze my perception of the Holocaust, I find myself at a fork in the road. One direction leads me on a journey where I attempt to interpret another's meaning. . . . While traveling [in] the other direction from the fork in the road, I find myself able to focus mainly on my own internal perceptions . . . asking questions about the roles of perpetrators and victims . . . never finding any answers. Whichever direction I choose, I'm unable to reach the expected destination.

This student's interview partner took a different approach to her own self-reflection:

Amy Shapiro

Doing the interview exercise did not interfere with my learning but rather enhanced it because it showed me how we all have our own narrative, psychological, and historical truths. It's in listening to others and sharing our truths that, hopefully, we can come to a new and deeper understanding of what it means to be human. . . . I realized how much our personal experience and perspectives were of a common nature. It's when we run up against experience that is so different from our own that I feel we need to make that extra effort and consciously invoke the ideas of equality, compassion, and tolerance. We're probably all guilty of letting these ideals turn to stone through complacency at times as we go about our lives.

One can see two different agendas and two different responses to a shared experience. The interview allowed both students to hear each other and to voice their own thoughts. As another student put it:

During an interviewing process [you are] able to articulate what is inside your head. Being interviewed [like] this is almost like therapy because when you are allowed to talk about what you [have] read or have seen through videos, you are putting this information in order through your own perception, and thus [you learn] about [yourself] and [realize] how [the other has] reacted to the information.

That last phrase, about taking in the listener's reaction, contains a precious bit of insight. I make a case for recognizing affect and using students' affective responses because those responses play a part in epistemology. When a student can put her reactions into words and acknowledge the emotional and psychological filters that play a role in how she comes to know what she knows, the student is better able to know, can ask more questions, and can realize the assumptions that are at work in her approach to the material. Studying the Holocaust and absorbing the material to be learned can have—and perhaps, at times, should have—a temporarily crippling effects on the student. One could even argue that the student's failure to respond emotionally would be a failure to grasp the significance and scope of the material. Whether the student's emotions are on the

206

surface or buried inside, it makes pedagogical sense to enlist them in furthering the student's learning.

It is also important to realize that students who respond with powerful emotions are at risk in their learning. When studying the Holocaust, many students feel very raw, and they report feeling psychologically exposed and emotionally on edge. Their known worlds often collide with their new knowledge. For this reason, it becomes crucial to safeguard their learning by providing a classroom environment that acknowledges the intensity of these often nonverbal responses and that provides a situation in which they are personally protected from exposure.

With a Holocaust course, as with any other, the potential is always there for the student to walk away and never think about it again. In regard to study of the Holocaust, this reaction could result from lack of stimulation, a need to shut the information out, or various other reasons having to do with the way a student learns. It could also be a consequence of the instructor's never providing a way for students to develop their own understanding and relate it to how they experience themselves in the world. If I can stimulate my students to want to read and explore further, I think I have been quite successful. I am even more successful if students also learn about themselves—as learners, as thinkers, as people with emotions. Thus knowledge of the Holocaust contributes to students' way of continuously knowing the world; it informs their personal epistemologies. Regardless of how much college professors want to argue that students' learning must be "objective" and information-based, the pedagogy of the Holocaust shows us that, no matter what we believe, students will have affective responses to the material.

I cannot number the times I have encountered alumni who have told me how much they remember from my course on the Holocaust. Years later, they are still asking questions regarding ethics in the world around them, in light of questions about the Holocaust. Many of them have continued reading in the field, and three even came with me on a Holocaust travel course, many years after having taken the original course (one of them had graduated ten years earlier). It is gratifying to know that, with some prodding of students' affective responses, their articulations of their understanding can encourage their learning and deepen their grasp of the significance of studying the Holocaust for the rest of their lives.

NOTES

1. The educational design of Alverno College is governed by the belief that learning is developmental, and that better learning takes place when disciplines are grounded in a clear articulation of the abilities needed for grasping the practices of each discipline.

2. Terence Des Pres, *The Survivor: Anatomy of Life in the Death Camps* (New York: Oxford University Press, 1976).

3. Carol Rittner and John K. Roth, eds., *Different Voices: Women and the Holocaust* (New York: Paragon House, 1993).

4. *One Survivor Remembers,* directed by Jon Else (Los Angeles: HBO Films, 1996).

5. *Diamonds in the Snow,* directed by Mira Reym Binford (New York: WMHT Educational Telecommunications/Connecticut Public Broadcasting, 1994).

6. Anxiety is part of what students must feel in order to move on. It is through relating their thoughts and feelings that they begin to realize that their responses are not as singular in nature as they think, and that they share with others many responses that are similar, though not the same.

12

Keeping the Faith

Exploring the Holocaust with Christian Students

MARY TODD

Teaching is ultimately about decision making and therefore can be considered to have its own ethic(s). Before she enters her classroom, each teacher begins in and from her own context, within which the endless decisions about her teaching are made, and by which those decisions are informed if not directly influenced. My personal context begins with my discipline, my history, my faith perspective (Christian), and the institution in which I taught, a church-related university where people are trained for careers as teachers and church workers as well as for multiple vocations in the secular world. Teaching in that context often means reteaching, introducing new ways of looking at ideas, to students who arrive on campus with fairly narrow constructs, knowledge, and points of view. Teaching the Holocaust in that setting means confronting the fact that the Shoah is part of Christian history—indeed, is a watershed in that history. Where does one begin in developing an ethic of teaching the Holocaust?

One place to begin might be to build on students' prior learning. What can colleges and universities assume about the knowledge base of their incoming students? As a historian, I know that most high school classes in American history cover World War II, but I am not assured that I can expect the Holocaust to have been included in that coverage. Twenty states have adopted legislation encouraging Holocaust education, but inconsistency blunts the implementation of legislative support from state to state. Only six states go so far as to mandate the teaching of the Holocaust, but by what rubric or agency are those mandates assessed or enforced?

The state where I taught, Illinois, was the first to adopt a mandate for Holocaust education: "Every public elementary and high school shall include in its curriculum a unit of instruction studying the events of the Nazi atrocities of 1933 to 1945. This period in world history is known as the Holocaust."[1] The mandate goes on to reaffirm the commitment that such an event will never again occur. But if anecdotal evidence can be used to determine informally whether the mandate (which contains no standards for enforcement) is being observed in the elementary and secondary schools in Illinois, I found very few in-state students (a population comprising half the student body) who had received any introduction whatsoever to the subject before arriving on campus. Moreover, because about one-third of the students come from private, mostly Lutheran, schools that are not subject to state mandates, what they know about the Holocaust is minimal at best.

At any rate, college teachers face a dilemma, regarding not only the type and degree of prior exposure that students may have had to the Holocaust but also the question of the courses in which the subject should be introduced. The reader might expect a historian to insist that the Holocaust be included in a course on European history, world history, or twentieth-century history. It often is included in such courses. In church-related colleges that offer courses on the Holocaust, the history department is the one where such courses are most frequently found.[2] History often provides the necessary context, which Lawrence Langer suggests is the only thing that "can discourage the uninformed student from leaping to judgment"[3]; but the study of history is really only the beginning of Holocaust studies.

Perhaps more than any other event in history, the Holocaust is embedded in questions of ethics and moral dilemmas.[4] The history teacher, if her approach to teaching is at all holistic, will move from questions of what happened and how and why it happened to the only real question of history: "So what that this happened?" Thus a course based on a historical episode becomes much more. Arguably, teaching the Holocaust is by nature, like the topic itself, interdisciplinary if not omnidisciplinary.

Before developing an honors course on the history and literature of the Holocaust, I had taught the subject only as a two-week unit in a humanities seminar that was required in an adult degree-completion program at another university. I found that I not only had to cast the subject differently for traditional college students, as opposed to returning learners, but also that I had to make countless decisions about how ambitious to be in terms of readings, assignments, course content, and course direction.

The church-related university at which I taught is one of ten schools affiliated with the more conservative branch of American Lutherans, the Lutheran Church–Missouri Synod. Concordia's signature education program reflects its heritage as a teachers college. In addition, as already mentioned, the university is noted for training church-work professionals. The prevalence of preprofessional church-work students contributes to a student population that is far more theologically and politically conservative than the faculty. But, because Concordia understands itself as a university based in the liberal arts, the student body also includes many students who are neither Lutheran nor planning careers in either church work or education.

So how does a historian who teaches teachers—a Christian who teaches mostly Christian students, many of whom come from conservative theological backgrounds—approach the teaching of the Holocaust? I structured my course on the Christian response to the Holocaust by blending the university's mission statement (which locates Concordia both in the Lutheran Christian tradition and in the tradition of the liberal arts) with a teaching philosophy that challenged students not only to think differently but also to take the lessons from the course into their lives.

The ideological foundation for the Holocaust begins with the difficult history of the Christian attitude of contempt for Jews. I began the course by examining anti-Judaism over the course of Christian history. We read excerpts from the letters of Paul and the gospels in the Christian scripture, and then we read from Martin Luther's pejorative treatise "On the Jews and Their Lies."[5] For many Lutheran students, the Luther reading was profoundly disturbing, since they were not far removed from the concentrated study of his catechism that they had undertaken in their confirmation instruction, and many considered him a hero of the faith.

I took care to differentiate Luther's medieval diatribe from the political antisemitism of the late nineteenth century that more directly fueled the racism of the Third Reich; nevertheless, I found the Luther "discovery" to be difficult for some students, particularly church-work preprofessionals, to overcome.

To study the Holocaust is to no longer have the option of being a bystander. Yet a frustration I repeatedly encountered, even among honors students, was students' reticence to offer their opinions upon confronting a text or information. Beyond my first frustration, however, was a greater one, which involved students' resistance to provocative readings and ideas regarding the nature of the Holocaust as a Christian event.

Christian students also tend to hold the conventional supersessionist view: that Christianity replaced Judaism because the Jews had rejected Jesus Christ. Disabusing my students of this dominant viewpoint became a challenge, one that required me to do some reteaching about Christian origins as well as some theological explication about the relationship between Jews and Christians historically.[6] All this was complicated by the absence, in the sponsoring church body, of interfaith dialogue between Lutherans and Jews—the only honest answer to students who inquire about what the church says.

The teaching of twentieth-century history is greatly enhanced by the fact that the century was captured on film. I have watched students respond to filmed historical events in ways that differ from how they respond to reading or hearing about events (perhaps the best example of this phenomenon is students' reactions to witnessing the events of the civil rights movement as portrayed in the remarkable video series *Eyes on the Prize*). Therefore, I relied heavily on videos in my teaching. The first third of the documentary *The Longest Hatred*,[7] a segment titled "From the Cross to the Swastika," sets antisemitism in historical context as the anti-Judaism that became a necessary condition for the Holocaust. As a "bookend" at the conclusion of the course, I showed *Shadow on the Cross*,[8] which challenges viewers on Christianity's exclusion of and evangelism toward Jews. *Shadow on the Cross* begins and ends with a scene meant to shock: the arrest of Jesus by the SS. Nevertheless, I believe it is important in teaching the Holocaust not only to indict Christianity but also to affirm episodes of remarkable witness that Christians performed, often at great personal risk. My students were especially moved by the story of the French village of Le Chambon as told in Pierre Sauvage's film *Weapons of the Spirit.*[9] Of particular significance in the context of Concordia was Sauvage's reference to the descendants of the Protestant Huguenots as "fundamentalist" Christians, who took seriously both their biblical understanding of the Jews as people of God and their duty as Christians to resist a regime that demanded silence and compliance in the face of injustice.

A persistent question that runs through a course on the Holocaust is how the Shoah could have happened. Building on the history of anti-Judaism with which we began, I tried to keep before my students the issue of how we treat the Other. Some resisted this issue, wondering why we had to talk about other humans *as* "other." A blissful naiveté tends to lead some Christian students to protest the existence of discrimination until they are challenged to acknowledge it, not only in history but also in current events, or even as it manifests itself on campus (usually through the words or actions of another student). Such an incident generally moves a class to a consideration of what the Christian response should be when any people are targeted for risk or harm because of their identity. Again, youthful idealism prevents some students from recognizing the seductive power of a charismatic leader who appeals to national pride, as Hitler did. Holocaust educators differ on whether to ask students how they might have responded to certain developments during the Shoah,[10] but an examination of the responses of actual people moves a discussion from the speculative to the specific. Again, the story of Le Chambon, as told in *Weapons of the Spirit,* was instructive as the students heard the words of a sermon preached by Pastor Andre Trocmé the day after the fall of France:

> The duty of the Christian[s] is to resist the violence that will be brought to bear on their conscience through the weapons of the spirit. We will resist whenever our adversaries will demand of us obedience contrary to the order of the gospel. We will do so without fear, but also without pride and without hate.

In response to this sermon, Le Chambon became "a conspiracy of goodness" during the war as five thousand Jews were hidden by three thousand villagers. The story of Le Chambon offers an important counter-point of hope to the grimness that tends to overarch a course on the Holocaust, and it presented my students with evidence of an ethic of con-viction and risk taking in the face of daunting darkness.[11] Adapting Stephen Haynes's question to his own students—whether there was anything in their institution's mission, environment, or curriculum that would make its graduates "Nazi-proof"[12]—I asked mine if there was anything about our campus culture that would make our graduates Le Chambon–prone. It is one thing to admire courage, another to practice it.

Talking about "the Christian response" to the Holocaust becomes prob-lematic when left in the abstract. In order to focus students on one par-ticular aspect of this response, the second time I taught the course I used Simon Wiesenthal's powerful story *The Sunflower: On the Possibility and Limitations of Forgiveness.*[13] For years after the war, Wiesenthal remained haunted by his action toward a dying SS man who had wanted the for-giveness of a Jew, and so Wiesenthal posed to a diverse group of indi-viduals the question "What would you have done?" The fifty-three responses to Wiesenthal's challenge make *The Sunflower* an invaluable text as readers are introduced to the contextual differences among the diverse respondents. Given my students' previous reluctance to engage in discussion of ethical issues, I introduced them to an exercise called "Fishbowl," to encourage their involvement in discussing *The Sunflower*. In "Fishbowl," discussion is limited to a few volunteers who sit at the front or in the center of the classroom—a class within a class—but others are allowed to participate when ready. In order to join the conversation, a student who had previously been only watching and listening had to get up and "tag" or trade places with one of the students in the so-called fishbowl. From a sense of fairness and restraint, I held myself to the same rules but made sure to end the exercise with adequate time to allow the larger group to debrief. Responses to the exercise varied. Some students became very animated, and others criticized the method for leaving them out. With this particular class, I learned I couldn't win; but, as usually happens when I teach, I learned something else as well: the students had misread several of the fifty-three responses to Wiesenthal's question because they had never been exposed to such theological concepts as "cheap grace" and theodicy.

The students' limited understanding of what it means to be a Christian in a particular faith tradition became apparent when I presented them with Leon Stein's essay "A Parting at the Cross," which contrasts the behavior of Danish and German Lutherans toward Jews in their respective countries.[14] Stein's essay raises important distinctions about the influence of culture on the practice of believers, and it challenged the students to consider multiple dimensions of what it means to be Lutheran. I intend to use Stein's work again because he identifies so well the essence of Lutheranism. If Lutheranism is the way in which at least half of those at Concordia "did" Christianity, then to take seriously the different responses of the Danes, who opposed Nazi persecution of the Jews, and the Germans, few of whom spoke out against such persecution, was also and necessarily to take seriously the differences among Lutherans today. We may not casually dismiss others who act differently from within a tradition that we share.

Stein argues for "how seemingly similar Christian religious beliefs and practices can be interpreted and exercised in radically different ways by distinctive national cultures that can result in opposite impacts," offering "a warning for the future as to how Christian ideas and institutions can be shaped for purposes of prejudice, hate, and indifference—or instead put to the service of humanitarian, tolerant, and life-saving ends."[15] Particularly insightful is his differentiation of ethnic and civic nationalisms, as displayed in Germany and Denmark, and the interplay of Christian values with national culture that created "a culture of intolerance and illiberalism" in Germany. Because the historic roots of Missouri Synod Lutherans are German, Stein's essay was especially challenging to my students' understanding of the tradition from which many of them came, and in which the university stands. Finally—what is perhaps most important from the perspective of ethics—Stein asks whether history is made "by structures or conditions" or "by men and women who make decisions and choices."[16]

Thus far my discussion of teaching the Holocaust has been about antecedents and responses, but what of the Shoah itself? To teach about the camps, I used literature, asking students to read and compare Elie Wiesel's *Night* and Tadeusz Borowski's *This Way for the Gas, Ladies and Gentlemen*. One difference students readily noted is how steeped in religion Wiesel's text is. One of the most poignant stories that Wiesel relates is of camp inmates observing a hanging and debating where God is. I played an audiotape of Wiesel reading that story and then shared with the class another story he tells elsewhere, of rabbis who put God on trial in Auschwitz.[17] The class, troubled by the very idea, insisted on knowing what the charges were. "Silence and absence," I responded, and then reported that the rabbis had found God guilty. That believers could be angry or argue with God was a concept most of the students refused to accept, though I explained that it was not only a long-standing Jewish tradition but also one I myself practiced, especially in light of the then recent sudden death of my husband.

A contested aspect of Holocaust education is whether to teach about Holocaust denial. I firmly believe that it is essential to do so, though I know colleagues who just as firmly disagree. Because honors courses at Concordia intentionally emphasize the development of critical-thinking skills, I asked students to look critically at the language and the arguments used in the literature and the rhetoric of Holocaust deniers. We discussed the importance of evaluating primary sources as historical evidence, including the testimonies of Holocaust survivors. We did all this shortly after the class had been visited by two Holocaust survivors, both of whom spoke eloquently about the threat that Holocaust deniers pose to the memories they had just recounted. The survivors—children during the war—told me later that they were wearying of telling their stories so often; though the urgency they felt to speak about their experiences had not diminished, they were aging. I wonder, and so I asked my students, whether literature will suffice to teach the Shoah once the last survivor is dead. Interestingly, students tended to respond differently to the question before they had heard the survivors speak.

To teach a course on the Holocaust is to take a journey into darkness. I remain determined not to leave us there, and so I tried to keep hope before the class. One powerful way of doing that is to observe the Day of Remembrance in the spring with a *Yom HaShoah* liturgy. I asked student volunteers to serve as readers, using a liturgy that included readings from course texts as well as poems and prayers and that had been adapted from an interreligious service in Elie Wiesel and Albert H. Friedlander's book *The Six Days of Destruction*.[18] Students generally found the liturgy to be a moving experience, though a narrow understanding of interfaith activities had led some students to misunderstand the activity.

Even more hopeful than sharing a liturgy together, however, was the preparation and presentation of the culminating activity for the "Introduction to Honors" class: an exhibit through which the class shared with the rest of the university community what it had learned. The underlying philosophy of the honors program, the course, and the exhibit is that one has an obligation not to keep one's learning to oneself. The students worked in groups on segments of the exhibit, which has since become an anticipated feature of finals week on campus. The segment of the exhibit that was most often commented on by visitors was a display and brochure on Luther and the Jews. Another segment marked off a narrow space representing one in which eight people had hidden from the Nazis for days at a time, a space that didn't look so small until eight students stood in it to have a photograph taken. The exhibit offered students the opportunity first to focus on an aspect of the Holocaust that was of particular interest to them and then to figure out a creative way to present their learning. In so doing, they learned about public history, about representation and memory, and about teaching by doing. With the exhibit, the course ended, but the learning did not and does not. As Lawrence Langer reminds us, "Teaching and learning about the Holocaust is . . . a double journey, a temporary excursion that concludes with the end of a class or a course, and a ceaseless encounter with evil that raises a multitude of unsettling questions about history and human conduct."[19]

Stephen Haynes suggests that for Christian scholars who teach this subject, "the Holocaust is a matter of faith; . . . teaching the Holocaust is an act of faith, of religious self-criticism and of religious affirmation."[20] Yet, as in faith itself, tension is the inherent paradox in teaching the Holocaust. Each time I teach a course on the Holocaust, I am enriched. And each time I teach such a course, I agonize—over those especially frustrating class periods in which discussion seems burdened by too-easy answers spoken out of immature spiritual formation; over someone's resistance to considering a point of view based on a less literal, more complex reading of Scripture; over zealous, well-meaning, mission-minded young people who just want to convert non-Christians; over narrow conceptions of God; over judgmental twenty-year-olds. Should I spin the course a different way? Is it possible that one student was right when he complained on his course evaluation about there having been too much emphasis on the Christian response? I don't think so. Students who speak freely from the perspective of faith do so in all their classes, and often to the dismay of faculty who are looking for differently informed or more nuanced responses. To ask students to respond as Christians invites them to abandon the facile dualistic thinking so characteristic of entering college students, and to carefully examine their own faith traditions as well as those of others. But asking students to respond as Christians is not the same as issuing them an invitation to enter a comfort zone. One student wrote in her final paper that she often left class with "a headache and an unsettled frame of mind," and struggling: "This class raised questions that I need to consider and explore as I learn more about the world and myself." While recognizing that the questions would stay with her "for a long time, if not forever," she reported being amazed at the personal growth she saw in herself. Another student said simply, "This class has changed how I think about things and how I act."

The preamble to my syllabus includes this quote: "In studying the Holocaust, we study not only a particular society of the past but ourselves as well."[21] A fairly autobiographical teacher, I readily tell my students that study of the Holocaust has had a transformative effect on me. The subject has had a grip on me since I first saw a photo of a Dachau crematory, when I was about nine years old. But despite the fact that I have been at it longer and my immersion in the subject is far deeper, I hold out hope that their encounter with the Holocaust might be transformative as well. One semester, during finals week, I found a note on my office door that fed my hope. A student had torn some pages from her personal journal and left them for me. In our work together in the course, Rachel had discovered something about herself—she was seeing things differently. And it was, she believed, because "you mean to change us."

The final question I ask students to write on is one I have borrowed from John Roth, who asks what it means to be Christian after Auschwitz.[22] Their responses give me further hope: "I need to pay more attention to what is going on in the world," wrote one young man. "The Holocaust must inspire us to change," said another. "I can refuse to be a bystander," said a third, a young woman. To her teacher, she expressed the essence of what it means to be a Christian, especially after Auschwitz.

NOTES

1. School Code (State of Illinois, 1990), sec. 27–20.3

2. Stephen R. Haynes, *Holocaust Education and the Church-Related College: Restoring Ruptured Traditions* (Westport, Conn.: Greenwood Press, 1997), 167.

3. Lawrence L. Langer, "Opening Locked Doors: Reflections on Teaching the Holocaust," in *Preempting the Holocaust* (New Haven, Conn.: Yale University Press, 1998), 191.

4. On Holocaust education and ethics, see John K. Roth, *Holocaust Politics* (Louisville, Ky.: Westminster John Knox Press, 2001).

5. Jaroslav Pelikan and Helmut T. Lehman, eds., *Luther's Works,* vol. 47 (St. Louis, Mo.: Concordia Publishing House/Fortress Press, 1955–1986), 123–306.

6. See, for example, Mary C. Boys, *Has God Only One Blessing? Judaism as a Source of Christian Self-Understanding* (New York: Paulist Press, 2000); Tikva Frymer-Kensky et al., eds., *Christianity in Jewish Terms* (Boulder, Colo.: Westview Press, 2000).

7. *The Longest Hatred: A Revealing History of Anti-Semitism,* directed by Rex Bloomstein (Boston: WGBH, 1991).

8. *Shadow on the Cross,* directed by Malcolm Feuerstein (Falls Church, Va: Landmark Films, 1990).

9. *Weapons of the Spirit,* directed by Pierre Sauvage (Los Angeles: Chambon Foundation, 1990).

10. See, for example, Langer, *Preempting the Holocaust,* especially the essay on the dilemma presented in Simon Wiesenthal's *The Sunflower* and responses to it.

11. For a discussion of the discovery of the story of Le Chambon and subsequent research on the village, see Philip Paul Hallie, *In the Eye of the Hurricane: Tales of Good and Evil, Help and Harm* (Middletown, Conn.: Wesleyan University Press, 2001); Philip Paul Hallie, *Lest Innocent Blood Be Shed: The Story of the Village of Le Chambon and How Goodness Happened There* (New York: Harper Colophon, 1979).

12. Haynes, *Holocaust Education and the Church-Related College,* 131.

13. Simon Wiesenthal, *The Sunflower: On the Possibility and Limitations of Forgiveness* (New York: Schocken Books, 1997).

14. Leon Stein, "A Parting at the Cross: The Contrasting National Cultures of Lutheranism in Germany and Denmark during the Holocaust," in John K. Roth and Elizabeth Maxwell, eds., *Remembering for the Future: The Holocaust in an Age of Genocides,* vol. 2 (New York: Palgrave Macmillan, 2001), 618–34.

15. Ibid., 618.

16. Ibid., 619.

17. Elie Wiesel, *The Trial of God* (New York: Schocken Books, 1995).

18. Eugene J. Fisher and Leon Klenicki, "From Death to Hope: An Interreligious Service," in Elie Wiesel and Albert H. Friedlander, *The Six Days of Destruction: Meditations Toward Hope* (New York: Paulist Press, 1988). See also Marcia Sachs Littell and Sharon Weissman Gutman, eds., *Liturgies on the Holocaust: An Interfaith Anthology* (Valley Forge, Pa.: Trinity Press International, 1996).

19. Langer, *Preempting the Holocaust,* 196.

20. Haynes, *Holocaust Education and the Church-Related College,* xxii.

21. Peter J. Haas, *Morality after Auschwitz: The Radical Challenge of the Nazi Ethic* (Philadelphia: Fortress Press, 1988), 232.

22. John K. Roth, "What Does the Holocaust Have to Do with Christianity?" in Carol Rittner, Stephen D. Smith, and Irena Steinfeldt, eds., *The Holocaust and the Christian World: Reflections on the Past, Challenges for the Future* (New York: Continuum, 2000), 10.

13

Teaching Theology after Auschwitz

A Political-Theological Perspective

JUERGEN MANEMANN

After World War II, the Catholic theologian Johann-Baptist Metz developed a new political theology. In opposition to Carl Schmitt (1888–1985)— Adolf Hitler's "crown jurist," who had worked out a political theology based on the Catholic traditionalists of the nineteenth century, and who had focused on the institution of the Catholic Church in terms of its power—Metz's question was that of keeping religion from political instrumentalization. Therefore, he took the opposite perspective to Schmitt's; that is, he adopted a positive view of the Enlightenment and modern freedom of thought, but at the same time he worked out an eschatological reservation with regard to all stages of progress and emancipation in history. For this political theology, the term "theology" means "speaking of God" in our time. Speaking of God in our time always means giving a diagnosis of our time and finding out what is going on in history and society. Thus speaking of God means diagnosing the so-called signs of our time (Vatican II)—and the sign without which no Christian in our context should speak of God today is Auschwitz. Hence political theology is explicitly worked out as a theology after Auschwitz.[1]

As a theology, an "after Auschwitz" political theology does not refer to yet another field in the diversity of fields, schools, streams, or tendencies within Catholic theology; at least, it should not refer only to this. (That has been the traditional way of thinking about different theological approaches, the so-called genitive theologies.) Rather, it refers to a different way of thinking about Christian theology itself. From this perspective, Metz formulated the following axiom:

> What Christian theologians can *do* for the murdered of Auschwitz, and thereby for a true Christian-Jewish ecumenism, is, in every case, to never again do theology in such a way that its construction remains unaffected, or could remain unaffected, by Auschwitz. In this sense, I make available to my students an apparently very simple but in fact extremely demanding criterion for evaluating the theological scene: I ask them if the theology they are learning is such that it could remain unchanged before and after Auschwitz. "If this is the case," I tell them, "be on your guard!"[2]

According to Metz, the theological insights to be sought demand an inability to be successfully distanced from the suffering of others. Therefore, he argues, the so-called question of theodicy must be the foundation of contemporary "God talk" because only then can Christianity protest the catastrophes of history, by developing the idea that God—and not, as Hegel said, *Weltgeschichte* (world history)—is the tribunal of history. Political theology, as a self-critical theology, forces the Catholic Church to work itself out as an institution of the memory of suffering. Such a memory is a dangerous one, calling the church into question, because it demands a remembrance of the most radical protest against Christianity: Auschwitz. As such an institution of memory, the Catholic Church would have its interest not in self-preservation but in the victims of history and society.

The new political theology is not a concept of some order, nor is it a system; rather, it is a *subjective* concept, one that suggests a use for the recognition that our findings are missing a certain something. Questions are much more important than answers. Therefore, theology is not a tool for guaranteeing security and the unity of society. As already mentioned, the new political theology is not grounded in representation but in eschatology. Based on the presupposition of Theodor W. Adorno (1903–1969) that the need to lend a voice to suffering is the precondition of all truth,[3] the new political theology works for an anamnestic culture, a culture of remembrance based on memory of suffering.[4] The memory of suffering leads to the premise that there is no true knowledge without compassion. The first epistemological principle is not the Cartesian "Cogito, ergo sum"; it is "You suffer; therefore, I am!" Or, to formulate it in another way, it says that becoming a subject in history and society means being responsible for the Other. Being responsible means acknowledging the Other in his or her Otherness—or, to use another term, in his or her nonidentity. The capacity to enlighten reason about itself depends on the ability to perceive the nonidentity of the object of knowledge because reason is in danger of projecting or facing the object in another way: as an object of knowledge. To face an unintentional truth means to interrupt our way of projecting the world around us.

In this respect, political theology works theology out as a way for human beings to become subjects in history and society. But is there any chance, in contemporary society, to work out such a narrative-memorial theology? Collective memory is bimodal: it contains both communicative memory and cultural memory.[5] Working on and teaching such a theology at a German state university, I am confronted with a radical shift of remembrance: we have been entering a situation in which communicative memory of the Holocaust must be transformed into cultural memory. Facing this process, we recognize that the more we communicate about the struggle and discuss the past in the present, the more will be remembered in the cultural memory of the future. In other words, cultural memory depends on the communicative energy we invest in it. But is there any chance for the transformation of *memoria passionis* into cultural memory? Klaus Ahlheim and Bardo Heger, both of whom teach pedagogy at the University of Essen, have analyzed how students in present-day Germany think about the past. In 2002, they published the survey results, which are most challenging: 61 percent of the German students who were surveyed called for "gesundes Nationalbewusstsein" ("a healthy national identity"), and 36 percent voted for a "Schlusstrich" (indicating that they thought it was time to "close the book").[6] Ahlheim and Heger have also diagnosed what they call a secondary antisemitism among these students.

Teaching theology after Auschwitz from a political-theological perspective means resisting the evolutions of amnesia. But how? Political theology reveals the political dimensions and impact of doing theology, which means that, first of all, the teaching of theology after Auschwitz should be based on a critical reflexivity, what Pierre Bourdieu (1930–2002) has called "reflexartige Reflexivität" (reflective reflection), a methodology that enables the teacher to perceive and control the effects of the social structures that frame the teaching situation.[7] The adjective "reflective" underlines the necessity to ponder these effects while teaching the topic. It is a permanent challenge, one that has to be dealt with *within* the teaching situation. This reflection will help the teacher interrupt the hierarchical structure of the teacher-student-relationship—but of course it will never completely abolish every hierarchical element of that relationship because, ultimately, the teacher has to evaluate the students. Teaching with such a methodology is essential for a democratic society because democracy aims at a relationship between teacher and students that is based on fairness and not on dependency. According to John Rawls, justice understood as fairness is the foundation of a liberal democracy.[8]

It is obvious that education after Auschwitz is grounded in the regulative idea of a communication process that is free of violence. The aim of this process is to help students become subjects, and becoming a subject means being able to say no. The way I as a teacher ask questions, and the questions I raise, are ways for me to enter into the thoughts of students, ways that could become the beginning of a communicative process—or the end of it. Therefore, I have to be very careful in dealing, for example, with the results presented by Ahlheim and Heger. Without such critical reflectivity, I would be in danger of treating the students in my courses not as individuals but only as representatives of the image of German students offered by these two researchers. Furthermore, as a political theologian, I should be very sensitive to the antidemocratic tendencies in surveys that are based on standardized questions. Teaching theology after Auschwitz, I should not begin to raise questions; on the contrary, as a teacher I should help students articulate their own questions. Thus the task of the teacher can be described as that of a midwife, of someone who enables the other to express himself or herself, to express his or her feelings and thoughts. Another way to describe this project is to say that my role is to help each student become a narrative self because in order to express himself or herself, the student must have a story to tell. Stories are not coherent; they are fragmented, and they

inherit self-transcended moments. The teacher must refrain from analyzing the stories according to criteria of truth or of right and wrong. If
students tell their own stories and listen to the stories of others, they will
be challenged with a plurality and diversity of stories.

Teaching the capacity to face these different stories is to teach tolerance of ambiguity,[9] which is the precondition for people's ability to live
together without fear. And there is one more important aspect, a paradox to be considered: to tell one's own story does not mean to tell *only*
one's story, because to tell about oneself is at the same time to speak about
others. If a theologian does not offer the place and the time for students
to communicate stories, students won't develop a consciousness of being
entangled in stories. That's why I offer students a colloquium every two
weeks, in the evening, without the constraints of class time. The participants in this colloquium raise questions, and they themselves try to find
the answers without referring to texts. The communication process is
the center of this meeting. No one is required to find solutions, but all
those present have to bring themselves into the discussion. Students
need the experience of nonhierarchical discourse, a mode of discourse
that requires them to listen to others and respond from their individual
perspectives. Such a colloquium is a way to extend our understanding of
justice as fairness because it perceives justice as a deepening of the ability to acknowledge the other in his or her singularity.

For a political theologian, compassion is the foundation of speaking of
God after Auschwitz. It was Adorno, in his famous essay "Erziehung nach
Auschwitz," who questioned the educational value of hardship. According
to Adorno, to educate in order to harden is to give reason for violence:
"People who are hard toward themselves think they have the right to be
hard toward others as well and avenge themselves for the pain they were
not permitted to show and had to repress."[10] Adorno pleaded for an education in which fear is not repressed: "When fear is not repressed, when
one admits actually having as much fear as the reality of the situation
deserves, then precisely in this way much of the destructive effect of unconscious and displaced fear will probably disappear."[11] He criticized coldness:

> If coldness were not a basic feature of anthropology, thus of the nature
> of people as they in fact are in our society, and thus if they were not deeply

indifferent toward what happens with all other persons except for the few with whom they are closely connected and even connected by obvious interests, Auschwitz would not have been possible and people would not have accepted it. . . . The inability to empathize was unquestionably the most important psychological condition for the occurrence of something like Auschwitz amidst fairly civilized and harmless people.[12]

On the basis of these reflections, the teaching of theology after Auschwitz has to resist processes of evading emotions; on the contrary, feelings and emotions are of the highest importance for theology because they prevent us from worldlessness and from evading society. As Agnes Heller writes, "To feel means being involved."[13] Moral imperatives are not bodiless; pain is not something we simply feel. It possesses at the same time a cognitive dimension: pain should *not be*!

To think about and teach theology after Auschwitz without reflecting praxis, without thinking, without working for a more just society, is hypocrisy. But what is the foundation of a just society? Compassion. Liberals define justice as fairness and equality. But the focus of equality should not be concentrated only on the perspective of the generalized Other—as in John Rawls's theory, for example—but also on the perspective of the individual. The second perspective is very important where equality is concerned, because criticisms and complaints of individuals are the foundations of a new understanding of equality—but only if we try to justify the complaints of the individual by referring to what he or she is suffering.[14] Such an approach could be universalized, because everyone who articulates his or her suffering wills that everyone else take that suffering into consideration. As a suffering person, I will that no one else affirm my suffering. Transforming our understanding of equality from the perspective of the suffering individual presupposes proximity. A self-reflective egalitarian liberal perspective is rooted in a feeling of solidarity, which itself possesses a bodily character because it is based on a somatic impulse from which is derived the imperative that suffering shouldn't exist. To sum up very briefly: compassion is, in a general sense, the foundation of living in a human society; therefore, it is necessary to teach students how to educate children in such a way as to deepen their capacity to empathize with the suffering Other. But to empathize does not mean to identify!

Reflecting on morality in our society, and in order to become aware of the ethical dimensions of ordinary everyday life, students should also learn to consider what Tzvetan Todorov has written about social interactions in the concentration camps:

> Today at least two ideological models preside over the sphere of human interactions. The first model, a modern version of classical heroism, dominates and suffuses the *public* sphere. . . . The other model . . . governs the *private* sphere. . . . These two models account for the simultaneous presence of heroic virtues (valued in the public sphere) and ordinary virtues (appreciated in the private sphere).[15]

Todorov focuses on ordinary virtues in the concentration camps, the first of which is dignity and the second of which is caring. Here, students will learn that the popular understanding of Hobbes's doctrine is not true, because, as Todorov indicates, individuals in extreme circumstances do not necessarily behave like wolves; on the contrary, they communicate with one another, they help one another, and they distinguish good from evil.[16]

In light of these insights, the teaching of theology after Auschwitz has to account for the subject in the Levinasian sense, which means that this teaching has to work at the deconstruction of what we call a subject. The subject we often talk about is a middle-class subject, one that privatizes values in such a way that they make no public demands. Religion, instead of collaborating in this privatization of our values, should have a different task—namely, to

> remind individuals and modern societies that morality can only exist as an intersubjective normative structure and that individual choices only attain a "moral" dimension when they are guided or informed by intersubjective, interpersonal norms. Reduced to the private sphere of the individual self, morality must necessarily dissolve into arbitrary decisionism. By bringing publicity into the private moral sphere and by bringing into

the public sphere issues of private morality, religions force modern societies to confront the task of reconstructing reflexively and collectively their own normative foundations.[17]

This is very important, especially for a theology after Auschwitz, because, in view of privatization, tradition makes no sense to the modern ideology of free and autonomous use of reason. On the foundation of a radical understanding of modern privatization, an evolutionary consciousness arises, with all its prejudices against tradition:

> Evolutionary logic denies corporeality, a corporeality composed of sufferings, of memories, of hopes, as well as of desires, longings, and needs. It smooths the passions of human life, replacing the pains and ecstasy of time-filled existence with the control and management of timeless reality.[18]

According to Walter Benjamin (1892–1940), whose philosophy is very important for a theology after Auschwitz, "The concept of progress should be grounded on the idea of catastrophe. That things 'just keep on going' *is* the catastrophe."[19] Political theology after Auschwitz analyzes the destruction of historical consciousness through this logic. The memory of suffering interrupts our so-called higher-order interests; it is a fissure in a society that is preoccupied with the future, a future that is not a *novum* but a prolongation of the present. In order to become sensitive to the importance of an amnestic solidarity,[20] which thinks of the future in a universal way—the future for the dead and for future generations— students have to think about their relationship to the dead. In my courses, a poem by Mascha Kaléko has been very helpful in teaching students to gain such an understanding because it expresses both the burden and the necessity of memory of the dead:

> Vor dem eignen Tod ist mir nicht bang,
> Nur vor dem Tod derer, die mir nah sind.
> Wie soll ich leben, wenn sie nicht mehr da sind?
> Allein im Nebel tast ich tod entlang
> Und lass mich willig in das Dunkel treiben.
> Das Gehen schmerzt nicht halb so wie das Bleiben.

Teaching Theology after Auschwitz

Der weiß es wohl, dem gleiches widerfuhr;
—Und die es trugen, mögen mir vergeben.
Bedenkt: den eignen Tod, den stirbt man nur,
Doch mit dem Tod der andern muss man leben.

I'm not afraid of my own death,
Only of the death of those who are close to me.
How am I supposed to live if they are no longer here?
Alone in the fog, I grope my way along death
And let myself be driven willingly into the dark.
Going doesn't hurt half as much as staying.
Anyone who's suffered the same knows it well;
—and may those who bore it forgive me.
Consider: your own death you merely have to die,
but you must live with the deaths of the others.[21]

Reflecting on the death of the Other, students may gain some awareness of the anthropological centrality of the memory of the dead. The very notion of humanity derives from the Latin word *humare,* to bury. A human being is someone who possesses the capacity to bury another person. According to David Blumenthal, this capacity is foundational for our morality: "The ultimate act of human grace is burying someone, for the dead can no longer do us favour. To bury a dead person is to act without expectation of any tangible reward."[22]

From this perspective, theology after Auschwitz could function as a way for us to broaden and deepen our understanding of a liberal democracy:

It is obvious that tradition is only democracy extended through time. . . . Tradition may be defined as an extension of the franchise. Tradition means giving votes to the most obscure of all classes, our ancestors. It is the democracy of the dead. Tradition refuses to submit to the small and arrogant oligarchy of those who merely happen to be walking about. All democrats object to men being disqualified by the accident of birth; tradition objects to their being disqualified by the accident of death. Democracy tells us not to neglect a good man's opinion, even if he is our groom; tradition asks us not to neglect a good man's opinion, even if he is our father.

229

I, at any rate, cannot separate the two ideas of democracy and tradition;
it seems evident to me that they are the same idea. We will have the dead
at our councils. The ancient Greeks voted by stones; these shall vote by
tombstones. It is all quite regular and official, for most tombstones, like
most ballot papers, are marked with a cross.[23]

Here, the students should be confronted with the *gravelessness* of Auschwitz:
"The Jews who were annihilated in the Holocaust have no graves either—
they lie deep in our memory."[24] Compassion and tradition—the central
elements of doing and teaching theology after Auschwitz—belong
together like two sides of a coin. In order to show the interrelationship
between both, I like to refer to Walter Benjamin's call for an empathetic
memory that forces us to break with our bourgeois, evolutionistically colored consciousness:

> History is not just science but also a form of memoration [*eine Form des
> Eingedenkens*]. What science has "established," memoration can modify.
> Memoration can make the incomplete (happiness) into something com-
> plete, and the complete (suffering) into something incomplete. That is the-
> ology; but in memoration we discover the experience [*Erfahrung*] that forbids
> us to conceive history as thoroughly a-theological, even though we barely
> dare not attempt to write it according to literally theological concepts.[25]

In order for students to be taught, and educated to become subjects based
on such empathetic memory, teacher and students alike must first of all
regard the university not only as a complex of classrooms but also as a living space. The university is a place of social learning, in a double sense: a
place where we teach theories of social interaction, and a place of social
interaction itself. Here, students must reflect on the dimension of compassion with respect to their ways of living and learning. The lectures that
teachers deliver, and the courses that they teach, are elements of this context.

COURSE STRUCTURE

Generally speaking, I approach the course on the Holocaust with a threefold structure in mind.

Teaching Theology after Auschwitz

Speaking, Listening, and Motivating

In order to learn to become a teacher, the student must deliver a paper while other students are forced to train their ability to listen to the reflections of their colleague. The student who speaks to the whole group also has the task of motivating the others to communicate their ideas about the topic, and he or she must lead the discussion. Here, the student presenting the paper should use scientific tools in order to present results of historical, sociological, and theological research—or, in other words, he or she should try to give answers.

Reading

In this phase of the course, students in very small groups read texts by victims of the Holocaust and discuss the texts within their groups. Discussion of these testimonies does not take place in the whole group because reading should be understood as a kind of listening to victims. Here, students should work out perspectives that make them unable to distance themselves from the suffering of others. But the students also have to recognize that the attempt to look at the topic from "the" perspective of a victim does not mean to identify with the victim. The testimonies make students sensitive to what Adorno and Horkheimer have defined as the "dialectics of the enlightenment."[26] On the basis of their reading, students will be able to question the answers offered by other students who have presented papers. They now have to face insights that they are unable to deal with; that is, reading the stories of victims is a critical task that requires students to take account of insights that are difficult to handle. For example, reading Elie Wiesel, a Christian has to keep in mind what Wiesel said in an interview: thoughtful Christians understand it was Christianity, not the Jewish people, that died in Auschwitz. I, for example, as a Catholic and a German, can never make the memories of the victims my own. What I should make my own instead is the true interests of others, which are expressed in their stories. My story is first of all the story of the perpetrators and bystanders, but this does not mean that I should not remember the stories of the victims. Through the memory of the victims' stories, we can view our own story!

And then we will see if our tradition, with its stories, is able to face the stories of the others.

Round Table

Round-table group discussion of topics should remind students of the aim of a liberal democracy: to take every perspective into consideration. In this situation, students realize that one perspective at the table needs an attorney: the perspective of the victim. In this part of the course, students are asked to develop questions that were not raised at the beginning of the course.

A REFLECTION ON COURSE STRUCTURE

The organization of a course on theology after Auschwitz has to be open to the threefold process. This means that the teacher is responsible for creating an atmosphere that allows students not only to raise questions but also to question the teacher. That's why, in addition to formal class meetings, it is also necessary to offer colloquia where students and teachers can communicate without the pressure of time and similar constraints. The teacher must give students opportunities to get to know one another and must teach them from the beginning of their study that political institutions do not always secure freedom and justice. When political institutions fail, the only protection against barbarity may be memory.

NOTES

1. Johann-Baptist, Metz, "Christen und Juden nach Auschwitz. Auch eine Betrachtung über das Ende bürgerlicher Religion," in Johann-Baptist Metz, *Jenseits bürgerlicher Religion. Reden über die Zukunft des Christentums* (Mainz: Grünewald-Verlag, 1980), 29–50; Juergen Manemann, *"Weil es nicht nur Geschichte ist." Die Begründung der Notwendigkeit einer fragmentarischen Historiographie des Nationalsozialismus aus politisch-theologischer Sicht* (Muenster: Lit-

Verlag, 1995); Juergen Manemann, *Carl Schmitt und die Politische Theologie. Politischer Anti-Monotheismus* (Muenster: Aschendorff-Verlag, 2002).

2. Metz, "Christen und Juden nach Auschwitz," 29–50, 42.

3. Theodor. W. Adorno, *Negative Dialekti* (Frankfurt: Suhrkamp-Verlag, 1974), 29.

4. Juergen Manemann, "Being Entangled in Stories: The 'Logic' of Catholic Tradition in a Post-traditional Society," in Edward Kessler, John Pawlikowski, and Judy Banki, eds., *Jews and Christians in Conversation: Crossing Cultures and Generations* (Cambridge: Orchard Academic, 2002), 105–22.

5. Jan Assmann, *Das kulturelle Gedächtnis. Schrift, Erinnerung und politische Identität in frühen Hochkulturen* (Muenster: Beck-Verlag, 1992).

6. Karl Ahlheim and Bardo Heger, *Die unbequeme Vergangenheit—NS-Vergangenheit, Holocaust und die Schwierigkeiten des Erinnerns* (Schwalbach: Wochenschau-Verlag, 2002).

7. Pierre Bourdieu et al., *Das Elend der Welt. Zeugnisse und Diagnosen alltäglichen Leidens an der Gesellschaft* (Konstanz: Universitätsverlag Konstanz, 1998).

8. John Rawls, *A Theory of Justice,* rev. ed. (Cambridge, Mass.: Belknap Press of Harvard University Press, 1999).

9. Karl Ernst Nipkow, *Grundfragen der Religionspädagogik,* vol. 2: *Das pädagogische Handeln der Kirche* (Gütersloh: Gütersloher Verlagshaus, 1990), 166.

10. Theodor W. Adorno, "Education After Auschwitz," in Helmut Schreier and Mattias Heyl, eds., *Never Again! The Holocaust's Challenge for Educators* (Hamburg: Krämer, 1997), 11–20.

11. Ibid.

12. Ibid.

13. Agnes Heller, *Theorie der Gefühle* (Hamburg: VSA-Verlag, 1980), 19.

14. Christolph Menke, *Spiegelungen der Gleichheit* (Berlin: Akademie-Verlag, 2000).

15. Tzvetan Todorov, *Facing the Extreme: Moral Life in the Concentration Camps* (New York: Henry Holt/Metropolitan, 1996), 52.

16. Ibid., 39.

17. José Casanova, *Public Religions in the Modern World* (Chicago: University of Chicago Press, 1994), 229, 230.

18. Rebecca S. Chopp, *The Praxis of Suffering* (Maryknoll, N.Y.: Orbis Books, 1986).

19. Walter Benjamin, *Das Passagen-Werk* (Frankfurt: Suhrkamp-Verlag, 1983), 11n9a.

20. Helmut Peukert, *Wissenschaftstheorie-Handlungstheorie-Fundamentale Theologie. Analysen zu Ansatz und Status theologischer Theoriebildung* (Frankfurt: Suhrkmap-Verlag, 1976), 308–10.

21. Mascha Kaléko, "Memento," in *Verse für Zeitgenossen* (Reinbek: Rowohlt, 1980). The translation is by Timothy Bennett.

22. David R. Blumenthal, *The Place of Faith and Grace in Judaism* (Dayton, Ohio: Center for Judaic-Christian Studies, 1985), 18.

23. Karl Gilbert Chesterton, *Orthodoxie. Eine Handreichung für die Ungläubgien* (Frankfurt: Eichborn- Verlag, 2001), 99–100.

24. Simon Wiesenthal, *Every Day Remembrance Day: A Chronicle of Jewish Martyrdom* (New York: Henry Holt, 1987), 2.

25. Benjamin, *Das Passagen-Werk*, 1.

26. Max Horkheimer and Theodor. W. Adorno, *Dialektik der Aufklärung. Philosophische Fragmente* (Frankfurt: Fischer-Taschenbuchverlag, 1986).

PART THREE

PROGRESS AND PROCESS

HIGHER EDUCATION, MUSEUMS,

AND MEMORIALS

T his section of the book moves the subject of the Holocaust from the classroom to the institution: the university, the surrounding community, the community college, the museum or memorial, and the endowed symposium. The chapters explore the issue of Holocaust education as, on the one hand, an unwelcome addition to the campus and its surrounding community and, on the other, a welcome permanence. Responses to Holocaust education can be disturbing but are more often gratifying.

In chapter 14, Laurinda Stryker presents her very difficult and ultimately losing battle with university colleagues and administrators who refused to accept the Holocaust as a legitimate subject of study. Her former university, in a community that cradled Nazism in the 1930s, has a documented history of antisemitism. In these uneasy surroundings, Stryker's situation was untenable and very costly, monetarily and professionally. Her case, although unique, is not unprecedented.

Marilyn J. Harran, in chapter 15, leads us through a story with an unlikely and very happy ending. Her denominational university is a liberal bastion in Orange County, California, an area known for its intolerance and conservatism. Harran, seizing an opportunity and imbued with passion for teaching the subject, and with the conviction that it should be taught, inspired support from the university and the community. The Holocaust program she envisioned and implemented is exemplary.

Myrna Goldenberg, a longtime community college professor, argues in chapter 16 that the community college is the appropriate academic setting for exposing students to the Holocaust. Its high enrollments and its diverse populations of students, populations particularly students from oppressive countries, render the community college ideal as a setting for teaching a course that focuses on moral choices, victimization by the state, perversion of language, and the obligations of free citizens. Students who confront the issues raised by studying the Holocaust are helped to think critically and provided with a narrative that proves that individuals not only make a difference but also can change their community.

In chapter 17, Stephen D. Smith describes the impact of a realized vision. Beth Shalom, established by his brother and himself in the heart of England, has set a high standard for respecting and memorializing the victims of the Holocaust. Smith also sees Beth Shalom's mission as that of an educational institution, with a mandate to inform the public about the catastrophe. He takes his responsibility as an educator seriously, and his endeavors are reflected in the large number of school visitors who come to Beth Shalom. He works with schools to develop contextualized histories of the Holocaust. Through its Aegis Institute, Beth Shalom now monitors oppressive societies around the globe and prepares educational materials about them.

Leonard Grob and Henry F. Knight, in chapter 18, trace the history of the Pastora Goldner Symposium, which is responsible for inspiring and guiding this book, and from which most of its contributors came. Grob and Knight narrate the origins and progress of the symposium's dynamics, and they document their responses to participants' criticisms and interests. They are the symposium's "parents," and it is their vision that has been supported by generous funding from Pastora Goldner and from Fairleigh Dickinson University. They take only modest credit, but their persistence and energy have clearly contributed to the productivity of the symposium. This book and four others are products of that vision, testaments to its success and its positive impact on symposium participants. Through the ethic of caring, Grob and Knight have created a community of scholar-activists.

14

The Tensions of Teaching

Truth and Consequences

LAURINDA STRYKER

When *Commentary's* Gabriel Schoenfeld attacked academics for their Holocaust scholarship, apparently denouncing any approach to the study of the Shoah with which he did not personally agree, he vowed that he would stop all scholars doing such research "in their tenure-tracks."[1] As senior editor of a conservative monthly, Schoenfeld is of course in no position to do any such thing. His patently unfair attacks—made elsewhere as well as in *Commentary,* and echoed by other critics—have hurt and angered individuals, but Schoenfeld cannot directly sabotage careers. Indeed, because the scholars denounced by Schoenfeld include some of the leading researchers in the field, to be singled out by him is to be placed in distinguished company.

Nevertheless, the acrimonious nature of Schoenfeld's remarks does point to a characteristic of Holocaust studies: it can be controversial, and in a number of different ways. As someone who was a junior faculty member teaching and writing about the Shoah, I have learned that work in this field does indeed carry risks to promotion and tenure. Articles in a recent book on Holocaust pedagogy in North American departments of German suggest that this is true at a variety of institutions; one contributor, in fact, states that she considers herself wise not to have engaged in Holocaust scholarship and teaching before receiving tenure.[2]

One potential set of problems stems from students' responses to courses on the Shoah. In the years I have taught such courses, nearly all students have been committed and responsive. Nevertheless, tensions occur. Some of these derive from students' religious backgrounds. At neither of the two universities at which I taught full-time—first at the University of Brighton, in England, and then at St. Cloud State University (SCSU), in Minnesota—was there more than a handful of Jewish students on campus. In my eight years of teaching courses on the Shoah, only three of my students identified themselves as Jewish. At SCSU, especially, committed Christians appeared to be in the great majority. Many such students find it difficult or even offensive to be exposed to the Christian roots of antisemitism. Similarly, although they generally find it interesting to learn about Judaism, there is among them some consternation over the Jewish nonacceptance of the messianic and divine status of Jesus. Questions concerning forgiveness, on which traditional Christian and Jewish outlooks differ fundamentally, can also be problematic: any demonstrated refusal to forgive those who perpetrated the Holocaust can give rise to students' condemnation.

Discussion of these reactions, either with students in person or through responses to their journal entries, is generally effective in helping students assess and analyze such feelings. Some college students, however, may be hostile to Holocaust education per se, for other reasons. There are those who take great pride in their German ancestry and who perceive Holocaust education to be anti-German. Others have been brought up to harbor the suspicion that accounts of Jewish suffering purposely obscure the experience of non-Jewish Poles in the Second World War.[3] Some students are simply antisemitic.[4] Some may be admirers of the Nazis.[5] Others may themselves be right-wing extremists.[6] Students on the left may view any account of the Holocaust as, at root, an apologetic for Israeli governmental policies toward Palestinians.[7]

Most students who have these sorts of views are unlikely to take a course in Holocaust studies unless it is required. From a variety of motivations, however, some—and not all—will negotiate their feelings through discussion, notes, and journals. The possibility of official complaints is a real one. One Canadian professor has written an account of how an antisemitic student in her course launched an official complaint that went all the way to the president's office because the student was unhappy about the inclusion of Holocaust subjects in a German composition and conversation course.[8] In dealing with students, my own experiences were happier ones: the students who took my course on the Holocaust were among those who were most supportive of my position and work at SCSU.[9] I am aware, however, that nontenured faculty are particularly vulnerable when students complain; whether such complaints are legitimate or not, nontenured faculty who are the targets are not viewed favorably by university administrators.

It may be argued that the transitory liverishness of administrators should be of little concern to any junior faculty member with an intact backbone. That is a valid argument, of course, if one is confident—and soundly so—of general support from colleagues and the administration. Unfortunately, however, students are not the only source of criticism and hostility at some institutions. If one set of tensions facing the nontenured professor teaching about the Shoah stems from possible student reactions, another set potentially arises from the attitudes and actions of those who work with and assess the faculty member without tenure.

Academic politics are notoriously brutal, and education does not necessarily improve character.[10] These are truisms, certainly, but also reasons for suspecting that perhaps it is indeed unwise to become identified with Holocaust studies before gaining tenure. In writing this account, I draw upon my own experiences at SCSU, but I am aware that what I write may have all too much resonance elsewhere. My predecessor in the SCSU history department, who also taught the history of the Holocaust, lost her job; a colleague in another department who teaches about antisemitism and genocide had first his tenure and then his promotion jeopardized; and a colleague abroad who is a preeminent researcher on the Shoah was forced out of his academic post. This is anecdotal evidence, of course; but, given the rhetoric in the wider world about stopping people "in their tenure-tracks," it gives junior faculty pause.

One cannot assume that one's colleagues and supervisors will agree that Holocaust education is important, and that a commitment to teaching and writing about the Holocaust is of any particular value in a faculty member. This attitude can be the result of ignorance: one former colleague, whose specialty was American history, had difficulty dating the Holocaust even approximately and indeed believed that Germany's mass murder of Europe's Jews had begun in the course of the World War I. Although this is an isolated example, it does point to a more wide-spread problem: those who are unfamiliar with any but the roughest out-lines of events are unlikely to recognize the magnitude of those events' implications. In contrast, however, those who do know more about the Shoah may find an individual scholar's preoccupation with such horrors perverse. I've been told by others that they "could never do" what I do, since they would find the emotional burden unbearable. Coming from the mouths of people sitting on committees for retention, promotion, and tenure, what compliment there is in such a statement is worryingly backhanded.

Other responses indicate that even in parts of academe there is hos-tility to the subject itself. Gabriel Schoenfeld views Holocaust studies as agenda-driven; there are people on campuses who share his perspective. In my first year at scsu, articles and editorials echoing the Schoenfeld line were placed, anonymously, in my campus mailbox. Initially on cam-pus as a visiting professor, I learned in my first conversation with my departmental chair that he viewed Holocaust studies as a field with no academic legitimacy. In a subsequent interview for a tenure-track posi-tion in that department, I heard him reiterate this view and state that if I were hired, I would not be permitted to continue offering courses in Holocaust history. (I continued to do so, however, because by then he had resigned his chairship.)

Such animosity to Holocaust scholarship and teaching may be rooted in personal antipathy toward specific approaches, such as gender analy-sis or comparative genocide studies. It may also involve antisemitism. And where this is the case, even non-Jewish probationary faculty mem-bers may find themselves highly vulnerable. Antisemitism in academe remains a fact. Higher education does not necessarily mean increased tol-erance, let alone increased respect. American universities have a history of antisemitism, and it is not all in the past.[11] As a Holocaust scholar, one feels obligated to take stands against such prejudice; doing so, how-ever, will not necessarily contribute to one's prospects for tenure.

scsu may be an extreme case in this regard. It is a large public com-prehensive university in central Minnesota, a region historically populated by people of German and Polish ethnicity, and the city of St. Cloud has a "checkered past in its relations with Jews. In the 1940s it served as head-quarters to the American Nazi Party. In 1989, following the still-unsolved kidnapping of 11-year-old Jacob Wetterling, flyers appeared throughout the city headlined, 'Where are our missing Children? Jewish Ritual Murder,' alluding to the centuries old blood-libel charges against Jews."[12] The scsu Center for Holocaust and Genocide Education was founded in response to this charge of ritual murder that circulated after the abduction, but unresolved debates continue about the removal of stonework swastikas ornamenting the exterior of the city's Catholic cathedral, completed in the early 1930s. Incoming scsu students are warned by university administrators that the area is a regional center for neo-Nazism.

The university itself has been charged in the past with antisemitic practices. Very few Jewish students enroll; some who have enrolled have quickly transferred elsewhere. Jewish faculty, too, in many instances seek new jobs elsewhere.[13] It is also reported that complaints filed with the university's office of affirmative action and alleging antisemitism are not acted on appropriately.[14]

In the spring of 2000, several events on campus brought anti-semitism to public attention. The *University Chronicle*, the student newspaper, accepted a paid insert from the so-called Committee for Open Debate of the Holocaust, a major Holocaust-denial organization. A rally against antisemitism and Holocaust denial was organized in response and was well attended; notably, however, the faculty advisor for the newspaper offered excuses but no substantive apology for the circulation of the Holocaust-denial insert. Concurrently, an Israeli-born fixed-term colleague in the history department, who had not been interviewed for a new tenure-track position in his field, filed an official complaint of anti-semitism on campus, in response to which investigations were launched by the scsu office of affirmative action and, ultimately, the office of the state university system's administration.[15] Over the summer, I testified to these offices, at length and in detail, about the antisemitism and other forms of discrimination of which I'd been informed, or which I had witnessed. Retaliation for my having done so began when I returned to scsu for the fall semester. My performance reviews, previously excellent, now alleged incompetence in all areas of my work; my chair and my dean, tacitly supported by the vice president for academic affairs, made repeated attempts to dismiss me from my position at SCSU through the retention/promotion/tenure processes.[16] When my quick removal proved difficult to effect, the dean accused me of academic misconduct, appointed another administrator to investigate my entire academic career in the hope of finding something to use against me, and hand-picked a committee of faculty members to conduct a hearing and decide the case.[17] At this point, I hired a lawyer and filed a complaint with the Equal Employment Opportunity Commission, as my Israeli-born colleague and another Jewish faculty member from a different SCSU division had also done. In the autumn of 2001, we filed a class action suit against the university.

The events at SCSU received attention in the local, national, and international media, but the issues were not resolved. Retaliation continued— and was even directed against students in response to their outspoken and organized support for me.[18] The president of the university, from the beginning informed about the retaliation by concerned colleagues at other universities and by Jewish organizations in Minneapolis and St. Paul, did not intervene, although he did invite the Jewish Community Relations Council to conduct an "environmental scan" concerning antisemitism. The findings of the "scan" were that antisemitism is indeed a concern at SCSU.[19] Antisemitism is now, for the first time, officially listed as a form of discrimination that will not be tolerated at SCSU; nevertheless, those who have spoken out against it, as against other forms of discrimination, were targeted.[20]

Had my own experiences at SCSU been entirely anomalous, they would not have a place in this volume, which deals more generally with the tensions of teaching about the Holocaust. As already noted, however, other faculty members, in North America and abroad, have expressed concern about the impact on a fledgling academic career of work in Holocaust studies, or they have experienced such negative effects themselves. This is not coincidental, given the subject. Holocaust studies is itself controversial in some settings. It raises questions about antisemitism that are not easily compartmentalized. Perhaps most important, the very nature of Holocaust studies places moral demands on scholars and students who are active in this field. The lessons that can be learned from the Shoah surely include those about the moral indefensibility of being a bystander to injustice. In settings where discrimination and injustice are systemic, however, speaking out can carry a high price.

In July 2002, I was summoned to a settlement conference dealing with the class-action lawsuit concerning antisemitism in which I was a named plaintiff. A settlement was reached. The settlement was a good one, if not just. SCSU was required to change its retention/promotion/tenure procedures to give greater protection to junior faculty, whatever the cause of a negative career decision. It was also required to investigate its "academic misconduct" procedures (this requirement was due in no small part to an unrelated lawsuit filed by an African-born professor who had also been targeted in this way). In addition, SCSU was urged to hire a rabbi to devise extracurricular programming and, perhaps, academic programs to expose non-Jewish students to Jewish culture and history. In short, there are to be institutional changes. And although there was no admission of wrongdoing, there was its intimation.[21]

And yet, the SCSU Department of History, where I worked, advertised for my replacement—for a twentieth-century Europeanist—without specifying any interest in, let alone expertise in, Holocaust studies, although a professional interest in the two world wars was sought. There was thus no institutional commitment to Holocaust history, despite the existence of a center for education on this topic.

So is it indeed wise for academics to steer clear of Holocaust studies until they have safely navigated the tenure track? Quite possibly; yet for those of us struck by the enormity of the Holocaust, there is something distasteful in such caution. The Shoah demands our committed pedagogical, intellectual, and moral response. For myself, I am glad to have done the work and taken the stands I have taken, though clearly I wish the consequences had been different. Aware of those consequences, I would still make the same choices. I'd counsel other junior Holocaust scholars about the wisdom of hiring a good lawyer, but above all I would advise them to make sure their bank accounts are fortified against possible lean days.

In the end, I sent the following letter to the university's student newspaper:

As someone who played a role in filing the lawsuit about anti-Semitism, I would like to express my appreciation for and support of the *University*

Chronicle editorial statement ["Lawsuit Was a Last Resort"] about the legal settlement Thursday.

Lawsuits should indeed be seen as a last resort. When state universities are increasingly strapped for cash and when students are expected to reduce the shortfall by huge hikes in tuition, million-dollar settlements are offensive—whatever the worth of centers or programs which are set up by those means. Things shouldn't come to such an end. I'd hoped they wouldn't.

About two years ago, I spoke out against anti-Semitism, homophobia and other forms of discrimination and then immediately began to be denigrated by my chair and by my dean, despite previous praise from them. I tried to resolve things in a low-key manner and use the mechanisms available to me on campus. I asked for mediation, a process in which people sit down with each other and a trained mediator and talk through a problematic situation. However, despite Dean Richard Lewis's official leadership role as a member of the scsu Mediation Coordinating Committee, he did not agree to this nonadversarial, local solution to the situation which had arisen between us.

Nevertheless, I continued to try to work within the system. Only when it became clear that some administrators were intent upon terminating my employment at scsu by means of illegally noncontractual (and, to my mind, unethical) actions did I hire an attorney.

My hope was that by doing so I would be able to continue to teach at scsu. I had no interest in a financial settlement for myself. As the editorial writer notes, financial reparations do not mend all injustices suffered.

I continue to have difficulty accepting what has occurred. I was summoned to a settlement conference in July. At that conference, I was made the so-called "offer I couldn't refuse." Either I had to accept the settlement proposal or be fired, effective the next day, and have to hire another lawyer and then file yet another lawsuit for wrongful dismissal. This was how the "offer" was presented to me by the state university system and scsu.

So I signed.

My scheduled courses for this semester were oversubscribed; I've taught some of the students who had registered for them since they were freshmen and I was looking forward to seeing them through their senior year and celebrating their graduation with them. I wanted more than anything to return to the classroom.

Instead, I was told that I must submit a letter of resignation which would be effective August 2003 and not teach at all during this academic year. Beyond that—unbelievably to me—I was to vacate my office before the beginning of the semester, months prior to receiving a written offer of settlement. Again, if I didn't do so I would be fired immediately.

I'm now on paid study leave, which costs the university not only my salary, but salaries for those who are teaching "my" classes.

I'm no longer in St. Cloud. I no longer teach the discipline I'm passionate about to students I respect and whose company I enjoy. I no longer have the opportunity to teach about where injustice may lead—genocide— or about Jewish history and culture, or about women's history, or about the two World Wars, or about the philosophical foundations of human rights.

I miss doing so; I miss scsu. No, financial remuneration is not a way to mend injustices. The editorial writer is astute.[22]

NOTES

This chapter is dedicated to the members and supporters of the St. Cloud State University Student Coalition Against Racism, whose willingness to act conscientiously and courageously against all forms of discrimination deserves highest praise.

1. Gabriel Schoenfeld, "Auschwitz and the Professors," *Commentary* 105:6 (June 1998), 43–48.

2. Dagmar C. G. Lorenz, "The Difficulty of Breaking the Silence: Teaching the Holocaust in a Program of German Literature and Culture," in Nancy A. Lauckner and Miriam Jokiniemi, eds., *Shedding Light on the Darkness: A Guide to Teaching the Holocaust* (New York: Berghahn Books, 2000), 61.

3. See, for example, the following three essays in Lauckner and Jokiniemi, eds., *Shedding Light on the Darkness:* Miriam Jokiniemi, "The Holocaust in an Introductory German Literature Course," 200–201; Thomas Freeman, "Victims and Perpetrators," 32; and Linda Feldman, "Designing within and around Limits: The Holocaust, Madonna, and Me," 52.

4. The line between ignorance and antisemitism is, of course, a blurred one: "jewed down" is a term frequently used at St. Cloud State University by faculty as well as students; Jewish students report being aggressively targeted for conversion by other students, being asked to let peers feel their horns, and coming home to their dorm rooms to find swastikas drawn on their doors and on the doors of friends, or antiSemitic notes and drawings pushed under their doors.

5. In my first year at scsu, a survivor who was visiting my class asked a graduate student why he was taking a course on the Holocaust. "I really admire the SS," he replied. "They were so efficient."

6. For a discussion of the presence of right-wing extremist students in Holocaust courses, see Lorenz, "The Difficulty of Breaking the Silence," 69–70.

7. In my experience, this is especially true in Britain, where leftist anti-Zionism not infrequently takes the place of more traditional forms of antisemitism.

8. See Karin Doerr, "The Nazi Period, the Holocaust, and German-Jewish Issues as Integral Subjects in a German Language Course," in Lauckner and Jokiniemi, eds., *Shedding Light on the Darkness,* 195–6.

9. The only semiformal criticism of my Holocaust course has been one line on one student's course evaluation. In the scsu history department, however, all course evaluations are routed first through the chair, who is then able to use any comments—positive or negative—selectively in making recommendations for retention, promotion, and tenure.

10. See Laurinda Stryker, "The Holocaust and Liberal Education," in B. Brecher, O. Fleischmann, and J. Holliday, eds., *The University in a Liberal State* (Aldershot, England: Avebury, 1996), 7–20, especially 15, where I examine the obligation of morality in higher education: "Reason reveals ethical principles; these demands must then be fulfilled in thought and action. Moral neutrality therefore is not possible; the life of the mind is by necessity ethically committed. For it to be otherwise is for it to betray itself."

11. See, for example, Edward C. Siegal and Stephen R. Silberfarb, eds., *Anti-Semitism at St. Cloud State University as Perceived by Selected Jewish and Non-Jewish Faculty, Students and Staff* (Minneapolis, Minn.: Jewish Community Relations Council of Minnesota and the Dakotas, 2001), available at http://condor.stcloudstate.edu/jcrc/report.html (accessed Feb. 3, 2006). See also the U.S. Equal Employment Opportunity Commission report available at http://condor.stcloudstate.edu/eeoc/ (accessed Feb. 3, 2006) and the Nichols and Associates cultural audit available at http://www.stcloudstate.edu/documents/nichols/ (accessed Feb. 3, 2006).

12. Amy Klein, "Prof's Bias Suit Casts Cloud Over Minnesota Campus:

Teachers, Students Allege Anti-Semitic Harassment at College," *Forward,* Nov. 17, 2000, available at http://www.forward.com/issues/2000/00.11.17/news4.html (accessed Feb. 3, 2006).

13. See Siegal and Silberfarb, eds., *Anti-Semitism at St. Cloud State University,* 10, 14: "Virtually all professors [who volunteered to be interviewed by the Jewish Community Relations Council investigators] thought there was discrimination with regard to opportunity," and one Jewish faculty member said, "Part of the problem is that the University will not and does not accept responsibility for ever doing anything wrong. No one is ever punished for anything." The same informant stated that nine Jewish faculty members either had been forced or had chosen to leave because of the climate toward Jews at scsu, further noting that this was a large number, given the few Jewish faculty members on campus. I have been unable either to corroborate or refute these figures.

14. See Siegal and Silberfarb, eds., *Anti-Semitism at St. Cloud State University,* 13.

15. See the statement by Stephen R. Silberfarb, executive director of the Jewish Community Relations Council of Minnesota and the Dakotas, who cites "the discrimination case against St. Cloud State University by a former professor . . . and the general climate on campus toward Jews" and states that the "discrimination case . . . is shedding light on the untold story of anti-Semitism at scsu. It is a story of inattention, inactions and insensitivity on the part of the past administrations and it is a story that has caused pain to Jewish faculty and students, and stained the reputation of the largest school in the NMSCU system" (press release, Oct. 26, 2000). See also Klein, "Prof's Bias Suit Casts Cloud Over Minnesota Campus."

16. In an interesting move, one ground on which I was faulted with respect to teaching had to do with the enthusiasm that students expressed for my Holocaust courses. I was admonished because the excellent evaluations for my other courses did not reach the superlative status of the evaluations for the Holocaust courses—whose subject is, after all, my academic specialty.

17. The hearing was postponed, partly because of a resolution passed by the faculty senate, which criticized the tainted nature of the investigatory process. An almost identical case, brought by another dean against a colleague in another department—like me, a lesbian—was dropped; my case, however, remains on hold.

18. One student, who was taking an independent study course with me, found it necessary to hire a lawyer in order to receive a grade and credit for the course.

19. See Siegal and Silberfarb, eds., *Anti-Semitism at St. Cloud State University.*

20. This despite the presence on campus of the Center for Holocaust and Genocide Education, whose funds come from outside the university. The center's role has been problematic: it is not itself activist on issues concerning anti-semitism or racism, but its presence on campus is pointed to by the university administration as proof of institutional goodwill.

21. On December 3, 2002, President Roy Saigo of scsu sent an e-mail message to the university community, stating that a "tentative settlement in the current anti-Semitism case that was brought against the University by former and current members of our faculty" had been reached. The agreement, he said, "while not an admission of wrongdoing or liability, . . . avoids further expense, inconvenience and the distraction of burdensome and protracted litigation." Saigo further stressed that he and the university administration "strongly oppose[d] anti-Semitism and any other form of discrimination and deeply regret[ted]" instances in which anyone had felt the experience of any kind of discrimination at scsu. Moreover, he said, the university was "participating in the agreement in order to make a good-faith effort to communicate to all people, and especially to those who identify with the Jewish religion, that they are welcome at scsu." Part of the tentative agreement included "developing a Jewish Culture and Resource Center, clearly, a positive step forward in making Jewish members of our community and the St. Cloud community feel more welcome." Saigo concluded by saying that the university had "developed a plan for conducting exit interviews with faculty members who leave St. Cloud State University to determine the reason for their departure" because he was interested in knowing why any employee felt "uncomfortable" at the university.

22. Laurinda Stryker, letter to the editor, *University Chronicle,* Feb. 17, 2003.

15

An Unlikely Setting

Holocaust Education in Orange County

MARILYN J. HARRAN

While Los Angeles has been at the forefront of Holocaust education and remembrance—the city is home to UCLA's Center for Jewish Studies, with the first endowed professorship in Holocaust studies in the United States; to the Simon Wiesenthal Center and Museum of Tolerance; to the Los Angeles Museum of the Holocaust; and to the University of Judaism, with its Sigi Ziering Center for the Study of the Holocaust and Ethics— the reputation of Orange County, located approximately thirty miles east of Los Angeles, has been quite different. Unfortunately, Orange County has all too often been seen in a negative light, a fact linked to the self-described Holocaust "revisionist" Institute for Historical Review (IHR), in Costa Mesa. The Anti-Defamation League describes the IHR as "the world's single most important outlet for Holocaust-denial propaganda."[1] In recent years, however—thanks to a visionary university president, generous donors, interested and engaged students, and an intensely supportive survivor community—Orange County's reputation with respect to Holocaust education and remembrance has undergone a dramatic and very positive transformation. In this chapter, I will outline the extraordinary journey that has taken place, what has been achieved, and what goals lie ahead and will suggest some insights that may be applicable to other institutions, particularly private ones, seeking to initiate and develop programs in Holocaust education.

Chapman University, in the town of Orange, California, is the largest independent university in the county. The student body is composed of approximately 3,700 undergraduates and about 1,200 graduate students. While a revived Hillel organization is now making its presence felt on campus, few of the university's students are Jewish, and only 3.5 percent designate their religious preference as Jewish in the 2002 Higher Education Research Institute/Cooperative Institutional Research Program (HERI/CIRP) annual survey of freshmen. In the fall of 1994, when a course on the Holocaust was offered on campus for the first time, it was unclear whether there would be sustained interest in this topic among our students, especially given the extraordinary difficulty of the subject matter. Would there be sufficient interest to allow for the development of more than one course? If we sought to develop a more public forum for discussion of the Holocaust, with lectures by survivors and scholars, would there be interest within the wider university and the surrounding community?

The answer to all these questions has proved to be a resounding yes. Holocaust courses, now taught every semester, fill up quickly, and our three lecture series, bringing distinguished scholars and inspiring Holocaust survivors to campus, are attended by hundreds of people— not only our own students and faculty but others as well, from many walks of life, who are interested in learning more about the Holocaust and the profound ethical questions it raises.[2] The Holocaust courses have contributed a new dimension to the university's curriculum, while our lecture series, our observance of Holocaust Remembrance Day, and our annual art and writing contests for middle and high school students have strengthened our connection to our surrounding community. To the surprise of some in Orange County and beyond, a non-Jewish institution has become a leader in Holocaust education in southern California, preparing young people to become witnesses to the future, fostering discussion of the social, political, historical, and economic causes of genocide, and encouraging young people to become active and informed citizens.

Orange County is often regarded as a politically conservative county, but Chapman University, since its founding as Chapman College, has been at the forefront of issues of social justice. The denomination with which the university is affiliated, the Disciples of Christ, has a remarkable record of ecumenism and social activism. Chapman University's forerunner, Hesperian College, founded in 1861, demonstrated dedication to equality and human rights by welcoming applications from students of all races, all religious and ethnic groups, and both genders. In more recent decades, the ideal of "reverence for life," articulated by Albert Schweitzer, has become central to our articulation of our mission and to our identity as an institution. Chapman College welcomed as speakers Ralph Bunche in 1956, Eleanor Roosevelt in 1959, and Martin Luther King Jr. in 1961. Chapman began to offer courses in peace studies in the 1930s. A minor in peace studies was established in 1981; a major, in 1989. The innovative "Freshman Seminar Program on War, Peace, and Justice," which is required of all entering students and uses a common syllabus, was established in 1989; in 1995, the course theme was changed to "The Global Citizen," a focus that continued through the fall of 2001. In short, throughout its history, and in a variety of ways, Chapman has been notable for its commitment to preparing students to lead informed, ethical lives of service to others.

But would this institutional ethos translate into interest and support for a program in Holocaust studies? How could our students—few of whose families had been affected by these events—connect to this history and the difficult issues it raises? With the benefit of hindsight, I wish I could claim to have had a carefully formulated strategic plan in place for establishing a program in Holocaust studies, but that was not the case. Our first steps into Holocaust education were modest ones, taken in our freshman seminar program, in which a section focused on the Holocaust. Students read Elie Wiesel's *Night* and sections from Adolf Hitler's *Mein Kampf,* and they considered the topic of obedience to authority. Our first speakers were Alfons Heck, who, as a member of the Hitler Youth, had experienced the lure of Nazism at first hand and was dedicated to educating young people about the dangers of blind obedience to authority, and Elisabeth Mann, an Auschwitz survivor, who had lost her whole family in the Holocaust and come face to face with the so-called Angel of Death himself, Josef Mengele. These two exceptional speakers gave faces and voices to experiences that were far distant from the sunny culture of southern California.

Marilyn J. Harran

In 1994, several Chapman University students indicated an interest in enrolling in a course where they could study the Holocaust in more depth and detail than was possible in the freshman seminar program. The film *Schindler's List,* released in the spring of 1993, had sparked enormous interest among the students. At the time, I wondered whether this interest would continue when the film was no longer such a frequent topic of conversation, and I was concerned that the complexity and intensity of the Holocaust could overwhelm the students. "Germany and the Holocaust: From Antisemitism to Final Solutions" is a course that is demanding, in every sense of the word. Students read ten to twelve books, and they write essay examinations as well as research and analysis papers, but what they find most challenging is the subject matter itself. Indeed, it is material that cannot be neatly compartmentalized into scheduled study time; instead, it opens up complex and lingering questions about human nature and about our capacity for good and evil, for apathy and altruism. I remember several of that first group of students telling me that their friends and families had asked them if this was the only course they were taking, since they seemed to spend all their time on it.

I have often pondered why students choose to enroll in this and the other Holocaust courses that we now offer. I think they are drawn by a desire to understand how people could participate in such evil, how a plan to exterminate millions could be developed by intelligent people in a civilized country, how so many could remain silent in the face of the growing persecution of their neighbors, and at the same time how people could face the horrific circumstances of those years with such courage and humanity. While the number of victims is overwhelming—1.5 million Jewish children alone—equally overwhelming in quite another way is the experience of meeting a survivor, a person who defines himself or herself as a witness, not a victim. That experience has proved to be a life-changing one for many of our students, and, at the same time, I believe, the interaction with students has proved to be extremely meaningful to survivors, who discover that young people who have no family connections to the Holocaust, and who often do not share the survivors' religious tradition, are nonetheless committed to remembrance and witness. Students from diverse majors, from film to art to economics, have chosen to study the Holocaust; their willingness to grapple with this complex history led to the development of two more courses, one in the spring of 1996 and the other in the spring of 2001, and, in 2003, to the establishment of a twenty-one-unit minor in the history department.

With our academic courses in place, we questioned whether we could do more, and if so, what? There was little response to our initial efforts to raise even a modest amount of funding for students to travel as a class by bus to the Museum of Tolerance, and for us to cover travel costs for speakers. Those to whom we appealed for funds often said they were "Holocausted out," by which they meant that they felt that too much attention was being focused on this event, or that they had received too many appeals, or that they had already given generously, often to Jewish institutions and organizations, which they saw as bearing a special responsibility for Holocaust remembrance and education. While we remained committed to offering Holocaust courses as long as there was student interest, it seemed unlikely that we would be able to do more.

Perhaps it was our years of remaining steadfast in educating our students about the Holocaust that enabled us to reach several of the goals that initially had seemed so unattainable. In 1999, a generous donor pledged support for a lecture series that would bring Holocaust survivors as well as Holocaust scholars to campus. Thanks to the initiative and commitment of the university's president, we were able to offer a full-tuition scholarship to Christoph Meili, the former security guard at Union Bank, in Zurich, whose courageous act in January 1997 had prevented the destruction of Holocaust-era records. Our desire to help Christoph and his family start a new life in southern California led to a partnership with the 1939 Club. The club, one of the largest and most active Holocaust survivor organizations in the United States, offered enormous support to the Meili family, allowing the Meilis to begin their new life on the West Coast.

The generosity of the 1939 Club enabled us to initiate a second lecture series and to launch a Holocaust art and writing contest for middle and high school students throughout southern California. The presence of 1939 Club members on our campus has given our students as well as those from surrounding local schools remarkable opportunities to learn about the complexity of the Holocaust and to be inspired by the courage and humanity of those who survived and who continue to relive their experiences so that others can learn. Chapman students attend the semiannual banquets of the 1939 Club, and several have joined the organization.

In February 2000, a generous donation led to the endowment of the Rodgers Center for Holocaust Education, and a few months later, in September, a major gift resulted in the establishment of the Stern Chair in Holocaust Education. A single course, taught for the first time in the fall of 1994, had now grown into a distinctive, multifaceted program. A foundation grant led to the establishment of the Leopold Page Memorial Righteous Rescuers Lecture Series, our third such series, and another gift made possible an annual communitywide observance of Holocaust Remembrance Day.[3]

Over the last decade, our focus has been primarily on developing a strong curricular and co-curricular program. Yet, as our program grew, it became increasingly evident that we needed a dedicated space—a place where our students could meet with visiting scholars and Holocaust witnesses, and where teachers could attend workshops and local school students, as well as our own students, could conduct research in primary and secondary sources. In the spring of 2005, that dream was realized with the establishment of the Sala and Aron Samueli Holocaust Memorial Library on the fourth floor of our university's new library building.[4] The library includes a permanent exhibit that introduces visitors to the themes and chronology of the Holocaust. Artifacts—some on loan from individuals and museums, many others donated—range from letters returned to the sender marked "address unknown" to a shoe worn by a child murdered in Majdanek. They bring home to students the vitality of Jewish culture before the Holocaust, the destruction of individual lives and of so much promise, and the courageous actions of those who chose rescue and resistance in all their forms. The library includes space for approximately five thousand volumes, and our goal is to develop a small but excellent reference library, with an emphasis on survivor memoirs. Two endowments for collection development have been established and will, in time, provide annual funding for books, journals, and other materials. Thanks to the 1939 Club, we have some sixty DVDs of interviews conducted during the 1980s at UCLA with Holocaust survivors. A recent gift has enabled us to partner with a distinguished photographer and with the 1939 Club in creating a permanent exhibit of photographic portraits and synopses of memoirs from one hundred Holocaust witnesses, most of whom are members of the 1939 Club. Students in our Holocaust courses are also partners in this project, working in teams to research and edit the survivors' accounts. They find the project challenging and rewarding as they become active contributors to remembrance and witness.

The response to our programs from the Orange County community has been quite astounding. Between three hundred fifty and one thousand people—Jews and non-Jews, witnesses to the Holocaust, teachers, university and school students, and interested people from throughout the community—attend the lecture series. Seventy-five middle and high schools from throughout southern California, private and public, entered the 2005 art and writing contest, with some three thousand students participating. The contest has flourished in large part because of the support of both the Orange County Department of Education and the Roman Catholic Diocese of Orange. Teachers regularly contact our Center for Holocaust Education to ask for information about the Holocaust and names of possible speakers. A university once viewed as uninterested in the Holocaust, in a county all too often equated with Holocaust denial, is now regarded as an institution actively committed to remembrance and witness.

THE DEFINING PHILOSOPHY: WE MUST ALL STAND

Our efforts in Holocaust education have been guided by the belief that while the Holocaust overwhelmingly targeted Jews, it is not a "Jewish issue." It is an issue for humanity. If the responsibility for remembrance and witness is left with the Jewish community alone, the wider meaning of these events is not being grasped. Thus our lecture series focus on themes that not only are central to the Holocaust but also challenge us to reflection and action today, themes such as "Conscience and Community: Choices of Courage" and "Moments of Decision: Perpetrators, Witnesses, Rescuers." Recently the lecture series has included speakers on the genocides in Rwanda and Darfur. Students come to understand that they cannot study the Holocaust, on the one hand, and, on the other, remain disengaged from events in the world around them. Not to read a newspaper, not to be aware of and connected to events in the world today, is to follow in the footsteps of those who chose not to know during the time of the Holocaust. I think the winning poem in the middle school division of our 2001 writing contest summarizes very well this bridging of past and present:

> When it seems everyone is sitting still for cruelty and hatred,
> I will stand.
> Against violence, such as Columbine, and tyranny such as Hitler,
> I will stand.
> When it seems that ignorance and prejudice are holding us down,
> I will stand.
> When we ignore each other's basic needs for compassion,
> I will stand.
> When I walk into school,
> I tell violence it has not won.
> When I learn and share the knowledge,
> I tell ignorance to go away.
> When I celebrate the differences between human beings,
> I tell prejudice to fade.
> For our world, our lives, and our future,
> We must all stand.[5]

IDEAS AND APPLICATIONS

Are there lessons here for others seeking to initiate and expand Holocaust programs? What have been the essential factors in our success? Certainly geography has been a big help. Southern California offers a multitude of resources, from the Museum of Tolerance to the presence of a large Holocaust survivor community in Orange County, Long Beach, and, of course, Los Angeles. Airports are close and convenient, and the climate is always a positive factor in drawing speakers. Thanks to university support and generous donors, we now have the resources to bring to the campus well-known speakers whose presence continues to draw attention to the program.

Significant challenges remain. The greatest of these is to establish a solid endowment for all aspects of our program, from library collection to lecture series to art and writing contests. Our growing program needs more faculty and staff. The Center for Holocaust Education remains small, with one full-time and one part-time staff person in addition to myself, although we are fortunate to have wonderful volunteers—students, faculty, and staff from the university as well as community members. Building connections with local-area schools from year to year continues to be a time-consuming and labor-intensive effort. In order to keep the connections strong, we need to do more year-round programming specifically directed to teachers. Fundraising remains essential and can be daunting at times. Now that we have a dedicated space, we must bring it to life, with events such as book readings and informal discussions, and we need to be able to keep the library open more hours to encourage research.

We also hope to increase the number of students enrolling in our minor and to consider the possibility of developing a major. We need to strengthen the connection between the minor and other departments and disciplines of the university, including peace studies, political science, and film. While continuing to focus centrally on the Holocaust, our courses and lectures need to include more study of subsequent acts of genocide and contemporary challenges to human rights. We also continue to work with student government and other groups to build co-curricular connections so that students have the opportunity to translate knowledge into civic action. It would be a terrible mistake for the minor in Holocaust history to become an isolated segment of the curriculum. And, although this reality is a painful one to consider, our curriculum must also take into account the fact that within a very few decades there will be no survivors left to tell our students about their experiences. That fact underlines the urgent need to make survivor testimony a vital part of our current curriculum as we seek to prepare students who can bear witness to subsequent generations. Giving students a chance to talk informally with survivors, enabling students to engage in more formal interviews with survivors, arranging for students to work in groups with a survivor to compile an oral history—these are all vital activities.

Partnerships, both internal and external, are crucial to building a successful program. Our annual Holocaust art and writing contest would never have become a reality without the extraordinary commitment and innovative ideas of a faculty member in the School of Education. We have been fortunate to involve many teachers as partners, to gain the active support of the survivor community, and to develop excellent working relationships with such organizations as the Facing History and Ourselves National Foundation, the Anti-Defamation League, and the United States Holocaust Memorial Museum, which held its second annual Southern California Teacher Forum on our campus in spring 2002. Early on, we established an advisory board of local community leaders whose perspectives, expertise, and knowledge have been invaluable, and who have further strengthened our connection to our community.

Our partnership with local-area teachers and schools is especially meaningful. Recently we were able to bring to campus students from two local high schools so they could hear Sobibor survivor Thomas Blatt speak. After the event, two teachers shared their reflections on this event and what it meant to their students, many of whom are recent immigrants or children of immigrants:

> This experience provoked deep and empathetic thought in our students. . . . As teachers, we grew excited by the many moments in Thomas Blatt's testimony when we felt our students would feel a special connection to the speaker and the content. . . . The preface to [his] lecture, [when he asked] the audience to excuse his heavy accent, is one such example. . . . We knew our students, many [of whom] similarly speak in accented English, would be able to relate. Another is when Thomas Blatt spoke of crossing perilous borders and the use of guides. Our students made personal connections to Blatt's plight, relating experiences with "coyotes" to his experience with his guide. . . . Many of our students have also crossed borders, facing humiliation and even risking their lives in many cases, to be where they are today.[6]

Such a learning encounter not only teaches students about the Holocaust, it also empowers them to value their own experience and to see the connections that bridge religious, social, and ethnic differences. It inspires them to remember that each person can make a difference, as the stories of the villagers of Le Chambon in France, of Raoul Wallenberg in Hungary, and of Mordechai Anieliewicz and Irene Gut Opdyke in Poland all testify. It teaches them that silence and apathy in the face of injustice have terrible consequences, and that evil will not triumph when we affirm our common humanity and the value of every human being. At Chapman University, we are teaching new generations—our students and those from schools throughout southern California—who will carry on the survivors' witness, and who will proudly say that they represent the true spirit of Orange County.

NOTES

1. See http://www.adl.org/holocaust/ihr.asp (accessed Feb. 20, 2006).

2. The Schwartz Holocaust Lecture series was established in 1999. The 1939 Club Lecture Series was established in the fall of 2000. The 1939 Club's Leopold Page Memorial Righteous Rescuers Lecture Series began in the fall of 2001, thanks to a five-year grant from the Righteous Persons Foundation.

3. From 2001 to 2005, the Kenneth and Laura Honig Foundation supported our annual observance of Holocaust Remembrance Day. Beginning in April 2005, a generous grant from the Lodzer Organization has made this occasion possible.

4. A major gift from the Samueli Foundation established the library, which was dedicated by Elie Wiesel in April 2005.

5. Erin Poole, "I Will Stand," second annual Holocaust Writing Contest, sponsored by Chapman University and the 1939 Club, including Shoah survivors of Orange County and Long Beach, California.

6. Letter to the author from Debra Russell and Erica Vicario, teachers at Century High School, Santa Ana, California, Nov. 26, 2002.

16

The Importance of Teaching
the Holocaust in Community Colleges

Democratizing the Study of the Holocaust

MYRNA GOLDENBERG

In 1946, President Harry S. Truman issued a report that established community college education as a right for every American. He set into motion a system that facilitated upward mobility for all U.S. residents. His goal—to have every resident in the nation live within commuting distance of postsecondary education—may not have been fully realized, but his action did enable reasonable access to some college education for nearly everyone.[1] Truman led the way for the community college to be, conceivably, the most democratic institution of higher education in the nation, if not on the entire continent. Its open-enrollment policy has leveled differences and provided unprecedented opportunities, especially for those for whom a college education would have been unattainable because it would have been unaffordable.[2] The effect of this policy, which is to provide broad access to virtually everyone, is one of several reasons why the Holocaust should be taught in community colleges.

Before we discuss why it is important to teach about the Holocaust in community college, we need to understand and acknowledge why it is an important subject. The Holocaust was a disruption of civilization. It was not an aberration but rather the result of various complex elements that led to a major genocide in what was, at the time, arguably the most cultured country in the Western world, maybe even in the whole world. It happened in full view of that country's citizens and in full view of the

citizens of other countries. Much of the world witnessed a singular political, spiritual, ethical, physical, and cultural catastrophe and—because
of fear, indifference, or complicity—stood by and watched a government
institutionalize and thereby sanction the murder of a segment of its population (that is, people who were labeled as "Other"). Mass murder, even
genocide, was not new in the 1930s. What was new was its codification
into law and its visibility. Hitler's speeches, writings, and actions were
accessible to anyone who wanted to know.

Moreover, while genocides have occurred since the Holocaust, they
should never happen again—and, clearly, they should never happen as
a result of inaction on the part of an indifferent or complicit nation or
group of nations. We know that even education does not guarantee that
genocide won't happen again. After all, almost all the major perpetrators, and particularly those who sat around the table at the Wannsee
Conference, had advanced academic degrees, and still they agreed to
implement the Final Solution. At the same time, however, we also believe
that education and a sharp awareness of the conditions that allowed this
genocide and, by extension, other mass murders and genocides is perhaps our only safeguard. We must try to make a difference: we cannot
not teach about it.

Given that academics generally agree that the Holocaust is an important subject in its own right, we can also agree that it is an important
subject in the disciplines of American and European history, twentieth-
century and contemporary literature, ethics and philosophy, sociology,
psychology (particularly social psychology and the subject of victimization), film studies, political science, and art history, all of which are fields
in which courses are normally offered in community colleges that include
programs for transferring academic credit to four-year institutions of
higher education. Demographically, pedagogically, and morally speaking, courses on the Holocaust should be responsibly offered in every community college. I say "responsibly" as a way of alluding to the qualifications
of the faculty member who teaches the subject, and "morally" because
the Holocaust and other genocides result from complicated choices made
by individuals and by local and global communities. That is, genocides
don't just happen. They require people's deliberate action and inaction,
leaders and followers whose decisions may or may not be informed. The

community college movement is an activist movement. It is committed to educating vast numbers of people, encouraging students to change their own destiny, and empowering them to become engaged in and responsible for their own future and the future of their communities. It is reasonable, and probably idealistic, to assume that students who are informed about genocide will be motivated to become activists in the prevention of genocide. It is reasonable because there is no alternative.

The numbers, too, support the case for teaching the Holocaust in community colleges. Currently there are 1,171 community colleges in the United States, of which 992 are public. Total enrollment in community colleges is 10.4 million; more than half of the students (5.4 million) are enrolled for academic credit. These 10+ million students comprise 44 percent of all U.S. undergraduates, or 45 percent of first-time college freshmen. Of the total number of African American undergraduates in the United States, 46 percent are enrolled in community colleges. There are parallel statistics for other minorities: 55 percent of all Hispanic college students are at community colleges, as are 46 percent of Asian students and 55 percent of Native American students.[3]

The point, of course, is that close to half of all college students in this country attend community colleges. Community colleges comprise more than one-fourth of the 4,070 accredited degree-granting institutions in the United States, and students seeking degrees from community colleges make up about one-third of all matriculating undergraduates in this nation.

In some ways, these impressive statistics constitute a mandate for Holocaust education. Obviously, community college faculty teach a great number of students from a variety of economic, cultural, and political backgrounds. About one-half of all minority college students attend community colleges. Indeed, if we are looking for ways to teach vast numbers of students about the Holocaust, we must turn to community colleges because that's where so many of the students are. Those of us who feel compelled to teach this subject know intuitively that our students will be changed by Holocaust courses, even though there are no hard data to support that intuition. We know from anecdotal research and personal experience that our Holocaust courses help our students become acutely aware of the historical, sociological, political, and economic circumstances that can lead to genocide or, at the very least, informed about the kinds of political and social environments in which tyrants gain both popularity and control. Moreover, students can and do learn that genocides may happen when people—bystanders and others—relinquish the civic and moral responsibility to make a difference. We've all heard our students tell us at the end of our courses that Holocaust education should be required of every student at the colleges where we teach. Our students do learn the effects of indifference.

Let me cite the discipline of nursing as a case in point. There are currently 2.7 million persons in the United States who are licensed to practice nursing. About 40 percent of these 2.7 million licensed nurses were trained in community colleges. In fact, 65 percent of all new health care workers in the United States currently get their training from community colleges. Nurses and other health care workers were very involved in T4, the euthanasia program in Nazi Germany. When interrogated, these professionals, like almost all the other perpetrators, pleaded "not guilty" on the grounds that they were just following orders.[4] In interviews twenty years after the Holocaust, Susan Benedict found that half said that they "still didn't see anything wrong"[5] with what they had done, that they were "just following orders";[6] "It was legal . . . we were alleviating the suffering."[7] In large measure, nurses' training in Germany focused on obedience to authority and on racial hygiene—in this case, a deadly combination. Benedict explains that people who were different were devalued while "obedience was emphasized." Thus, when the nurses were ordered to kill, they did so believing that those they killed were people who were not worthy to live.[8] Nevertheless, while it would have been unthinkable to question orders to kill, it would not have been at all out of the ordinary to recuse oneself in these circumstances. We know from the work of Christopher Browning and others that withdrawing from this duty entailed virtually no substantive repercussions.[9] To be sure, peer pressure may have influenced the decision to participate; but peer pressure is a weak excuse for immoral behavior in the face of training that begins with the injunction "First, do no harm." Moreover, Benedict reminds us, "there is no case yet identified where a nurse was punished for refusing although it was uncommon to do so."[10] Indeed, she continues, nursing curricula in the Germany of 1939 had no content in ethics, nor do most undergraduate and graduate nursing curricula today offer separate courses in ethics. Some Ph.D. nursing programs do, but only if the faculty members involved are also actively involved in Holocaust or genocide studies. Benedict found that no major undergraduate nursing texts refer to the Holocaust at all, although there are oblique references to it in mentions of the Nuremberg Code as the trigger for "informed consent." Clearly, a course in nursing ethics should be one of the requirements for a nursing degree, and these ethics courses should uniformly include case studies stemming from Nazi Germany. Such case studies would also have applications to assisted suicide and euthanasia, controversial topics in the late twentieth and early twenty-first centuries. I don't suggest that the inclusion of ethics in health care workers' training in 1930s Germany would have prevented the T4 program, but I do suggest that some nurses, if they had been required as students to discuss the moral implications of euthanasia, might have had reason to pause before they murdered their patients, particularly since the victims of the T4 program were not terminally ill or even sick at all. As we community college faculty sit on curriculum committees in our respective colleges, might we not lobby for such courses, especially since many nursing students do not go on to four-year programs? And, of course, most nurses don't enter doctoral programs.

This discussion of nursing courses leads me to other discipline-related matters. For the most part, the current generation of American college students—and probably the preceding generation as well—is "history challenged." We know that most of our students are woefully ignorant about American history as well as world history. The sooner they become comfortable with the idea of history, as well as with the subject itself, the sooner they will be able to contextualize the humanities and the social sciences, which will undoubtedly continue to comprise a healthy component of the associate and bachelor's degrees. Holocaust study begins with history, no matter where a particular Holocaust course is situated in the departmentalized academic landscape. Most community colleges that require a core of courses in general education include courses in American history or Western civilization in that core. Further, the more that undergraduate courses are infused with historical data and interpretation, the more familiar with history our students will become. In courses on modern history, study of the Holocaust is inescapable—or should be. However, whether our students learn about the Holocaust obliquely through their literature, film, philosophy, sociology, or psychology courses, or more directly through general history courses, or most directly through courses on the Holocaust, they will become exposed to it. They will, we hope, make wiser, more humane choices for themselves and their communities.

Most specifically, the bread-and-butter course of just about every community college is English composition. Over twenty-five years ago, when I chaired my college's English department, we hit a benchmark of 10,000 students enrolled in EN 101 in one academic year. Nationwide, we now have a different student population, which demands sophisticated redirection into appropriate courses that are more delineated, such as English for speakers of other languages (ESOL) and developmental writing. Although these courses may have flattened the number of enrollments in EN 101, it is safe to say that many more students than ever before are taking some form of composition course. A composition course typically includes units or modules on the use and abuse of language, on propaganda, on persuasive writing, and on connotation. These topics are natural contexts for teaching about Nazi "doublespeak" and euphemism. We can begin with the Nuremberg Laws, move on to Eichmann's *Wannsee Protocol,* and then teach techniques for analyzing Hitler's or Himmler's or Goebbels's speeches. In terms of words having an impact on the population, these texts have few if any rivals. They engage students' critical-thinking skills, the development of which is one of the latest initiatives in all sectors of education. And these skills are at least as relevant today as they were in the 1930s. Reading is another course that is becoming a standard offering in community colleges. Here, too, there are numerous Holocaust-related texts from which to choose. Mid-level and advanced-level classes might explore Bernhard Schlink's *The Reader.* Although it is a historically unlikely narrative, since Germany at the time in which it is set had the highest literacy rate in the world, it is a story that confronts moral choices and is a book that probably no one is going to forget. It seems obvious to me that Holocaust-inspired or Holocaust-related memoirs, poetry, plays, and fiction can be readily and appropriately taught in contemporary literature courses.

Community colleges are far less rigid than four-year colleges about the separation of departments and disciplines, a fact that invites team teaching and linked or paired courses. The study of the Holocaust lends itself to such enriched teaching and learning across boundaries. With few exceptions, the college instructor teaching a Holocaust course is likely to be the sole such scholar in his or her field at that college, but team teaching alleviates this kind of isolation. It is helpful to develop linked courses with faculty members who have some knowledge of the Holocaust by dint of their expertise in their fields (for example, faculty in European history or in the German department). Thus a course on Holocaust history can be linked naturally with one on contemporary literature or film, and a course on Holocaust literature can be linked smoothly with a composition course or a course on ethics.

Nationwide there is a pronounced trend, supported by state and federal funds, to develop teacher-preparation programs at community colleges and to build 2 + 2 + 2 articulation agreements; that is, from high school through the associate degree and on to the bachelor's degree, young men and women are being trained to teach. For the last twenty years, however, U.S. education majors have learned much more about how to teach than about what to teach, and so American students are relatively ignorant of general knowledge. It is painfully clear that our colleges of education have become proficient in using technology to deliver instruction, but course content has apparently been sacrificed in favor of methods courses. (There is only so much we can cram into an education.) The Robert C. Byrd Honors Scholarship Program, which, among other activities, awards grants to improve the teaching of American history, is testament to the vagueness and superficiality of history instruction. I can vouch for that. I was involved in a million-dollar Byrd grant disseminated by the U.S. Department of Education to teach elementary school teachers enough history so that they could teach their own students enough history for them to pass the fourth- and fifth-grade state-mandated history tests. (The county in which I live enjoys an excellent reputation for progressiveness and is known for its exceptionally high education level, yet only one-quarter of the county's fourth- and fifth-grade teachers took any college-level history course.) I also served as the evaluator for another grant, this one intended to infuse education courses with the humanities at fourteen community colleges. In this case, I restrained myself from slipping Holocaust history and literature into the reading material because I also recognize that a little knowledge is a dangerous thing. But the opportunity to do so is there. With so many education majors now beginning their postsecondary studies at community colleges, we can raise the level of general knowledge and help these future teachers and their students understand the implications of long-held cultural and political hatreds and their connections to genocide. Certainly, we can make them aware that a reading of Anne Frank's diary only begins to introduce the subject of the Holocaust. Our teachers at every level need to recognize and respect the complexity of the subject.

I harbor the notion that integrating Holocaust history and literature into general education courses at our community colleges is more important than offering separate courses on the topic. Inclusion of Holocaust-related content in the general education courses constitutes de facto recognition of its importance and its influence in the broad body of knowledge that we teach. However, a Holocaust course that enrolls many students is also quite likely to attract attention and move other faculty toward learning enough about the topic to incorporate Holocaust-related materials into their own work, especially if those of us who teach about the Holocaust offer ourselves as guest lecturers in their classes. As a result of my making myself available, one of my colleagues in philosophy now includes a unit on Wiesel's *Night;* another colleague who teaches a course on women's studies and film includes *Aimée and Jaguar, The Night Porter,* and discussions about Leni Riefenstahl. She made it a point to immerse herself in the field of Holocaust films, and the impact is evident.

My focus on general education courses provides the opportunity to raise serious, consequential issues at the beginning of students' academic careers—issues that will influence their interpretations of past and current information. It is also important to note that Holocaust courses, by their very nature, provide grounding in ethical decisions that we all have to make. They may also help to shape students' understanding of their other subjects.

Particularly because popular culture bombards people between the ages of eighteen and forty-nine with images of the Holocaust (the television and film industries cater to this age group, and the average community

college student is twenty-nine years old), we have an obligation to contextualize and correct what is "out there." Whether it's the History
Channel, *Schindler's List, Life Is Beautiful, The Producers, Sophie's Choice,*
or *The Pianist,* all of which are engaging and popular, we will need to
teach them how to "read" a film rooted in historical reality. Ultimately,
these blockbuster movies represent "teachable moments." At the least,
they are provocative films that provoke emotions and questions. At their
best, they hone students' critical-thinking/viewing skills.[11]

For me, one of the most compelling reasons to teach Holocaust literature at my college was the diversity of our students—and that diversity is mirrored in virtually all community colleges, more so than in
four-year colleges and universities. As I stated earlier, about half of community college students nationwide belong to racial and ethnic minority groups, and many community colleges have even higher minority
enrollments. For the past ten years, there have been as many Asian,
Hispanic, and Eastern European students enrolled in my courses as there
were American-born Caucasian students. Almost half of my students who
belong to racial or ethnic minorities escaped from countries that had mass
murder in their recent pasts. Many of these students have witnessed the
horrors of famine, torture, random and targeted killing, disappearances,
and the like. They read *Night* and Art Spiegelman's *Maus* and feel Elie's
and Vladek's pain—and their own. Sometimes they stare in amazement
at the naive American students who express incredulity at the fact of
tyranny or state-supported violence. These minority students verify the
reality and impact of political repression and killing. They are good teachers for their classmates and are wise beyond their years. They are also a
bit surprised by the history of the Holocaust. Asians have not studied
the Holocaust in their home countries. Eastern European students have
learned a version of the Shoah that we in the West don't recognize. Students in both groups are like sponges, but they challenge the texts and
me. And we all learn.

It is this mix or diversity of students, coupled with our passion for
the subject, that keeps us persistent. "How Can We Not Teach the Holocaust?" was the title of a back-page commentary in an issue of the
Chronicle of Higher Education that was published about fifteen years ago.
While the Holocaust is, as Hubert Locke writes in his preface to the present

volume, "a topic . . . laden with the malevolent . . . subject matter that does not elevate but depresses, a history that is not inspiring but rather is filled with accounts of the worst of which the human species is capable," it is also a topic that demands to be taught because it is a critically important topic, particularly in the face of the relentless parade of genocides throughout the second half of the twentieth century and into the twenty-first.

Finally, I feel it necessary to acknowledge that Holocaust courses are difficult to teach because the topic provokes not only intellectual but also emotional responses. Anyone who has taught these courses has had to respond to students' doubts and anxieties about their own potential for violence and evil and has had to help some students, particularly those of German ancestry, address a perceived sense of guilt. Indeed, I prefer to teach Holocaust courses in the spring semester because we begin to learn in the winter and complete the course in the spring—when I reintroduce the subject of moral choices, rescuers, and resisters. We cannot impose a "happy ending" on such courses, but we can lead students to become involved in their communities and commit themselves to social activism. In this way, we can also reinforce the idea that it is necessary for them to choose to take responsibility for their society. And, frankly, it is less stressful for me as the instructor to teach the course in the spring semester because I identify spring with hopefulness and renewal.

I believe, as most Holocaust teachers must also believe, that each of us is morally and ethically obliged to continue the work of *tikkun olam,* repair of the world. Therefore, we must do no less than inspire our students to do the same and to make a difference.

NOTES

1. President Harry Truman established a commission in 1946 to "reexamine our system of higher education in terms of its objectives, methods, and facilities, and in the light of the social role it has to play." The commission issued the *Report of the President's Commission on Higher Education for American Democracy* in six volumes from December 1947 through February 1948. Known

as the Truman Commission Report, it declared, "The time has come to make education through the fourteenth grade available in the same way that high school education is available"; see John S. Brubacher and Willis Rudy, *Higher Education in Transition: A History of American Colleges and Universities, 1636–1976* (New York: Harper and Row, 1976), 234, 257–58.

2. Even now, however, despite these advances, populations underserved by institutions of higher education usually don't aspire to professional levels of career achievement, because the goal of attaining the required credential (the baccalaureate degree) is unrealistic.

3. Telephone conversation with Kent Phillippe, Research Unit, American Association of Community Colleges (AACC), Washington, D.C., Feb. 23, 2004. All the statistics about community colleges quoted in this chapter were provided and confirmed by the AACC in conversations with Kent Phillippe and Cynthia Vervena. See also http://www.aacc.nche.edu (accessed Feb. 16, 2006).

4. Susan Benedict, "Caring While Killing: Nursing in the Euthanasia Movement," in Elizabeth R. Baer and Myrna Goldenberg, eds., *Experience and Expression: Women, the Nazis, and the Holocaust* (Detroit: Wayne State University Press, 2003), 95–110; Mary D. Lagerwey, "The Nurses' Trial at Hadamar and the Ethical Implications of Health Care Values," in Elizabeth R. Baer and Myrna Goldenberg, eds., *Experience and Expression: Women, the Nazis, and the Holocaust* (Detroit: Wayne State University Press, 2003), 111–26.

5. Benedict, "Caring While Killing," 106.

6. Ibid., 104.

7. Ibid., 107.

8. Ibid., 104.

9. Christopher Browning, *Ordinary Men: Reserve Police Battalion 101 and the Final Solution in Poland* (New York: HarperCollins, 1992).

10. Benedict, "Caring While Killing," 105.

11. The significance of films as propaganda, and hence the need to teach students to read films, cannot be overestimated. Indeed, Veit Harlan, the director of *Jud Suess,* was tried for war crimes on the grounds that his film techniques, including the positioning of images, "affirm the true . . . anti-Semitic voice of the director"; see Judith Doneson, "The Use of Film in Teaching About the Holocaust," in Gideon Shimoni, ed., *The Holocaust in University Teaching* (New York: Pergamon Press, 1991), 17.

17

Teaching about the Holocaust
in the Setting of Museums and Memorials

STEPHEN D. SMITH

There is a link between sites where specific acts of history occurred and sites such as museums where those acts of history are represented. But they are not identical. This chapter explores the experience of visiting Holocaust museums as a learning experience. It explores how perceptions are influenced, learning is engaged, and personal responses are developed in relation to such museums. It looks at the role of museums at historical sites and museums that are geographically displaced, since they raise slightly different issues. It also attempts to explore the complexities of teaching about historical events through memorials and museums, the types of narrative they expound, the ideology that infuses them, and the contexts in which they exist. It asks whether such museums have an educational role and how their outcomes might be evaluated.

VISITING HISTORICAL SITES

Whatever the destination, places can play an important role in shaping our understanding of events and their consequences. Such sites, which may be scenes of destruction, heroism, martyrdom, or legend, are artifacts in their own right. Like any other artifacts, they have specific features to be observed, points to be argued over, and stories to be told about them. These particular artifacts place history in three dimensions. The experiences of topography, geography, and physical structures augment other forms of documentary analysis, narrative history, and pictorial representation. With a drive through the Somme Valley, a walk around Wounded Knee, or a stroll along the beaches of the Normandy landings, history takes on topographical features not perceptible in its two-dimensional representations. At such sites, there is not only the actual space in which history occurred but also some of the ambience that may have accompanied it— sounds, smells, colors, horizons, and other physical, sensory features.

In such spaces, the visitor is placed within a partial reality of the events. The scenery that made up the theater in which the events occurred assists the imagination. There is also the sense of having "been there." That is, a substitution takes place in which the visitor in some way sees himself or herself as bound up more personally with the history because he or she has trod the actual ground where events took place. There is also a realigning of that history in relation to the space, and what the space and its physical features say about it. On my own first visit to Auschwitz-Birkenau, I was surprised by how large the area of the camp was, even though I could have recited its dimensions from my knowledge of the camp before I arrived there. I was also surprised to discover how physically small the area of the Belzec extermination camp was, even though I had previously seen sketch plans of it. These two observations, insignificant as they are, were extremely important for re-envisioning, in my own imagination, the concentration camp system and the way in which it worked physically at the time. The perception I have of the two sites is largely conditioned by my having actually been there, even though my knowledge is built largely on documentary sources.

The anthropologist Jonathan Webber ran a five-day program at the Auschwitz complex in which graduate students spent one day observing such details as the development of the so-called *Rampe,* the fence posts surrounding the camp, the brick construction of the gate tower of the entrance to Birkenau, and the railway lines that make up the spur into the camp. This list of details seems unusually trivial in light of what happened there. They seem to have little to do with the victims, their experiences there, and the unthinkable consequences. But through an investigation of these specifics, students became better informed about the camp's construction as well as about the philosophy, finances, and planning of the system that lay behind it. At the end of the exercise, they also knew a great deal more about the victims and the system that they had endured. Space, place, and three-dimensional objects informed this exercise in a manner that has to be physically explored and deduced in order for the site's history of human tragedy to be more fully understood.

Thus being there gives both texture and physical dimension to factual narrative. But another aspect of visiting historical sites is that of emotional experience. Traveling from one context, in which one's world is a known quantity, into another, which lies outside one's own personal experience, itself creates transition and informs the visitor. A visit to a site of human suffering should in some way extend beyond a factual explanation of what is purely functionary. Part of the experience is to grapple with understanding the meaning or meaninglessness of that suffering for its victims. Being there should in some manner encompass the identity of the suffering individual, beyond the cerebral exercise of deconstructing the event of his or her suffering.

The danger is that visiting a place and experiencing its physical features, visualizing the human suffering that occurred there, and formulating a personal response to it will not necessarily mean that the visitor knows a great deal more at the end of the visit. In fact, the experience may only serve to underscore misperceptions, calcify myths, and reinforce held stereotypes. Auschwitz has become a symbol of Nazi persecution. But it is a different symbol for different people for different reasons. Therefore, more than one Auschwitz exists in the minds of people before they arrive at the site. This is as true for young schoolchildren as it is for adults. In what way, then, does a visit to Auschwitz challenge, enhance, expand, and inform those varied perceptions? All visitors may well be moved, even overwhelmed by their experience, but does the act of visiting do any more than superficially confirm what they already think they know? With the fall of the Communist bloc, Holocaust sites are increasingly visited. The "dark tourism" visit to a site depicting or commemorating gruesome human history is a phenomenon that is now well documented. Holocaust sites may well be "dark tourism" destinations, but it appears that visits to former concentration and death camps do have an interesting dynamic, worthy of observation, since these sites have a particular role in personal history and educational experiences.

Survivors and the children of survivors go to such sites for reasons of personal history. Jewish people who are not survivors travel to them because of the correctly perceived indirect link to their own past. Young Israelis visit them because their elders have identified a message there for them about self-determination and survival. Teachers visit such sites because they wish to extend their own knowledge and experience in order to convey it more effectively to their pupils. There is also a variety of other groups of people who visit such sites under the auspices of schools, associations, and interest groups. In the majority of cases, then, people appear to travel to these sites with a purpose in mind, be it personal, educational, or ideological. And among them are the casual visitors, who are there only because they think the site might be "interesting."

The question is, to what extent do such sites, and their content, adequately fulfill their role as educational destinations? What is the visitor expected to encounter, experience, and conclude? That is, what is the visitor there to learn from the experience? Can such experiences and their associated learning be predetermined? Should they be? There are also questions regarding whether such sites exist as places of learning per se. If thousands, perhaps hundreds of thousands, of people were murdered at a site and have their final resting place there, is that site not principally a cemetery? Even if it is not a cemetery in the conventional sense, should it not simply stand as a memorial to those who died there? Is not the purpose of visiting a memorial site to pay one's respects to those commemorated there rather than to receive historical commentary about the life and times of the site's former existence? The concern frequently expressed about "tourism," which includes the educational visits attracted by sites such as Auschwitz, is that symbolic meaning and historical representations have apparently supplanted respect for and knowledge about the victims themselves. One does not leave the Auschwitz museum complex with a strong sense that visitors are encouraged to reflect on *who* was murdered there rather than on how they were murdered.

Such sites do increasingly have their own education departments, aimed at supporting young people who visit them and explore their history as part of a formal education. The program developed for students tends largely to revolve around the specific history of the site, its development, its routines, the number of deaths that occurred there, its hierarchy, its mechanics, and its liberation. Such a program, which often includes additional lectures, films, and presentations as well as specially constructed tours, provides students with a far greater range of resources than would normally be available to casual visitors. However, the underlying questions concern its rationale: What is the aim of teaching at such a site? Is it to describe what happened there, or why it came into being? How should the specific history of that particular site be related to the broader canvas of the Holocaust experience? What should be the balance between providing information and encouraging students to respond more personally? What outcomes do the members of the pedagogical team expect? How do they know if they have achieved them?

HOLOCAUST MEMORIAL MUSEUMS

The creation of Holocaust memorial museums outside Nazi-occupied territory, by contrast with the opening of historical sites for public visits, is a recent development. It has significant consequences for how the community of the principal victims of National Socialism, and the societies in which they now live, interpret the events. How and why have so many Holocaust museums emerged in places as far-flung as Los Angeles, Cape Town, Hiroshima, and Sydney? This is a complex question and one that is unique in museum history. There is, arguably, no other event depicted by so many dedicated museums that are displaced by geography and national contexts. The sprawling network of Holocaust memorial museums scattered around countries not formerly occupied by the Nazi regime is not entirely out of context, however. The displacement of the survivor community after the war, the well-established Jewish diaspora, the involvement of many countries in the Allied effort to overthrow Nazism, the growing literature (and hence market) for narratives relating to the Holocaust period—all these factors, among others, provide the cultural, political, and communal context in which such museums emerge. The question is, what are these museums there to accomplish?

Just as a historical site gives a physical context to events, one of the functions of a memorial museum is to give form to experience. What resulted from the Holocaust was a physical, cultural, anthropological, and memorial void in which only the essence of the events could be conveyed. The people who were its victims were destroyed; its survivors, scattered. It was therefore no longer possible for those who were its victims to mourn their losses at the sites where the events transpired. Nor were the territories in which the Holocaust took place the same territories where its survivors—and, most important, their families—were now living. To create physical objects was one way to transfer the memorial duty into the new territory of those who survived. This activity was carried out in part from a sense of obligation, as would ordinarily have occurred at an actual historical site; only this time, instead of focusing on a single event and a particular site, it commemorated as a single event the whole set of events that had gone to make up the Holocaust.

In addition to this memorial duty, there is also a strong sense of the Holocaust as a world event, which goes some way toward explaining why memorial *museums* emerged rather than just memorials. Along with the memorial features, the need to tell the story in order to be able to share it with a wider audience appears to be a fundamental principle. Thus memorial museums have pedagogy at the heart of their conceptualization. The logic here is straightforward. Those who know about or personally experienced the events of the Holocaust do not need to learn about the Holocaust in order to commemorate it effectively. For them, a memorial object would be sufficient representation to demonstrate the fulfillment of their duty. Because survivors either initiated or have an interest in many of the memorial museums that now exist, it is clear that they want their story to be told to others. Therefore, memorial museums exist to inform, and they are, by extension, inherently pedagogical, whatever the accompanying methodology.

Memorial museums have become, arguably, virtual or surrogate sites to which one can journey in order to experience something of the physical, emotional, and personal trauma of the events in a space dedicated to their memory. As in the historical sites, one is transported out of one's own environment and into one consumed by historical events, an environment in which spatial areas, visual representations, reconstructed environments, audiovisual presentations, and survivors' testimonies create a representational experience in public space.

The comparison with historical sites is important because, like visitors to historical sites, the visitor to a memorial museum is more interested in the experience than in details. Just as a visitor travels to a historical site to walk the landscape and feel the sense of inclusion in its past, visitors go to museums dedicated to the Holocaust because they wish to experience something about the events that surround it. The dilemma is that such museums are created to inform, but visitors visit in order to experience. Therefore, both the methodology and the scope of the pedagogy need to provide an educational experience instead of attempting to teach Holocaust studies in depth in the space of a three-hour visit.

Conversely, there is danger in the temptation to make the visit nothing more than an experience—that is, inadvertently to make its effects and impact as temporary as the duration of the visit itself. The fundamental question is, what does a memorial museum have to do in order to ensure that visitors have a memorable and engaging visit, the effects of which will last and become increasingly tangible once they have left? Curators and particularly museum educators need to ask what the measure of success is. Is it the number of visitors? The number of visitors who learn something? The number of visitors who learn something and retain it? The number of visitors who do something with what they have learned and retained? Even if any of these outcomes were being measured, and apart from the value of an entirely quantitative process of counting visitors, how could an assessment of outcomes assist educational practice? Would that information be compared with research in similar institutions, to evaluate the comparative effectiveness of programs and enhance good practice? The question is, do memorial museums really understand the educational standards to which they should aspire?

This question raises another, more fundamental one about what memorial museums aim to achieve. Because of the self-evident worthiness of such sites' existence, there is an assumption that their aims are equally worthy in terms of their delivery. However, nuances of interpretation or, in some cases, the blatant infusion of ideology into the environment of the museum may actually close off the experience rather than open up a new learning process. Sometimes both the text and the subtext of the learning experience are dominated by conclusions rather than incoherence, perpetrators rather than victims, the mechanics of death rather than the struggle to survive, the political subjugation of a closed text rather than unencumbered ideas. The result is an unintentionally didactic pedagogy rather than the facilitation of a more deductive, open, personal inquiry for visitors.

The creation of memorial museums has doubtless made more material about the Holocaust accessible to more people than ever before. Parallel to the development of these institutions has been the introduction of teaching about the Holocaust in schools, which may be another consequence of the same factors that led to the development of Holocaust museums. The presence of Holocaust education in schools has led in turn to greater interest in gaining access to museum resources that exist to enhance the learning experience of children, many of whom live in areas where teaching about the Holocaust is mandated. The problem, it appears, is that this large cohort of learners, who attend schools that generally have little time and few resources to devote to Holocaust education, receive only a superficial grounding in school. The schools then rely largely on the experience of the museum visit to provide the required educational experience. In isolation, such a visit is clearly insufficient, however inspiring it may be on the day it occurs. A visit to a Holocaust memorial museum must be one part of a wider educational experience in order to be able to make an effective contribution. That is, the memorial museum is no substitute for a program in Holocaust education. Thus the onus is on the teacher to create a meaningful program in conjunction with the museum. It seems, however, that the duty to encourage this practice lies with memorial museums themselves.

In teaching about the Holocaust today there is still too little knowledge of outcomes. There is an assumption that because the Holocaust is an important topic, its importance will be self-evident to the students who come to learn. However, research into the long-term effects of teaching and learning remains scant. Students may respond to a visit with meaningful comments in the visitors' book, moving poems, or inspiring essays, but how can one be certain that such a visit truly has an impact on what they know and who they are? Is there clarity in the field with respect to the kinds of perceptions being created, the level of knowledge being attained, and the degree of personal challenge being brought to students by the experience?

It seems that memorial museums need to expend greater resources on discovering more about the outcomes of visits. This research needs to begin by asking whether it is evident that students learn anything by visiting a museum, and it needs to clarify the nature of their learning. Museums need to understand more clearly the types of experience that have an impact on students' thinking. It may be that graphic museological representations have one impact, survivor testimony another, memorial representations another, and that all intermesh in different ways. It may be that an opportunity for discussion, personal reflection, thinking about consequences, and formulating questions has a greater impact on the student over time than does a visual representation. Research needs to be conducted into relative outcomes, on the basis of the types of programs in which students are engaged. What type of long-term effect is there if students merely visit a museum, with little support from their schools before or after? How do outcomes differ when students are in a more extended program? What types of themes inspire students to want to know more? What types of questions and challenges does one pose to students? At what age is it appropriate for students to be presented what topics, and at what depth?

Memorial museums also need to evaluate how they can best support and enhance the learning experience of teachers. This evaluation should form part of the museums' extension of their scope of influence into the schools. By offering services to schools, memorial museums will be making a commitment to the school community to support students in their learning experience. Therefore, there is an implied duty for museums to provide the resources to make that learning experience as fruitful as possible. The pedagogical team at the memorial museum needs to be familiar with the school curriculum, its opportunities, and its demands and to think carefully about how best to support teachers and students, using the resources available. It seems that too often there is unnecessary disconnection between memorial museums and their goals, on the one hand, and the targets of teachers, on the other. The more that teachers understand how a memorial museum's educational team can help them provide a valuable learning experience for their students, the more readily they will work to enhance the effectiveness of the museum's outreach to the schools.

Nevertheless, there are fundamental questions that the memorial museum has to ask in order to be able to deliver a coherent pedagogical program. The scope of the intended outcomes has to be clearly stated. Because a memorial museum is an entirely constructed representation, it is self-conscious about its identity. Someone decides where the museum will be built as well as what it will say, to what audience, on what basis, and with what intended set of outcomes. That is an inevitable part of the founding of such an entity. The museum's creation of a clear educational policy or rationale is a natural extension of its existence. One museum may draw the conclusion that it should teach the facts of Holocaust history in order to provide a historical grounding. Another may see its duty as having a more memorial character, and another may see its role as raising issues in today's society. Whatever the museum's rationale, its educational team needs to be explicit about the program's scope and clear about what is to be included and omitted. Such issues clearly also apply to historical sites, which are not so self-conscious in terms of their design and implementation, but which then, as a result, may miss the process of developing a clear rationale that they can relate to schools. Another potential pitfall for historical sites with education departments is that they can too easily develop the tendency to feel that they are there to contribute their "bit" of Holocaust history instead of supporting schools more broadly in teaching the subject.

It may be of some value here to cite my own experience in co-founding with my brother James, in 1995, the Beth Shalom Holocaust Centre in Nottinghamshire, England. The center, which I now direct, was established principally because there was no Holocaust memorial museum in the United Kingdom, and it seemed important that there should be a center of this kind. Although James and I are not Jewish, we felt that British society should confront the Holocaust. It seemed appropriate that people outside the Jewish community should attempt to convey the history of the Holocaust and to encourage others to remember the destruction of the Jews of Europe. The development of the center also coincided with teaching about the Holocaust being mandated in the national curriculum.

The Beth Shalom Holocaust Centre attempts to identify itself among the teaching fraternity as an institution engaged within the school system rather than loosely appended to it for the sake of convenience. That way, the center is not viewed as an interesting extracurricular destination for a visit but as an integral part of the curriculum. When students visit the center, they are not encouraged to feel that they are on a field trip but rather that they are visiting a place that is another setting for the work they have been doing in school and will continue to do upon their return. The materials they use during their visit are sent to the school in advance and are studied in school before and after the visit to the center. Part of their visit does involve work in the historical museum, but the center has also devised a program whereby most of the historical work needed to form the basis for their visit is accomplished in school before they arrive. This arrangement gives the students more time for reflection and workshops during their visit, and it avoids overloading the day of their visit with historical information. It is also clearly recognized that the better prepared the students are, the more they benefit from the experience.

During their visit to the Beth Shalom Centre, students are clearly told that they are not there to collect the information they need to answer their exam questions (although they are also encouraged to do that) but rather to formulate questions. They are encouraged to do so around three themes.

The first theme focuses on the role and identity of the people who formed the unfolding history. Who were they? Where did they come from? Why did they do what they did? How did they respond when it was done to them? What alternatives were there? Who might have helped mitigate the outcomes? The idea is to root the Holocaust within human history and encourage students to contextualize their learning with respect to the real lives of real people. The presence of survivor testimony in the exhibition, like the opportunity to spend time with a survivor at the center, sharpens this focus and provides important connections to actual consequences.

The second theme revolves around the type of history this was. Students are encouraged to ask questions about the nature of National Socialism. The attempt here is to provide a basis for understanding the Holocaust as an ordinary political event, but one with extraordinary consequences. As such, our hope is to demythologize the Holocaust as something outside the framework of the systems to which the students belong. If the Holocaust is underscored as a unique event without par-

allel, as an evil aberration, then students are distanced from its historical reality and from the possibility of its repetition in whatever form;
their ability to respond to its consequences with positive action is fore-
closed. But when the Holocaust is presented in the context of a history
that they know, and of people and systems they can understand, then
the possibility of another such event is made all the more real, and its
questions become more demanding.

The third theme is the consequences of the Holocaust, and we
attempt to stimulate discussion and help students formulate appropriate questions. The intention is for students to leave the center reflecting
on the difficulty of living with the legacy of genocide, on the loss of community, and on the pain of survival. We attempt to demonstrate to students the dilemmas that surround memorialization and the problem of
the lack of justice. We also seek to inspire some form of introspection,
to encourage students to engage in discussion about their own roles and
responsibilities. An inherent part of the experience is for students to spend
time in the memorial gardens so that personal reflection is understood
to be a part of the learning experience.

Most important, we recommend that the students' visit take place at
the beginning of their inquiry so that they can follow up with their own
questions and with further reading and study. By supporting students
and their teachers in school after their visit, and with further study later
in their learning, the Beth Shalom Holocaust Centre attempts to become
a part of their lives rather than just a day in their lives.

Historical sites and memorial museums have an important role to play
in developing and deploying Holocaust educational programs. They are
rich in resources and are able to provide a learning experience that has
the potential to stay with a younger visitor for many years. They have the
opportunity to develop the knowledge base of students and provide them
with personal challenges.

However, there are still serious deficiencies in the way in which some
of these institutions formulate their programs for students. There is an
assumption that students need do no more than visit in order to increase
their understanding of the context and consequences of the Holocaust.
Some presentations, particularly at the historical sites, are too mechan-

ical and leave students with no real insight into the human consequences of the Holocaust. Some museums rely too much on emotion, setting an impossible hurdle around which students cannot navigate without feeling overwhelmed or distanced.

In a broader sense, there is need for serious scholarly research into the long-term impact and effects of teaching about the Holocaust. If memorial museums are to play a role in the future, after the Holocaust has ceased to be contemporary history, then there must be a much clearer sense of how the resources available to historical sites and memorial museums can best be used in the service of meaningful long-term educational outcomes.

Dialogue at the Threshold

The Pastora Goldner Holocaust Symposium and the Work of Tikkun Olam

LEONARD GROB AND HENRY F. KNIGHT

Scholarly conferences typically provide academics with opportunities to present papers and to test ideas, sharing their scholarship with peers. They also provide moments of nurture and insight that grow out of the gatherings over meals or at coffee breaks in the interstices of these gatherings. Conversations begun over drinks overflow into hallways and are picked up, only to be suspended until the next coffee break. Or the conversation takes precedence as a session is skipped for colleagues to remain engaged with their dialogue until it ripens into intellectual fruition. The Pastora Goldner Holocaust Symposium, a biennial gathering of Holocaust scholars from seven countries, is unique in that it intentionally seeks to build its gatherings around liminal moments like these. Indeed, the Goldner Symposium began because of just such a serendipitous conversation.

THE SYMPOSIUM: A HISTORY

In 1995, Dr. Nicholas Baldwin, then director of Wroxton College, approached Dr. Leonard Grob of Fairleigh Dickinson University (FDU) and Dr. Henry Knight of the University of Tulsa with the idea of planning an internationally oriented conference on the Holocaust at Wroxton College in northern Oxfordshire, England. Baldwin's college, a British campus of FDU, was host to a biennial program for faculty of the University of Tulsa that was coordinated by Knight, a Holocaust scholar. Baldwin had recalled that Grob, director of a humanities core program at FDU, was also a scholar of the Holocaust. Aware of the common interest and friendship between his two colleagues, Baldwin suggested to his academic vice president that Grob and Knight consider collaborating on an international gathering of Holocaust scholars. When these two friends met to consider Baldwin's proposal, each was convinced that the Wroxton location and their common interests called for something special.

Grob was interested in academic work that was praxis-oriented. He wanted to make a difference, not simply in the scholarship that might be produced but also in the way in which the participants might affect the arenas in which they worked. He was convinced that study of what had happened during the Holocaust should help bring healing to the wounds left in its aftermath. Knight was similarly oriented. He, too, sought ways of structuring scholarly gatherings that would make a concrete, practical difference in the way the work of education on the Shoah proceeded, and on its impact in real-life settings. When Grob and Knight met to develop their ideas, they quickly found common ground and began to formulate their proposal: a praxis-oriented gathering of scholars across disciplines, generations, religious identities, and cultures, which would sustain its dialogue during and between regular gatherings of the group. Furthermore, both agreed that the gathering should be of sufficient size to provide a rich mix of people and yet small enough to encourage intensive and sustained dialogue at the thresholds of these scholars' work. They were convinced that the group, toward this end, should be sustained as much as possible with the same individuals over an extended period of time. The participants, they believed, should consider their time together as time set aside for support and challenge, with the two-year interims considered as time to work on projects in partnership with other participants. Finally, there would be no "stars," though, later on, some very outstanding scholars did express their desire to participate.

Funding would be needed for the project that was taking shape. Pastora Campos Goldner had been a student in Grob's course on the Holocaust at FDU and had also studied at Wroxton College. Grob knew of her passionate concern with the subject matter under consideration and of her positive feelings about Wroxton. He also knew that she was a person with means who could support such a venture. Ms. Goldner met with Grob and reviewed Grob's and Knight's funding proposal. The proposal was approved; the symposium was blessed with a donor.

Together, Grob and Knight crafted a plan to attract applicants, posing the challenge to prospective participants in a call for proposals that asked the following questions:

> How are we to respond, in word and deed, to a world radically transformed, in which "business as usual" no longer applies?
> How are we to utilize our learnings from the Shoah in order to face, responsibly, the genocidal potentials inherent in our own world?
> Do you want to join us in an intergenerational, interdisciplinary, international, and interfaith venture committed to post-Shoah healing and responsibility?

From more than eighty proposals, they selected thirty-six, and from this group they identified six thematic groups. Grob and Knight were to serve as symposium organizers and conveners, but all the participants would serve one another as both teachers and learners.

Goldner I

The first meeting of the Pastora Goldner Holocaust Symposium occurred in June 1996. The gathering was international, interfaith, interdisciplinary, and intergenerational, as intended. Participants made the commitment to return to Wroxton every two years and to continue the work of the symposium during the two-year period between symposia. And the setting, a modernized seventeenth-century Jacobean manor house, provided a unique retreat for considering some of the ugliest aspects of human nature and most tragic occurrences in modern history.

Participants were asked to reflect on how they could use their base in Shoah studies to inform their research and praxis in service of *tikkun olam,* the repair of the world. After an initial plenary session, during which each person told of how he or she had come to focus his or her work on the Holocaust, the participants were divided, on the basis of their central concerns, into six small working groups: post-Shoah ethics, post-Shoah theology, post-Shoah politics, post-Shoah models of healing, post-Shoah education, and art in the post-Shoah world. Plenary sessions were devoted to "reporting out" from the small groups to the "committee of the whole." From these groups, ideas for projects—both formal and informal—emerged. Our first publication, titled *Ethics after the Holocaust: Perspectives, Critiques, and Responses* and edited by John Roth, emerged from the ethics group. The ideas that led to the present volume were first aired in the education group. Other sessions were planned to nurture the shared life of the symposium and to honor the various religious and secular foundations from which our members approached their work.

The symposium concluded with strong, positive evaluations and suggestions to add another day of conversation. In addition, the participants, although they appreciated the small working groups, asked for ways of increasing the interaction among all the members of the symposium at the next gathering without sacrificing the depth and intensity that had been achieved in the first meeting.

Goldner II

The 1998 symposium saw several changes in format. The symposium was extended by one day, and more free time was incorporated into the schedule to allow for concentrated work on the continuing projects begun at the 1996 meeting. Knight and Grob, responding to many participants' wishes to meet more often in small groups with others outside their areas of disciplinary concern, asked each Goldner participant to pose a "focusing question," articulating an issue that illumined his or her primary engagement with the Shoah. Each person prepared a brief but extended reflection to flesh out this question. The reflections were shared with others prior to the June meeting. At the symposium, participants worked intensively in small-group meetings to pursue discussion surrounding the "focusing questions." An in-house publication, *Fragments from Wroxton*, emerged from the writing of the original questions, which had been further clarified by discussion during the small-group sessions.

With the added day, the 1998 symposium incorporated two new features: an open house in which twenty distinguished British guests who were engaged in Holocaust studies were invited to participate in a half-day of the symposium's activities; and the presence of a guest scholar, the late Professor Emil Fackenheim, who had been invited to join for the duration of the symposium and who participated in the small-group discussions and, later, addressed the symposium as a whole.

The focus of the 1998 gathering turned from discipline-based groups to conversations structured around the cutting-edge questions identified by Goldner colleagues. Relationships were deepened and extended as more members of the symposium discovered shared interests and made common cause with new friends among their colleagues. The Circle of Friends, a relatively open time set aside for building community that had been introduced in Goldner I, continued, as did formal interfaith observance of two Sabbaths, with the participants learning more about one another's deeper allegiances and personal passions.

As the second symposium concluded, several colleagues expressed mixed feelings about moving from the more traditional disciplinary-styled groupings of Goldner I to the extended conversations with a richer mix of colleagues that had been fostered by Goldner II. While these participants appreciated the increased collegiality and the stretching of their own boundaries, they were concerned not to lose touch with the discipline-oriented reflections of traditional scholarship, particularly in history, and with how such reflections affected their work as Shoah scholars.

Goldner III

As a result of the feedback from Goldner II, conversations for the 2000 gathering focused on disciplined attention to the driving passions in our work. The symposium had cultivated a number of areas at its last gathering, with deepened relationships and extended networks as its most tangible fruits. Indeed, there were already results that were clearly and directly linked to the way in which the sessions had been structured. This time, however, evaluations pointed to the need to be more disciplined with the wide-ranging concerns that are interrelated in the work of the Goldner Symposium.

To signal this focus, the symposium began with a brief meditation on the call for disciplined attention as it cuts across the more traditional notions of academic disciplines and subject matter. Continued awareness of disciplined attention was integrated with plenary and small-group conversations. In this way, the symposium pushed its members to think beyond the boundaries of their expertise, but without giving up their carefully honed, critical acumen in doing so.

As an additional encouragement, the symposium focused on participants' reading texts in common, with the goal of deepening individual and collective knowledge bases while fostering a creative interaction of perspectives and epistemological approaches to a fixed set of materials. The texts were distributed several months before the opening of the symposium so that break-out groups could be linked to plenary sessions for more in-depth discussion. Topics for the plenary sessions included "The Roma and Sinti Genocide," "An Examination of the Wannsee Protocols," and "Responding to Other Genocides in Our Time." There was also a panel composed of the contributors to *Ethics after the Holocaust,* our first symposium-generated text. In addition, workshops devoted to examining the role of texts in disciplined discussion were organized. One addressed a political text, another a sacred text, and two others engaged the world of art. Moreover, in an endeavor to provide more nondiscursive modes of relating to our common subject matter, one of our members performed a dramatic presentation from his play, *Remnants,* a text constructed from his listening to survivor testimony, stories recounted to him over the years in the context of counseling and therapy. Throughout, small working groups remained central, as did creative use of the plenary sessions.

The symposium also had to face the deaths of two members, whose lives were remembered in a specially focused Circle of Friends. Each of our deceased members was remembered by friends who recalled poignant vignettes and spoke of their gifts to others. Both of our missing colleagues were Jewish, and in a simple yet profound ritual of thanksgiving, the symposium concluded by saying Kaddish, the Jewish prayer for the dead, in gratitude for their lives. The ecumenical/interfaith worship experiment of observing two Sabbaths continued, this time pushing the boundaries significantly: Shavuot was remembered in a Sabbath meal on Friday night and in a Sabbath service the next morning, and Pentecost was celebrated by a Christian contingent with an experimental Eucharist that self-consciously sought to articulate sacramental Christian identity in a non-supersessionary way and in the presence of Jewish friends and colleagues.

The 2000 Symposium concluded with suggestions to extend its concerns to more personally difficult matters and to confront current genocidal conditions around the globe.

Goldner IV

For Goldner IV, new areas in aesthetics were identified, and sessions were planned to challenge boundaries of comfort while preserving members' continuing commitment to close and critical reading of texts. Discussions of the uniqueness of the Holocaust and the relationship of the Holocaust to other genocides continued, giving rise to creative tensions. Two other issues aroused emotions to test the Goldner waters: the Palestinian-Israeli conflict, and a rethinking of Holocaust studies in light of the events of September 11, 2001. In addition, a more general session on "identifying the minefields" focused on negotiating and coming to terms with emotional and value-laden topics like these. Finally, two sessions were devoted to the subject matter of Goldner works then in progress: the present volume, and an anthology on the themes of forgiveness, reconciliation, and justice in the post-Holocaust world. These two sessions were deliberately designed not to be "show and tell" events; instead, their goal was to extend to other members of the symposium the conversations that had begun with these two writing projects.

As in the past, time and structures were provided for those who were working on extended projects to meet and continue their work. In addition, the symposium, in plenary session, discussed and decided to implement a series of Goldner publications in association with an academic press.

Goldner V

Goldner V, which convened in 2004, opened with a dramatic reading composed of excerpts from memoirs of survivors of the Holocaust and other genocides. Two sessions continued our tradition of setting aside time to apply our learnings as Holocaust scholars to critical issues of the day: a plenary session was devoted to the topic of terrorism and genocide, and a second session explored issues of possible antisemitism in Mel Gibson's film *The Passion of the Christ*. The multiple ways in which we remember the Shoah were explored in some depth through an examination of how the Shoah is discussed on Internet sites, in memoirs and diaries, and in political manifestos. Later sessions were devoted to an exploration of pedagogies employed in teaching about the Holocaust, and these sessions included conversations based in substantial measure on essays included in this volume. Our ongoing commitment to explore genocides other than the Holocaust was further realized in a plenary session devoted to genocide in the Sudan.

For the first time, a half-day was set aside for "networking" groups to meet so that participants could plan joint projects or receive responses from colleagues regarding current or anticipated projects. At one of these sessions, abstracts were exchanged and discussed for an anthology to be titled *Anguished Hope: Holocaust Scholars Address the Israeli-Palestinian Conflict*. The arts continued to play an essential role in the work of the symposium as Goldner V concluded with a performance of selections from an opera in progress, based on a survivor's memoir titled *Lost Childhood*.

REFLECTIONS: THE SYMPOSIUM AS PROCESS

Planning for Thresholds

From the beginning, the heart of our[1] planning was to move the interstitial moments of other conferences to the center of our gatherings. Moreover, we wanted to do this while building community and a common vision of our work together. Clearly, we had to provide enough structure for symposium participants to meet and work together on previously identified projects. But we also had to identify structures that would solicit ownership of the process and support the open-endedness of true dialogue.

The first symposium reflected the kinds of projects that were submitted by our first group of scholars. We had both worked separately, and then together, to identify related projects by themes and establish six working groups. We added a facilitators' group, which the two of us would lead, and we placed ourselves as single participants in two of the working groups. Each of these groups was encouraged to provide time and space for individuals to identify their projects and then to develop their interests and concerns as they saw fit. The groups were scheduled to meet several times in the same configurations during the three days of the symposium. Occasional plenary gatherings were scheduled for general orientation to the symposium, for feedback, and for evaluation.

The final session of the first symposium focused on critical feedback regarding the work of the symposium and the process that had emerged. We noted some unevenness regarding the small-group meetings. Some gelled better than others; one was able to plan and project a book on post-Shoah ethics. The members of some of the small groups expressed concern about not getting to know everyone in the symposium as fully as they were able to get to know members of their own groups. How might more interaction among all participants be achieved? And how might we stay engaged with each other and with our projects over the interim, until the next gathering of the symposium?

Because we are building our gathering around thresholds, our structures and methods continue to evolve. The task is to identify those structures and methods that are still vital and essential for continuity while also ensuring that the will, needs, and interests of participants are articulated well enough to provide "focusing questions" that evoke our most thoughtful work. In this regard, the two of us stay in ongoing conversation with our colleagues with regard to topics and concerns raised by members of the symposium. However, we have not committed the planning process to democratic action, at least not in the sense in which the term "democratic" is usually understood. Rather, we have chosen to continue exercising our roles as organizers and conveners who call our colleagues into ongoing engagement with what appears as the next threshold for our work. We see our task as that of articulating those thresholds for our colleagues in a way that respects their capacities to resist and change what we offer them. Therefore, we typically share our proposed agendas in provisional form, allowing feedback from the participants to generate revisions and adjustments. Our task has been to listen not only closely to what our colleagues tell us but also alertly to what they communicate indirectly and by intimation. In response, we have sought to provide a setting for mutual engagement of shared concerns at the thresholds of our own and our colleagues' learning and expertise.

In this process, both of us have sought the assistance of as many of our colleagues as we could in sharing leadership functions throughout each gathering. As a result, a high percentage of our colleagues have taken their turns teaching and leading the rest, both in plenary and small-group sessions. We plan to continue this approach, viewing the education and leadership of the group as a shared enterprise that arises from the considerable expertise we assemble each time we meet. Our task is to keep this dynamic fluid—evolving and matched to the goals and structures of each symposium.

Structures of Hospitality

We have chosen to understand our role as that of conveners, viewing our role through the lens of hospitality and seeing that our work is to cultivate, as hosts, a gathering of gifted leaders who are served by a dynamic structure that taps into the varied strengths and passions they bring to a larger partnership on behalf of *tikkun olam.* At first glance, this conception of our role may seem antiegalitarian, but it is not. Rather, it is intentionally oriented toward discovering the maximum number of opportunities for sharing leadership roles among our colleagues. This sharing is made possible by our differentiating our own role as being more process-oriented than that of our colleagues. Equally important, perhaps more so, has been our commitment, from the very beginning, to build the symposium by cultivating our own partnership in the process and to ground the symposium in structures of hospitality. The two of us, as a Jew and a Christian drawn to this work from different intellectual, spiritual, and familial traditions, are able to explore in our own relationship the very dynamics that we claim are necessary in order for the work of *tikkun* in a post-Shoah world to proceed. As long as our partnership opens up in hospitality toward the other members of our symposium, we believe we are moving forward in our work. In the future, more partnerships will evolve, and we will be able to step farther back from the out-front role we now maintain. But our goal has been less to focus our attention on leadership structures than to foster a fluid structure that allows increasing numbers of our members to find their niches and voices and exercise leadership with their colleagues. How effectively we have met his goal will be known through the continued journey itself.

We have sought to share leadership with our colleagues so that we can shift in and out of the host/guest role and provide, as the primary hosts, the nurturing service that welcomes our guests into our domains of expertise and responsibility. Furthermore, by meeting as we do as an international gathering hosted by Americans on British soil, we have tried very self-consciously to remember and acknowledge that we are literally guests in another country, even setting aside time to invite other British scholars from the area to visit us for an afternoon and to build networks with them that might bear other fruit in the future.

Most important to our dynamics, however, is the fact that all Goldner participants have all been guests in one another's presence, taking turns serving as hosts to each other. We have focused on the issue of otherness, and the place we give it in our lives, as an essential component of living a responsible life in the aftermath of the Shoah. And we have built our symposium on structures and dynamics that honor the Eternal Other in our midst, respectful of the various traditions by which we do so.

Meals and other occasions with food and drink have been, in an inclusive sense, sacramental to the Goldner experience. Hospitality has been practiced keenly in these situations. Indeed, the entire four-day symposium reflects important dynamics of ritual process as identified by anthropologists like Victor Turner. Setting apart time and space for participants to separate themselves from their routines is an essential ingredient, as are mealtimes and other settings where food and drink can be shared in token fashion. Structures that break down status distinctions are also important features. All participants share leadership and take turns guiding their colleagues. Turner characterizes this kind of relationality as *communitas*. And, in fact, its accompanying feature of antistructure is also present as we work by consensus and with as little governing structure as possible. Though we do not articulate this idea explicitly, the experience is like a pilgrimage in which we draw apart to live for a time in a cloistered setting, one from another time and milieu—a time and a milieu that were not, as one of our number reminds, without significant oppression of their own devising. Even within this larger framework there are ritualized occasions that have become important to our gatherings: Sabbath liturgies, our Circle of Friends, and even late-night gatherings in the pub to tell stories and jokes in moments of camaraderie.

Dialogue, hospitality, and threshold conversations are distinguishing marks of the methodology employed by the Goldner Symposium. For this reason, the structures and processes are not democratically determined. But it would be wrong to interpret the symposium as being autocratic. Instead, as its conveners, we see our role as monitoring a process that depends on consensus and dialogue, to be shared by the largest number of participants that we can manage at any given time. Furthermore, the interventions we make are not made in order to direct the outcome of our dialogue but rather to ensure that the dialogue is unimpeded and that it occurs at the boundaries and thresholds of our knowing and growth. Nevertheless, before each gathering, criticism and suggestions are sought in various ways throughout the planning process. Indeed, they are solicited to ensure that the partnership we both share as conveners extends to the larger partnership that every member of the symposium has chosen to build and support.

Goldner in Review

Over the course of nearly ten years and five completed sessions, the Pastora Goldner Holocaust Symposium has taken on an evocative and creative personality. Our Wroxton gathering has become a touchstone for renewal in our work, a testing ground for our scholarship and for our various ways of working for *tikkun olam*. We think we have made a significant difference in the lives of the Goldner participants and, by way of that difference, in the lives of the many others with whom they work. Supportive relationships have been formed and have led to a wide variety of creative processes. Our work during the interim periods, in dialogue and in varied partnerships,[2] has generated sustained engagement on behalf of responsible citizenship in a genocidal world.

In short, the work of the Goldner Symposium continues,[3] whether in the environs of Wroxton Abbey, our biennial British home for four days every other June, or throughout the interim periods, as we correspond by e-mail and phone and collaborate on long-term projects. The network of the symposium enables various connections among us across disciplinary, cultural, religious, generational, and linguistic borders. And through that network we are able to bear witness to a different way of doing our work as post-Shoah scholars and teachers, a way that we believe builds *tikkun olam* in a wounded and traumatized world.

NOTES

1. In the remainder of this chapter, the use of first-person pronouns conveys the personal voices of this chapter's two co-authors rather than the collective voice of the Goldner Symposium. This shift in voice is intentional. It expresses the shared perceptions and reflections that the co-authors have developed over the several years they have worked together convening the symposium. It also reflects their common cause and mutual respect as well their sense of partnership in this venture.

2. At present count, five books in addition to this volume have been generated by the symposium. The first and most recent projects have already been mentioned; see John K. Roth, ed., *Ethics after the Holocaust: Perspectives, Critiques, and Responses* (St. Paul, Minn.: Paragon House, 1999) and Leonard Grob and John K. Roth, eds., *Anguished Hope: Holocaust Scholars Address the Israeli-Palestinian Conflict* (New York: Eerdmans, forthcoming). Two more anthologies have been published; see David Patterson and John K. Roth, eds., *After-Words: Post Holocaust Struggles with Forgiveness, Reconciliation, Justice* (Seattle: University of Washington Press, 2004) and David Patterson and John K. Roth, eds., *Fire in the Ashes: God, Evil, and the Holocaust* (Seattle: University of Washington Press, 2005). Not yet in print at the time of this writing is an individually authored work by David Patterson, *Open Wounds: The Crisis of Jewish Thought in the Aftermath of Auschwitz* (Seattle: University of Washington Press, forthcoming). Still more projects are in the pipeline, and some of them, like the present book, will be published by the University of Washington Press as volumes in the Pastora Goldner Series in Post-Holocaust Studies.

3. Beginning with our June 2008 meeting, and extending for a minimum period of ten years, the symposium will be funded by Stephen S. and Nancy

Weinstein. Thus the symposium will be renamed "The Stephen S. Weinstein Holocaust Symposium at Wroxton College." The University of Washington Press is considering renaming the series of volumes emerging from the Wroxton scholars "The Stephen S. Weinstein Series in Post-Holocaust Studies, formerly the Pastora Goldner Series."

About the Editors and Contributors

*An asterisk (*) indicates that the editor or contributor
is a member of the Pastora Goldner Holocaust Symposium.*

EDITORS

MYRNA GOLDENBERG* is one of the early contributors to the field of women and the Holocaust. Her seminal article "Different Horrors, Same Hell" has sparked controversy as has her book *Experience and Expression: Women, the Nazis, and the Holocaust,* co-edited with Elizabeth Baer. In addition to her work on women and the Holocaust, her research focuses on American Jewish women's poetry on the Holocaust, hunger during the Holocaust, and Annie Nathan Meyer, founder of Barnard College. She has contributed chapters to a variety of books on Jewish women and women in the Holocaust and has written numerous encyclopedia articles on Holocaust memoirs and novels as well as many reviews of feminist literature. Goldenberg is professor emerita at Montgomery College and founding director of the National Endowment for the Humanities–supported Paul Peck Humanities Institute at Montgomery. She is also adjunct professor at the University of Maryland and in the Johns Hopkins University graduate program. The recipient of several prestigious fellowships, she was the Ida E. King Distinguished Visiting Scholar on Holocaust Studies at Richard Stockton College in 2005–2006. In 1996 she was recognized as Outstanding Faculty Member by the Association of Community College Trustees.

ROCHELLE L. MILLEN* is professor of religion at Wittenberg University. The author of numerous articles, book chapters, and review essays, she served as co-editor of *New Perspectives on the Holocaust: A Guide for Teachers and Scholars* and is the author of *Women, Birth, and Death in Jewish Law and Practice*. The recipient of grants from the Lucius N. Littauer Foundation, the National Council for the Humanities, the Lilly Foundation, the American Jewish Archives, the Ohio Humanities Council, the Hadassah-Brandeis Institute, and the Columbus Jewish Foundation as well as from Wittenberg University, Millen is co-founder of the Religion, Holocaust, and Genocide Group of the American Academy of Religion and served as chair for seven years. She is a member of the Executive Board of the Ohio Council for Holocaust Education, and she received the Samuel Belkin Memorial Award for Professional Achievement from Stern College for Women, Yeshiva University.

CONTRIBUTORS

BETH HAWKINS BENEDIX is an associate professor of religious studies and literature at DePauw University. Her areas of focus and interest are modern European literature (primarily French and German), philosophy of literature (primarily existentialism), religious studies (primarily Jewish studies), phenomenology, and psychoanalysis. She is the author of *Reluctant Theologians: Kafka, Celan, Jabès* and has contributed to journals including *Shofar, Journal of Jewish Thought and Philosophy, Jewish Quarterly Review,* and *Journal of the Kafka Society of America*.

TIMOTHY A. BENNETT studied at the Johns Hopkins University, where he received his M.A. and Ph.D. An associate professor of German at Wittenberg University, Bennett teaches courses in German language, literature, and culture and has published on the imbrications of poetic and political consciousness in the works of Isolde Kurz and Heinrich Mann.

He has led student groups in studying ecumenism and interfaith dialogue at the World Council of Churches in Geneva, at the Vatican, in
the former German Democratic Republic, and in Hungary. Co-editor,
with Rochelle L. Millen, of *New Perspectives on the Holocaust: A Guide
for Teachers and Scholars,* he is currently working on a project involving
Stefan Heym's revision of the legend of the Wandering Jew. Along with
Millen, he created a learning community—"Germans and Jews: Culture,
Identity and Difference"—that studies the complex cultural history of
the relationship between Christians and Jews in Germany.

DAVID R. BLUMENTHAL* earned a B.A. from the University of
Pennsylvania and his Ph.D. from Columbia University. He teaches con-
structive Jewish theology, medieval Judaism, Jewish mysticism, and Holocaust studies at Emory University and writes on the same topics. His
published works include scholarly articles, reviews, and eleven books,
including the two-volume *Understanding Jewish Mysticism* as well as *God
at the Center* and *Facing the Abusing God: A Theology of Protest.* His most
recent book is *The Banality of Good and Evil: Moral Lessons from the Shoah
and Jewish Tradition.* Former director of the Fred R. Crawford Witness
to the Holocaust Project at Emory, and the recipient of several fellowships and awards, he has been a visiting professor at the Ecole Pratique
des Hautes Etudes in Paris and at the Gregorian Pontifical University in
Rome. He has also been a Skirball Fellow at the Oxford Centre for Post-
Graduate Jewish Studies.

STEPHEN FEINSTEIN* is professor emeritus of history at the University
of Wisconsin, River Falls, where he taught history from 1969 to 1999. He
is now director of the Center for Holocaust and Genocide Studies at the
University of Minnesota. He was curator of the traveling art exhibition "Witness and Legacy: Contemporary Art about the Holocaust" at
the Minnesota Museum of American Art and of "Absence/Presence: The
Artistic Memory of the Holocaust and Genocide" at the University of
Minnesota's Nash Gallery. Feinstein is co-editor, with Karen Schierman
and Marcie Littell, of *Confronting the Holocaust: A Mandate for the 21st
Century—Proceedings of the 27th Annual Scholars Conference on the German
Churches and the Holocaust* and is the author of many articles about post-

Holocaust art. His most recent edited collection is *Absence/Presence: Critical Essays on the Artistic Memory of the Holocaust.*

DONALD FELIPE is associate professor of philosophy and coordinator of the Liberal Studies Core at Golden Gate University, where he teaches ethics, critical thinking, and humanities to undergraduates in business and professional degree programs. Felipe holds a B.A in philosophy and Greek from the University of California, Berkeley, and an M.A. and Ph.D. in philosophy from the University of Texas, Austin. He has published articles on the theory and practice of disputation in Greek philosophy and later scholasticism and on other, related topics in the history of logic.

LEONARD GROB* is professor of philosophy at Fairleigh Dickinson University. He has published works on the philosophy of Martin Buber and that of Emmanuel Levinas and is co-editor of two anthologies, *Education for Peace: Testimonies from World Religions* and *Women's and Men's Liberation: Testimonies of Spirit.* Grob is the author of a memoir, "Goodbye Father," published in *Judaism* in the spring of 1990, which describes his "roots" journey to Ukraine in 1989. His experience in uncovering the history of the destruction of his father's family during the Holocaust led him to the field of Holocaust studies. He teaches a course each year at Fairleigh Dickinson titled "The Holocaust: Philosophy Issues." Additional works by Grob include articles titled "Higher Education in the Shadows of the Holocaust," "Rescue During the Holocaust—and Today," "Emmanuel Levinas and the Primacy of Ethics in Post-Holocaust Philosophy," "The Israeli-Palestinian Conflict: Just Reconciliation in the Shadows of the Holocaust," and "'Forgetting' the Holocaust: Ethical Dimensions of the Israeli-Palestinian Conflict." He recently co-edited the recent volume *Anguished Hope: Holocaust Scholars Confront the Israeli-Palestinian Conflict.* Grob is co-organizer, with Henry F. Knight, of the biennial Pastora Goldner Holocaust Symposium held at Wroxton College, Oxfordshire, England.

MARILYN J. HARRAN is Stern Professor of Holocaust Education and director of the Rodgers Center for Holocaust Education at Chapman

University. She holds a joint appointment as professor in the Departments of Religious Studies and History. Harran was a contributing writer to *The Holocaust Chronicle* and is the author or editor of three books on the history of Christianity. She has been a visiting scholar at the Hoover Institution for War, Revolution, and Peace at Stanford University and has been the recipient of fellowships from the National Endowment for the Humanities, the Mellon Foundation, and the International Research & Exchanges Board. She has been honored by the 1939 Club, a Holocaust survivor organization, with the Teacher of the Holocaust award and by the Anti-Defamation League of Orange County and Long Beach with the Leader of Distinction award.

HENRY F. KNIGHT is director of the Council for Holocaust Education in Tulsa, Oklahoma, a joint venture of educational outreach of the Jewish Federation of Tulsa and the Sherwin Miller Museum of Jewish Art. He was formerly on the faculty of the University of Tulsa, where he served as University chaplain and associate professor of Religion and, later, as applied associate professor of Hermeneutic and Holocaust Studies. He also served as chaplain and associate professor of Religion at Baldwin-Wallace College in Berea, Ohio, from 1979 to 1991. He is co-chair of the biennial Steven S. Weinstein Holocaust Symposium (formerly the Pastora Goldner Holocaust Symposium, which he and Leonard Grob of Fairleigh Dickenson University co-founded in 1996). Knight is the author of *Celebrating Holy Week in a Post-Holocaust World* (2005) and *Confessing Christ in a Post-Holocaust World* (Greenwood Press, 2000), and co-editor with Marcia Sachs Littell of *The Uses and Abuses of Knowledge* (1997).

PAUL A. LEVINE* is *Universitetslektor* (assistant professor) of Holocaust history at Uppsala University's Programme for Holocaust and Genocide Studies. Since receiving his doctorate, he has served in various capacities as an expert in Holocaust history for the Swedish government and as an adviser to the prime minister's office in organizing the Stockholm International Forum. He has also served on Sweden's delegation to the intergovernmental International Task Force on Holocaust Education, Remembrance and Research. He has taught at Rutgers University, organized numerous teacher-training seminars in Sweden, the Ukraine, and

Latvia, and was director of the education project at Uppsala titled "Improving the Teaching of History at Swedish Schools." Co-author of the widely read *Tell Ye Your Children: A Book about the Holocaust in Europe, 1933–1945,* he has also co-edited *Collaboration and Resistance during the Holocaust; Belarus, Estonia, Latvia, and Lithuania; Genocide; A Background Paper;* and *Bystanders to the Holocaust: A Re-Evaluation.* His recent articles include "Whither Holocaust Studies in Sweden? Some Thoughts on Levande *Historia* and Other Matters Swedish," "One Day during the Holocaust; An Analysis of Raoul Wallenberg's Budapest Report of 12 September 1944," "Swedish Neutrality during the Second World War: Tactical Success or Moral Failure?," and "Swedish Historiography and the Holocaust: A Generation Delayed."

JUERGEN MANEMANN* teaches Christian Worldview, Theory of Religion and Theory of Culture at the department of Catholic Theology at the State University of Erfurt, Germany. He wrote his PhD. dissertation on the German "Historikerstreit." He is the editor of *Jahrbuch Politische Theologie* and took a Coolidge-Fellowship of the ARIL at Columbia University in 1997. He earned his *Dr. theological habilitation* in 2000 with a dissertation on "Carl Schmitt and Political Theology." Manemann is the founder and organizer of the biennial "Ahauser Forum Politische Theologie." His numerous publications include *Weil es nicht nur Geschichte ist; Demokratiefähigkeit; Christologie nach Auschwits* (with Johann Baptist Metz); *Befristete Zeit; Carl Schmitt und die Politische Theologie; Religion und Terror/Stimmen zum 11.September aus Chistentum, Islam und Judentum* (with Hubertus Lutterbach); *Monotheismus;* and *Rettende Erinnerung an die Zukunft.*

RACHEL RAPPERPORT MUNN is an architect with over twelve years of professional experience and currently holds the title of Scholar at the Women's Studies Research Center, Brandeis University. Her principal area of academic interest is the architecture of memorials, memory, and the built environment. She has taught in the Graduate Consortium for Women's Studies at Harvard University's Radcliffe Institute for Advanced Study and in the Department of Architecture at Wentworth Institute of Technology. She has also lectured at several other Boston-area colleges and universities. She received a B.A. in anthropology and a certificate in women's studies from Princeton University and an M.A. in architecture from the Graduate School of Design, Harvard University. In 1997–1998 she was a Fulbright Fellow in Berlin, where she studied the history and built environment of that complex city. Since her return to the United States, she has continued her research, teaching, and reflections in these areas.

TAM K. PARKER teaches in the religion department at the University of the South. In 1997 she received a doctoral dissertation award from the National Foundation for Jewish Culture. She was a participant in the seminar on ethics after the Holocaust held in 2001 at the Center for Advanced Holocaust Studies, United States Holocaust Memorial Museum. Her primary research and writing are in the areas of ethics, modern Jewish thought, and genocide and Holocaust studies. Her current project, whose working title is "The Effort of the Good: Levinas, the Neighbor, and the Politics of Atrocity," is a Levinasian analysis of responses and failure to respond on the part of those who have witnessed acts of atrocity and genocide. Drawing from accounts of Holocaust rescue and bystanding, this project examines the interplay of social institutions, public moral rhetoric, and witnesses' responses. It is well known that institutions and moral rhetoric have been used extensively in acquiescing to and justifying genocidal atrocity; Parker's current project examines how some witnesses have turned the same kinds of institutions and rhetoric to the tasks of rescue and resistance.

DAVID PATTERSON* holds the Bornblum Chair in Judaic Studies at the University of Memphis and is director of the University's Bornblum Judaic Studies Program. A winner the Koret Jewish Book Award, he has published more than 125 articles and book chapters on philosophy, literature, Judaism, and Holocaust Studies. His more than two dozen books include two that are forthcoming, *Honey from the Rock: Jewish-Christian Dialogue—The Next Step* and *Open Wounds: The Crisis of Jewish Thought in the Aftermath of Auschwitz. Others are Wrestling with the Angel: Toward a Jewish Understanding of the Nazi Assault on the Name; Hebrew Language and Jewish Thought; Along the Edge of Annihilation; Sun Turned to Darkness; The Greatest Jewish Stories Ever Told; When Learned Men Murder; Exile;*

Pilgrimage of a Proselyte; The Shriek of Silence; In Dialogue and Dilemma with Elie Wiesel; Literature and Spirit: The Affirming Flame; and *Faith and Philosophy.* He is the editor and translator of the English edition of *The Complete Black Book of Russian Jewry* and co-editor, with Alan L. Berger, of the *Encyclopedia of Holocaust Literature* as well as co-editor, with John K. Roth, of *Fire in the Ashes: God, Evil, and the Holocaust* and *After-Words: Post-Holocaust Struggles with Forgiveness, Reconciliation, Justice.*

DIDIER POLLEFEYT* teaches catechetics, religious education, and Jewish-Christian dialogue in the Faculty of Theology of the Katholieke Universiteit Leuven, Belgium, where he is chair of the Center for Teacher Training in Religion and also serves as director of the Center for Peace Ethics. President of the Institutum Iudaicum Interuniversity Center for the Study of Judaism in Belgium, Pollefeyt focuses his research on the Holocaust in the Department of Pastoral Theology at the University of Leuven. His dissertation on Christian post-Holocaust ethics and theology was followed by two studies on the Jewish post-Holocaust thinking of Rubenstein and Fackenheim; both studies were recognized by the Auschwitz Foundation of Brussels. Pollefeyt's *Religious Teaching of the Holocaust* received the Belgian Prize of Peace. He edited *Jews and Christians: Rivals or Partners for the Kingdom of God?* That volume includes his chapter "Jews and Christians after Auschwitz: From Substitution to Interreligious Dialogue." He has also contributed chapters to a variety of books, including *Hyping the Holocaust: Scholars Answer Goldhagen; Confronting the Holocaust: A Mandate for the 21st Century; Problems Unique to the Holocaust; Anti-Judaism and the Fourth Gospel; Hermeneutics and Religious Education;* and *Incredible Forgiveness.*

AMY SHAPIRO* is professor and coordinator of the philosophy department at Alverno College. For six years she was also director of the Holocaust Education and Resource Center at Milwaukee's Coalition for Jewish Learning. Shapiro has given workshops and courses and published on Holocaust history and pedagogy, student-centered learning, and assessment-based education. Her students are her inspiration and help her continue to pursue a peaceful and just world. She has long been interested in pedagogical practice and is currently at work on a book about the philosophy of teaching the Holocaust, from which her chapter in this volume was adapted.

STEPHEN D. SMITH is co-founder and executive director of the Aegis Trust, a United Kingdom–based nongovernmental organization established in 2000 to examine genocide and its prevention. He is also chairman of the Beth Shalom Holocaust Centre, which he co-founded with his brother in 1995. Beth Shalom has received international recognition for its approach to keeping the memory of the Holocaust alive and to stimulating greater understanding of genocide. Smith has lectured and written widely on the Holocaust and genocide and on the issues of memorialization and education, both in the United Kingdom and abroad. He serves as adviser on memorials to Rwanda's Ministry of Youth, Culture and Sports and as special adviser on genocide to the Stockholm International Forum, office of the prime minister of Sweden.

LAURINDA STRYKER* undertook graduate work at Harvard Divinity School, earning a master's degree in theological studies with an emphasis on theology and social ethics, and at Cambridge University, where she earned a doctorate in history. At the University of Brighton, where she was a senior lecturer in the School of Historical and Critical Studies, she taught history, philosophy, cultural studies, and Holocaust studies. Until 2002, she was an assistant professor in the history department at St. Cloud State University, where she taught courses in Western civilization, modern European history, and the history of the Holocaust. Stryker was recruited as a historian for the Holocaust Victim Assets Programme of the International Organization for Migration, Geneva, where she researched Roma and Sinti claims on Swiss banks in 2003, working primarily on Polish and Hungarian claims.

MARY TODD currently serves as vice president for academic affairs and dean of the faculty at Ohio Dominican University, where she is also professor of history. A scholar of American history, she earned her Ph.D. from the University of Illinois, Chicago. Her areas of specialization include gender and women's studies, American religious history, and the Holocaust. She was a participant in the seminar on ethics after the Holocaust held in 2001 at the Center for Advanced Holocaust Studies, United States Holocaust Memorial Museum. Todd is a member of the executive board of the Ohio Council for Holocaust Education. She is the author of *Authority Vested: A Story of Identity and Change in the Lutheran Church–Missouri Synod* and past president of the Lutheran Historical Conference.

Index

Index

243; and student exhibitions, 217; study of local, 6; truth in, 161–62; uniqueness in, 175; use of, 62; witness, 103–14, 141

The History of Jewish Art and Architecture (video series), 35

Hitler, Adolf, 141; and art, 29, 30, 56, 57; authorization of, 121; catastrophic actions of, 21–22; historical circumstances of, 14; knowledge concerning, 261; *Mein Kampf*, 29, 251; and nationalism, 213; plans of, 162; and Schmitt, 221; speeches of, 265

Hitler Youth, 251

Hobbes, Thomas, 227

Hochhuth, Rolf, *The Deputy*, 157

Hoffman, Martin, 85–86, 101n37

holiness, 181–82

Holocaust denial, 10, 179, 216, 241, 249

Holocaust (docudrama miniseries), 5, 6, 10

Holocaust Educational Foundation, 9

Holocaust fatigue, 118, 124, 253

The Holocaust in Historical Contexts (Katz), 136–37

Holocaust Politics (Roth), 115n16

The Holocaust Project (Chicago), 49n11

Holocaust Remembrance Day, 144, 250, 254

hope, 194, 196, 216

Horkheimer, Max, 231

hospitality, 293–95

Huberband, Shimon, 138

Huizinga, Johan, 151

humanism, 14

humanity, 138, 139, 160, 161, 166, 169, 176, 177–79, 194, 252, 255

human rights, 127

humility, 86, 89

Hungary, 126

Iconoclastic Controversy (Kiefer), 44

ideals, 148

identification, 198, 231

identity: Aryan, 183; assaults on, 160, 213; images of, 152; and integrity, 91; and Jews, 76, 77, 80, 160–61, 178; and morality, 150–51; sense of, 161; shared, 86

ideology: and Berlin, 53, 54, 56, 57; criticism of, 175, 179, 182; and literature, 78; and museums, 277; and urban design, 53

If Not, Not (Kitaj), 40–41

IG Farben, 90, 92–93

imagination, 22, 30. *See also* art

In Bluebeard's Castle (Steiner), 156

indifference, 169, 225–26, 252, 261, 263

Institute for Historical Review, 249

"Integrating Ethics into the Business School Curriculum," (Dunfree and Robertson), 97n2

integrity, 88, 91, 92, 94

intellect, 194

interfaith activity, 212, 289. *See also* ecumenism

interview process, 196–97, 200–204

"In the Penal Colony" (Kafka), 67, 77–78

Ionesco, Eugène, 78, 80

Isherwood, Christopher, *Goodbye to Berlin*, 55

Israel, 11, 14, 173, 238, 274, 290. *See also* Zionism

Italy, 121

Nazis/Nazism *(continued)*
by, 265; racism of, 5, 29, 106, 108;
refusal of posthumous victory to,
145; and religion, 183; and Salomon,
31; and singularity of Holocaust,
136; and theodicy, 164; totalitarian
reach of, 21; war of on imagination, 30; Western aid to, 161–62.
See also perpetrator(s); SS soldiers
Nelson, Tim Blake, *The Grey Zone*,
27–28
neo-Nazism, 127, 175, 241
Netherlands, 121
new historicism, 136
New Testament, 31, 211
New York City, schools of, 8
Nietzsche, Friedrich, 78, 155–56
Night and Fog (film), 160
The Night Porter (Cavani), 28, 267
Night (Wiesel), 109, 140, 142, 143,
215–16, 251, 267, 268
1939 Club, 253–54
Nomberg-Przytyk, Sara, 143; *Ausch-
witz*, 147n24
non-identity, 223
Norway, 121, 126
Nuremberg Code, 264
Nuremberg Laws, 68, 265
nursing, 263–64
Nussbaum, Felix, *The Dance of
Death*, 31

obedience, 166–69, 251, 263
Obedience (film), 167
objectivity, 84, 87, 96, 104, 108, 177
"Of Rest and the Weary" (Blumen-
thal), 118
Olesky, Krystyna, 12
Oliner, Pearl, 168

Oliner, Samuel, 168
One Survivor Remembers (Klein), 200
"On the Jews and Their Lies" (Luther),
211–12
Opdyke, Irene Gut, 258
Orange County, California, 249,
250–51, 255, 256
Order Police, 105
Other: acknowledgment of, 225;
approach to, 87; death of, 229; facing of, 24, 190; generalized, 226;
in Germany, 261; and God, 180;
and Goldner Symposium, 294;
and identity, 151; and Judaism,
184; perspective of, 176; religious
claims of, 183; responsibility for,
223; suffering, 227; treatment of,
213

Palestinian-Israeli conflict, 238, 290
Palmer, Parker J., *The Courage to
Teach*, 150, 151
Park, Hun-Joon, "Can Business
Ethics Be Taught? 97n1
Parks, Sharon D., *Can Ethics Be
Taught?* 97n2, 99n16
"A Parting at the Cross" (Stein), 215
The Passion of Sacco and Vanzetti
(Shahn), 27
The Passion of the Christ (Gibson),
100n18
Passover, 43
Pastora Goldner Holocaust Sympo-
sium, 236, 284–96; *Fragments
from Wroxton*, 287; publications
of, 296n2
Pentecost, 289
perpetrator(s), 63, 231, 277; and acade-
mia, 261; and art, 33, 44, 48; and

business ethics, 90, 93; demoniza-
tion of, 87; and determinism, 181;
experiences of, 125; focus on, 10;
forgiveness of, 238; humanity and
inhumanity of, 177–78; and identity, 86, 112; judgment of, 103, 104,
105–9, 111; lessons from, 129; Levi
on, 122; obedience of, 166, 263;
perspective of, 176, 182; psychology
of, 100n18; stereotypes of, 149; in
Wiesel, 174. *See also* Nazis/Nazism
Persson, Göran, 14, 127
photography, 36, 46, 185
phronesis, 113
The Pianist (film), 268
Picasso, Pablo, *Guernica,* 27
Piper, Thomas R., *Can Ethics Be
Taught?* 97n2, 99n16
Pirandello, Luigi, *Six Characters in
Search of an Author,* 80
Plato, 140
poetic visions, 34
poetry, 27, 28, 29, 79
Poland, 6
Polish ancestry, 238, 240
political theology, 221–32
politics, 65, 68, 287, 289
popular culture, 267–68
*Portraits des élèves du C.E.S. des
Lentillères* (Boltanski), 46
Postconventional Moral Thinking
(Rest), 98n10
postmodernism, 85, 107, 136
postmodern society, 180
Potsdamer Platz (Berlin), 63
power, 69, 70, 75
The Power of Place (Hayden), 64n2
prayer, 137, 138
pregnancy, 138

prejudice, 73, 74, 75, 178
preservation, architectural, 58–59
private sphere, 227, 228
The Producers (film), 268
progress, concept of, 228
propaganda, 55, 57, 67, 265, 270n11.
See also language
psychology, 85, 194, 196
public sphere, 227

rabbinic tradition, 31, 163, 164, 165
racism, 5, 8, 29, 74, 104–5, 106, 108,
136
Rathenow, Hanns-Fred, 5–6
rationality, 156, 164, 177, 185
Rawls, John, 224, 226
reader(s), 66, 70, 71–72, 74, 75, 87,
93, 109, 111, 197, 214
The Reader (Schlink), 265
realism, 28, 36
reason, 154, 155, 223, 228. *See also*
knowledge
redemption, 164, 174
Reflections of a Post-Auschwitz Christian
(Cargas), 144
reflective reflection, 224
Reinharz, Jehuda, *The Jew in the
Modern World,* 152
relationality, 71, 72, 74, 80, 294
relationships, 85–86, 91
religion, 150; and absolutism, 183–
84; civil, 186; decline of, 155, 156;
dilemmas of, 175; as exclusive, 183;
and morality, 180, 186; and moral
relativism, 184; natural *vs.* positive,
154; and Nazis, 183; and Other, 183;
perspective of, 173–74; and prejudice, 8; and self-criticism, 217;
Steiner on, 156; students' back-

Index